BEST BOOKS
ON THE STOCK MARKET

EDITORIAL ADVISORY BOARD

BEST BOOKS ON THE STOCK MARKET

An Analytical Bibliography

Sheldon Zerden

R.R. BOWKER COMPANY
New York & London, 1972
A Xerox Education Company

XEROX

655842

Published by R. R. Bowker Co. (a Xerox Education Company)
1180 Avenue of the Americas, New York, N.Y. 10036

Printed and bound in the United States of America

Zerden, Sheldon.
  Best books on the stock market.

  1. Stock-exchange—Bibliography. 2. Investments—
Bibliography. I. Title.
Z7164.F5Z46   016.3326'42'0973   72-8275
ISBN 0-8352-0547-9

To Charlotte

CONTENTS

FOREWORD

In *Henry the Fourth*, *Part One*, Shakespeare has Glendower say, "I can call spirits from the vasty deep," to which Hotspur replies, "Why so can I, or so can any man; But will they come when you do call them?"

It's an illuminating dialogue, one a person interested in securities and financial markets can appreciate. Many people buy and sell stocks and bonds, and when they do, they are, in effect, making predictions as to the future. Like Glendower, they are trying to call spirits—prices and market tendencies—from the vasty deep—for this, read next week, month, or year. But as Hotspur correctly noted, many people can do this, and all who deal in securities make the effort, but few have good records, or methods of selection that truly work.

During the past two centuries literally thousands of books have been written about securities and exchanges, and the magazine articles, essays, and monographs are many times the number of books in the field. These range from works claiming almost magical knowledge and offering certain success if only the correct formula is applied to the markets, to arcane volumes unintelligible to all but a few who are versed in the language of higher mathematics, but divorced from the realities of the sweaty, complicated, and often irrational market places.

The novice in search of information or guidance in this field has no way to judge the merits of individual works, while the specialist or advanced student may wade through many volumes before finding the exact information he desires. But for the past few decades it has been almost impossible to keep up with the field by going through *all* the books, or even the more important works. And how can one distinguish significant from insignificant books? Hyperbole is the rule, not the exception, on Wall Street, and most new books are advertised as though they contained the distillation of all human knowledge regarding the markets.

There has long been a need for a guide to investment literature. But the task of assembling such a guide was awesome. The scholar would have to be familiar with all the many works in the field, select the best and most important through a reading of all, and then summarize and analyze their contents. Such a person would have to have a knowledge of all aspects of the securities industry. He would have to be a scholar as well. Finally, this person would by necessity possess an ability to write clearly.

Few such people exist. Most of those who know the markets are busily engaged in working at the job of buying and selling, managing or advising, and have no time left for the compilation of such a guide, even though they recognize the need for one. And those who have the time usually lack the knowledge to perform the task.

Sheldon Zerden is one of the few men on Wall Street who possess all the qualifications for this project. He has spent years in the financial profession, and has a record of success in the field. At the same time, he has a burning interest in the literature of investments, the history of the markets, and the various ways by which people have viewed them and tried to master the exchanges. He has spent years in the monumental task of ploughing through the books on investment. In his work, he has called upon other experts for assistance, but the job was his alone, and he has performed it admirably.

I am tempted to say that the result is the *best* guide to the literature of investment we have, but am halted from doing so by the fact that this is the *only* work of its kind. In it the reader will find evaluations of books on investment methods, the history of the markets, the psychology of investment, mutual funds, and many other fields, and all of these are evaluated with intelligence and skill.

Of course, new books on the subject appear every week, and by necessity such a compilation is dated the moment it is completed. Mr. Zerden's book will have to be updated regularly. But for the moment at least, we have a guide to the literature that every serious investor and scholar will have to have. All of us—students of finance, investors, and academicians—are in his debt.

Robert Sobel
Professor of History
New College of Hofstra

PREFACE

The significance of Wall Street's contribution to the country's economic welfare is rarely appreciated by the average American. This is true in spite of the fact that the latest estimate of stockholders in the United States is 30.5 million. Projections are 40 million for 1975 and 50 million for 1980. Common stock market values are now well in excess of a trillion dollars. This awesome statistic should reveal the importance of our securities markets and the vital necessity for the investor to be informed.

There are many hundreds of books that deal directly with Wall Street and the stock market, but until now there has not been one comprehensive educational guide to this literature. My research at various libraries convinced me that reference books and catalogs are difficult to handle, contain excessive duplication, and often prove to be a time-consuming study in futility. That is how the idea for this work was born.

With the help of major publishers and the fine reference shelves of the best business libraries, this book has evolved into a thorough, classified, and up-to-date bibliography of the stock market. The bibliographic material reveals the title, author, publisher, year of publication, page count, and price. Each book is analytically reviewed in order to acquaint the reader with its content. For those interested in a complete reading of the books represented here, they are all available from the publishers or in the better libraries throughout the country.

The main body of reviews consists of 150 books which are classified into six categories. A textbook and reference section and a supplementary list of unannotated titles round out and complete this first major compendium of the accumulated knowledge of Wall Street.

This work will prove helpful to the novice who wants to educate himself in the ways of the market, to the sophisticated investor who desires to sharpen his trading or investment techniques, and to the student who now has a single source from which to learn the history of the stock market or organize himself to do a thesis on any Wall Street subject. It will also be a boon to every banker, money manager, insurance company executive, investment analyst, and serious broker or investor who wants to develop a well-rounded view of the stock market through the wisdom of its greatest minds. Readers should note, however, that editorial choice has been exercised in the selection of titles for review, and

that neither the author nor the publisher intends the opinions expressed to be
construed as legal, accounting, investment, or any other business advice.

ACKNOWLEDGMENTS

Many thanks to the editors of R. R. Bowker and my Editorial Advisory Board.
Their enthusiasm and advice were most helpful and important in the development of this work. Many thanks are due to all the authors and publishers who
extended permission for the use of the quoted material present in the reviews.
The author is also grateful to Gerald M. Loeb for the interest he demonstrated in
this project. It is a manifestation of his unselfish devotion to the cause of Wall
Street. Finally, a humble apology to a patient and forebearing wife, who allowed me to spend thousands of hours at work when they could have been devoted to her.

METHODS OF INVESTING

TECHNICAL ANALYSIS

✓Edwards, Robert D., and Magee, John
   Technical Analysis of Stock Trends, 5th ed. Springfield, Mass.: John Magee,
   1967. 486 pp. $16.00

The durability of this work through the years has earned it the title "The Bible
of the Chartists." A technical analyst must be thoroughly familiar with the contents of Edwards and Magee to be sure he knows his craft. It would be valid to
attribute a great deal of the startling growth of the technical school of analysis
to this book. Securities research can be broadly broken down into two major
areas, the fundamental or statistical, and the technical. The fundamentalist depends on statements, balance sheets, earnings, and dividends. He analyzes management, monitors plant capacity and sales. In short, he collates all these factors
to determine if a stock is a good buy. The chartist or technical analyst studies
the action of the market itself. He studies the actual trading in graphic form—
the history of trading, price changes, and the volume of transactions in a stock.
The picture or pattern of that history indicates the probable future trend. This
book offers a thorough study of these patterns. It defines and elaborates the authors' basis for predicting a stock's behavior with the help of illustrations and
more than 150 sample charts.

   The average investor doesn't realize it, but the most widely followed indicator
in the stock market is technical in nature. The Dow Theory is the grandfather of
technical market studies. It is not infallible, but its record is impressive. The investor can't buy the averages, however, and it remains for this book to tell you
what stocks to buy, when to buy them, and when to sell them. That covers just
about all an investor must do to make money.

   Charts are the tools of the technical analyst. There are many kinds of charts.
For this book a simple daily chart is used. It records the price range (high and
low), the closing price, and volume each day. On the charts a vertical line con-
nects the high and low, and a horizontal bar or a "tick" is added to show the
closing level. Volume is shown at the base by drawing a vertical line. The au-

1

thors caution that there is no magic in the chart itself. It is simply a pictorial record of the history of the stock. It has been said that "there is nothing wrong with the charts—the trouble is with the chartists." It is not the chart but the interpretation that is important. Chart analysis is neither easy nor foolproof.

Stock prices move in trends just like the Dow. Sooner or later they change direction from down to up or up to down. When that happens a characteristic pattern shows up on the chart; it is called a "reversal formation." The most reliable reversal pattern is the "head and shoulders top." It consists of a strong rally on heavy volume that climaxes an extensive advance. A minor retreat follows on light volume. This forms the "left shoulder." Another high volume advance ensues which exceeds the level of the left shoulder, and a reaction carries the price to the level of the previous recession. This is the "head." A third rally on less volume fails to reach the height of the head before another decline sets in. This is the "right shoulder." Finally, a decline through the "neckline" (a line drawn across the bottoms of the reactions between the shoulders and the head) of 3 percent of the stock's price is the confirmation of a breakout on the downside. This may come on increased volume, but there is often a "pullback" to the neckline. This attempt usually fails and then prices turn lower on high volume. The minimum probable objective of the decline is equal to the number of points from the top of the head to the neckline. This number is figured from the penetration point at the neckline. The "head and shoulders" formation relates to the Dow Theory in that it sets up a sequence of lower tops and bottoms. It is important because of its frequency and dependability.

Reversal patterns include (1) head and shoulders tops and bottoms, (2) complex head and shoulders, (3) rounding turns, (4) symmetrical triangles, (5) right-angle triangles, (6) rectangles, and (7) double and triple tops and bottoms. Other reversal formations are (1) broadening formations, (2) the diamond, (3) (3) wedge formations, (4) one-day reversals, and (5) selling climax. All of these are explained in depth by the authors. There are also several chapters which are devoted to other technical phenomena such as consolidation formations, resistance and support, and trendlines and channels.

Chart interpretation is not a science but an art. It is not an exact science because all the rules have exceptions. It requires judgment in appraising many factors which are often in conflict. Still, to imply that there is need for genius is improper. The authors feel that technical analysis is a skill which can be acquired by anyone with ordinary intelligence. They observe that greater regulations and higher taxes have not provided more stable markets for the small investor. Higher margins have not prevented panic collapses. Markets are thinner on the downside and more vulnerable to drastic decline than they were prior to modern regulation. We still have the same bull and bear markets that we had fifty years ago. Although a few chart patterns are less common now, the chartist of 1907 would be right at home in today's market.

Many traders in the stock market have no basic strategy. They are in danger of being hurt by every panic, rumor, or tip. They are consequently worried, uncertain, and riddled with doubt and fear. This causes them to drop good stocks unnecessarily. The authors don't claim that the technical approach is infallible, but point out that in a majority of cases charts are dependable. If you follow chart signals you will not be wiped out, you will not be frozen into a weak market, and you can make decisions calmly. You will have peace of mind in spite of the fact that you will continue to have losses.

This book is not a sure road to riches nor does it guarantee profits at all times. It is a reference work for the trader that should be consulted over and over again. It deals not only with systems, but provides the insight necessary to understand the mechanics of the auction market. Technical analysis has grown in stature with the addition of Edwards and Magee to the literature of the stock market. Your comprehension of the value of this work will mature with experience, intelligence, and hard work. Your technical knowledge will then save you from buying at the top or selling at the bottom, which is the fate of the less disciplined investor.

Gann, William D.
45 Years in Wall Street: A Review of the 1937 Panic and 1942 Panic, 1946 Bull Market with New Time Rules and Percentage Rules with Charts for Determining the Trend on Stocks. Miami, Fla.: W. D. Gann, 1949. 149 pp.

The wisdom and experience of a successful stock market technician is distilled into this book. Gann develops a mass of statistics to help formulate valuable rules for the trader. Every page is full of practical advice which the author believes is necessary to be successful in the stock market. He concludes that his forty-seven years of experience have taught him that the most precious possession is time—the time to secure knowledge which is more valuable than money. Gann reveals his most valuable rules and secret discoveries in his classic twenty-four rules for trading:

1. Divide capital into ten equal parts.
2. Use stop-loss orders.
3. Never overtrade.
4. Never let a profit run into a loss. After you have a profit of three points or more raise your stop order so that you will have no loss of capital.
5. Do not buck the trend. Make sure of the trend before you buy.
6. When in doubt—get out, and don't get in.
7. Trade only in active stocks.
8. Trade in four or five stocks.
9. Buy and sell at the market.
10. Don't close your trades without a good reason.
11. Accumulate a surplus after a series of successful trades.
12. Never buy just to get a dividend.
13. Never average a loss.
14. Never get out of the market just because you have lost patience, or get into the market because you are anxious from waiting.
15. Avoid taking small profits and big losses.
16. Never cancel a stop order after you have placed it at the time of a trade.
17. Avoid getting in and out of the market too often.
18. Be just as willing to sell short. Stay with the trend.
19. Never buy just because the price of a stock is low or sell short just because the price is high.
20. Be careful not to pyramid at the wrong time.

21. Select stocks with small capitalizations to pyramid on the buy side and short those with large capitalizations.

22. Never hedge. If you are long of one stock and it goes down, don't sell another short as a hedge.

23. Never change your position in the market without a good reason.

24. Don't increase your trading after a long period of success or a period of profitable trades.

In addition to these rules there are many suggestions throughout the rest of the book. Gann doesn't approve of a joint account. He cautions the reader never to answer a margin call and not to gamble on hope. You must stop hoping and start thinking. Most traders don't want to hear the truth; they like to hear something that agrees with their hopes. When they buy a stock they believe all the rumors, views, and lies that are bullish. They refuse to believe the bad or unfavorable reports about the stock. It is the human element that is the trader's greatest weakness.

The object of Gann's book is not to paint a rosy picture of how easy it is to get rich. There is no easy road to riches. He has tried to give the reader practical rules that will work. If the trader or investor will study hard and have the patience to wait for the opportunities to buy and sell at the right time, he can be successful. However, all the rules in the world will be of no avail if the trader fails to follow them. If he works on hope or fear instead of facts, if he delays or becomes impatient, he is doomed to failure.

√ Hamilton, William P.
The Stock Market Barometer. New York: Harper, 1922. 325 pp.

The Dow Theory, popularly known to the public by an industrial average of thirty leading stocks, started out as a number of editorials in the *Wall Street Journal* written by Charles H. Dow, one of the founders of that superlative business newspaper. It remained for a man named S. A. Nelson to coin the phrase "the Dow Theory." He could not persuade Charles Dow to write a book about his theories, so he did the next best thing. He wrote a book of his own called *The ABC of Stock Speculation*, and included all he could find of Dow's editorials from the *Wall Street Journal*.

The author of this book, William P. Hamilton, was the first major successor to Charles Dow. He followed Sereno S. Pratt as editorial writer of the *Wall Street Journal*. He carried on the Dow tradition, expanding on the work Dow had started but could not complete because of his untimely death at the age of fifty-two. *The Stock Market Barometer* is Hamilton's clear affirmation of his belief in the efficacy of the Dow Theory. He proved to be a faithful disciple of Charles Dow and successfully used that stock market barometer to predict the bull and bear markets from 1903 until the 1929 crash.

Hamilton believed that psychology and emotion play a great role in the movement of the market. He felt that we need a "soulless" barometer to tell us where we are going. The Dow barometer has the ability to forecast that no other business record has ever approached. It can predict months ahead of time.

According to Dow, there is a triple movement in the market, and these three movements are in progress simultaneously. The primary movement is a major swing upward or downward. It tends to run at least a year and generally runs much longer. The secondary movement consists of sharp rallies in a primary bear market and sharp reactions in a primary bull market. The third concurrent movement is the day-to-day fluctuation of the market. It is important to understand that the industrial and rail averages must corroborate each other in order to confirm the existence of a major primary trend.

Hamilton discusses the history of the eventful years during his tenure as editorial writer for the *Wall Street Journal*. He includes profiles of many famous market operators such as James R. Keene, Russell Sage, E. H. Harriman, and James J. Hill. He studied their methods but avoided a close friendship with any one of them so that he could maintain his journalistic neutrality. Other chapters briefly describe the action of floor traders, the work of the specialist, bucketing, short selling, and other mechanics of the stock market.

Most people who come to Wall Street lose money. They then spend the rest of their lives denouncing the stock exchange as a gambling hell. But there is no law that compels them to trade in Wall Street if they do not choose to do so. Hamilton tries to educate the investor and make him feel that he has a fair chance to earn the prize which he seeks.

The Dow Theory is not a system to beat the market or a get-rich-quick-scheme. Hamilton believes that it is an excellent means of protecting the intelligent investor from the emotional and psychological pitfalls which normally lead him astray. He maintains that the "embryo investor" is deluged with a "chaos of knowledge" and "an almost inextricable confusion of opinion." To help the reader find his way through this maze, he presents the Dow Theory, which he calls "the stock market barometer," and claims that strict adherence to its principles is the surest road to success.

Jiler, William L.
  How Charts Can Help You in the Stock Market. New York: Trendline, 1962. 202 pp. $10.00

The presentation of an authoritative and clear explanation of technical analysis is invaluable for the investor who seeks the answer to stock trends. Hybrid chartists believe fundamentals should also be considered in any assessment of a stock's future action. The pure technician, however, is firm in his belief that the chart action reveals the fundamentals with a clarity that becomes obvious after the news is made public This primer on the technical aspect of the market has served the thousands of investors who want to know the story that charts tell us. The author stresses that charts are not the answer to certain success. There are no sure things in the stock market. They can provide the investor or trader with some clues to the trend of a particular stock and are an important first step in the process of analysis that can lead to investment success.

The illustration and explanation of reversal patterns show how the changes occur. The major reversal tops are called "head and shoulders," "double tops," "V formations," "island reversals," "line tops," and "saucer tops." These occur after an uptrend. The same patterns develop bottoms after a downtrend and signal a turnaround.

There is a discussion of support and resistance, showing how each is formed and how old resistance becomes new support. When the market runs up or down there usually tends to be a reaction or rally that retraces half of the ground won or lost. This is called the 50 percent rule.

Continuation and consolidation patterns occur during an uptrend or a downtrend. There are four types of triangles: symmetrical, ascending, descending, and inverted. Although the triangle is a continuation pattern, it can lead to a reversal about 40 percent of the time. Other continuation patterns which are more reliable are boxes, flags, pennants, wedges, and diamonds. Their names accurately describe their shape.

Gaps, reversal days, traps, and other unexpected changes that occur with news of a startling nature cause a rush of buy or sell orders in a stock or in the market as a whole. This possibility points out the frailty of prediction in the stock market, whether that prediction is fundamental or technical.

The balance of the book is confined to a surface treatment of some other indicators which add to the technician's fund of knowledge and serve to fortify his conviction when the majority of them point to a particular trend. Those mentioned are the advance-decline line (market breadth), the odd-lot index, Barron's confidence index, short interest ratio, and the 200 day moving average.

The importance of charts as a market way of life is not overstated by the author. In fact, he has taken pains to play down their accuracy and necessity. Though they are not infallible, it becomes obvious to the reader of this book that a thorough knowledge of the technical aspect of the market does help determine the trend, indicate when to buy and sell, and in short adds immeasureably to your chances for success.

✓**Livermore, Jesse L.**
How to Trade in Stocks: The Livermore Formula for Combining Time Element and Price. Original: New York: Duell, Sloan and Pearce, 1940. Reprint: Palisades Park, N.J.: Investors' Press, 1966. Distributed by Simon & Schuster. 112 pp. $6.95

Just before he tragically took his own life, Jesse Livermore, one of the most successful speculators in stock market history, wrote a short book that remains his legacy to the speculator for all time. He was no idle theoretician, but a fabled market operator who made and lost four multimillion dollar fortunes. He states his philosophy of trading and lays down a list of rules which have proven necessary in order to win at the speculative process. The list below is taken directly from Livermore's chapters:

1. Markets are never wrong. Profits take care of themselves; losses never do.
2. Investors are the big gamblers. They let their investments ride and if it goes wrong they lose it all.
3. Never buy on reactions and go short on rallies.
4. Never average losses.
5. When you see a danger signal, never argue with it—get out. You can always get back in.
6. Banish wishful thinking.

7. Steer your speculative ship along with the tide; do not argue or try to combat it.

8. Don't spread out all over the market; it is easier to watch a few stocks.

9. Confine your studies of movements to the leading stocks (the active issues).

10. There are fashions in the market just as in women's gowns, hats, and jewelry.

11. Follow the leader.

12. Never meet a margin call; close out your account.

13. Take one half of your profits in a successful trade and lock it up in a safe deposit box.

14. Draw out cash after a successful trade. Count it over. Have something in your hand. It has psychological value; it is real. Speculators rarely see their money; to them it is not real, not tangible.

A thorough explanation of the "pivotal point" is the subject of a whole chapter in which Livermore describes the precise point at which a stock breaks through on the upside or the downside. Technical analysts recognize this as a resistance area on the upside and a support level on the downside. It is obvious that the "Boy Plunger" had worked out his own system of charts to keep track of a stock's movement. When the signal he received was right, when the time element and price were in balance, he was ready to buy or sell a stock.

There is a section at the end of the book which contains charts and explanations of the Livermore market key. They are preceded by rules which graphically portray the system Livermore used to select his stocks. The special thirty-two page section contains reproductions of his actual worksheets, complete with Livermore's own comments on the system as applied to actual market action in specific stocks.

This valuable book by a Wall Street great is a collector's item. The sage advice represented by his rules are like commandments. The speculator who is emotionally able to follow them will win in the market, and his obedience to Livermore's philosophy will have been the most important factor in that success.

Neill, Humphrey Bancroft
Tape Reading and Market Tactics: The Three Steps to Successful Stock Trading. Original: New York: B. C. Forbes, 1931. Reprint: Burlington, Vt.: Fraser, 1970. 232 pp. $9.00

The astute market trader is aware of the importance of the tape. It is the composite action of all the people, the blend of their hopes and fears. The tape is therefore a true indicator of market trends and underlines the demand for individual stocks. If this explanation appears too simple, and causes you to wonder why you haven't thought of it before, don't berate yourself. The answers are here in Humphrey B. Neill's excellent analysis of how the tape tells you what to do, how to do it, and the all-important when to do it. I don't intend to imply that there is a magic formula. There is a great deal of common sense and help in distilling the problems of trading into their essential components. They are discussed in this book. Even when you are armed with the book's knowledge, however, you must do it yourself.

The emphasis throughout is on the human equation and how it relates to market action. The tape shows the trader what the crowd is doing. It also spotlights the individual stocks that are popular. This brings us to the importance of volume activity and how it helps us determine our course of action. There are three types of volume: (1) increasing volume during an advance with pauses to consolidate on light volume, indicating that demand exceeds supply and favors a resumption of the advance; (2) increased volume at the top of a rally with no appreciable gain, a churning of transactions without progress, indicating a turning point; (3) a tired advance with stocks up on light volume, showing a lack of demand and marking a "rounding turn" which may be followed by more volume on the downside.

This interpretation of market action crystallizes the investor's answer to the problem of ascertaining the trend of the whole market or his individual stocks. Selection of issues is avoided by Neill, but he does advise working with only three to five at the most and charting their moves until you know them intimately.

There are useful suggestions which bring home the reality that the paper Wall Street is selling you is worth money. Neill suggests that you try to think of each trade in terms of its dollar value rather than of the amount of points. This perspective will help you exert more care in your actions. Trade for the intermediate term so that you can allow a stock time to develop a mature move and make the most profit. The in and out trader can only last for a short time before he runs out of money.

Neill believes that to be successful you must be a cynic, not a pessimist. You should have an open mind without preconceived opinions. For that reason a bear or bull cannot trade successfully. Francis Bacon's "doubt all before you believe anything" applies to the stock market. You are playing the coldest, most bitter game in the world, and everything is fair. The whole idea is to outsmart the other fellow. You must resign from the public, which is always wrong, and diligently study, practice, and be prepared to take losses.

This short summary can't possibly cover the wealth of philosophy that forms the nucleus of this work. Neill does offer a list of "Ten Ways to Lose Money in Wall Street" which tells the reader what *not* to do if he wants to be successful in the stock market:

1. Put your trust in board-room gossip.
2. Believe everything you hear, especially tips.
3. If you don't know, guess.
4. Follow the public.
5. Be impatient.
6. Greedily hang on for the top eighth.
7. Trade on thin margins.
8. Hold to your opinion, right or wrong.
9. Never stay out of the market.
10. Accept small profits and large losses.

The message of this work is clear. You have it within your power to win in Wall Street. Neill has charted the way with a wisdom forged from experience. He clearly sets down the rules which you must follow in order to be successful. They are the maxims and tenets which have withstood the test of time. They represent the interplay of almost two centuries of human emotion. The complex character of today's stock market has not dimmed the excellence of this book. It will remain a classic reference for the trader who loses his market equilibrium. A fresh reading will immediately bring things back into their proper perspective.

Paris, Alexander Perry
  A Complete Guide to Trading Profits. Philadelphia: Whitmore, 1970. 196 pp. $5.95

In *A Complete Guide To Trading Profits*, the author provides the layman with a short course on the technical aspect of trading. There are lucid explanations of the various patterns with the inevitable diagrams showing what they look like on the charts. The only deviation in this normal progression is Paris' admission that he does not rely solely on charts, but allows for the fundamental factors which weigh heavily on the determination of a stock's direction. It is a far cry from the attitude of John Magee who seals himself into his office so that no outside influence of any kind can disrupt or affect his "technical vacuum."
  Technical analysis is classically defined as the study of stock market behavior through the use of a charting technique strictly dependent on the action of the market. Trading in the market connotes a short term approach and is most effective when market analysis is used as a tool.
  The "techno-fundamental" or hybrid approach has its adherents and is a compromise that the technician has made in his attempt to avoid a sterile and inflexible attitude that might trap him into uneducated decisions leading to inevitable failure. By using this method Paris merges both major market systems and improves his chances for investment success.

Scheinman, William X.
  Why Most Investors Are Mostly Wrong Most of the Time. New York: Weybright and Talley, 1970. 268 pp. $10.00

The ingredient in the recipe for stock market success which must be added to fundamental and technical knowledge is an understanding of the psychological factor. The author of this book calls it "divergence analysis," and claims that through the study of the human behavior producing the technical patterns it is possible to anticipate its effect on the market and thus improve the timing of your purchases.
  With a well-documented background that touches all bases, Scheinman points out why most investors are wrong most of the time. He includes among the losers many of the so-called experts, professional money managers, investment advisors, and others who are paid to be right.
  A discussion of the importance of money and inflation is part of this coverage, since the supply of money is an important indicator of stock market trends.

This brings the author to the meat of his subject, charts. The heart of his thesis is introduced by a long dissertation on the technical aspect of market measurement. Sophisticated and unsophisticated buying and selling are measured, along with the volume characteristics which accompany them. These measurements are then superimposed upon fundamental and other technical factors to arrive at conclusive decisions.

Divergence analysis and the timing of stock selections is in its infancy, and much more research must be done to refine its conculsions and improve its accuracy. It is to the author's credit that he does not claim his method to be infallible. By using divergence analysis it is nonetheless possible to gain some psychological insights into crowd behavior and thereby avoid the handicap that emotion places on our stock market decisions.

✓ **Rhea, Robert**
   The Dow Theory: An Explanation of its Development and an Attempt to Define its Usefulness as an Aid in Speculation. Colorado Springs, Colo.: Robert Rhea, 1932. 111 pp.

The third important member of the triumvirate which professed the validity of the Dow Theory was Robert Rhea. He followed Charles Dow and William P. Hamilton who both developed their ideas at the *Wall Street Journal*. Rhea was confined to bed as an invalid for ten years. He made exhaustive studies of the Dow's action and became firmly convinced that it was the only sure method of forecasting stock market movements. A good part of this book is devoted to the published wisdom of Hamilton, both from his *Wall Street Journal* editorials and *The Stock Market Barometer*. Rhea displays the zeal and fervor of a true believer, and his idols were obviously Dow and Hamilton. His devotion to their theory gave his broken life a purpose, and his contribution was a valuable addition to the study of the Dow Theory.

The history of Dow's reticence was stated by Hamilton. The ideas that he had formulated in his editorials were new and needed time to prove their merit. Dow refrained from making definite forecasts. As the years passed Hamilton's precision constantly improved. He made one bad mistake in 1926, thus proving that the Dow Theory is not infallible, a fact Hamilton stressed even when he was accurate with his forecasts. After ten years of study and an exchange of opinions and experiences with students of the theory from all over the country, Rhea defined the terminology of the theory. The successful use of the theory as an aid in stock speculation must be predicated upon the acceptance of several hypotheses:

Manipulation. The day-to-day movement of some stocks and, to some extent, secondary reactions can be manipulated. The primary trend, however, can never be manipulated. Hamilton said, "The market is bigger than all the pools and insiders put together."

The averages discount everything. The averages are a composite index of the hopes, the disappointments, and the knowledge of everyone.

The theory is not infallible. The Dow Theory is successful as an aid in speculation, but it is not infallible.

Dow's three movements. There are three movements which can be in progress at the same time. The first and most important is the primary trend—a bull or a bear market. It may last for several years. The second is the secondary reaction—an important decline in a primary bull market or a rally in a primary bear market. These reactions last from three weeks to three months. The third movement, the daily fluctuation, is unimportant.

Primary bull market. This is a broad upward movement interrupted by secondary reactions, and averaging longer than two years. Prices advance because of investment and speculative buying caused by improved business conditions. There are three phases: (1) revival of confidence; (2) response of stock prices to known improvement in corporate earnings; (3) rampant speculation and apparent inflation—a period when stocks advance on hope and expectations.

Primary bear market. This consists of a long downward movement interrupted by important rallies. It usually lasts 70 percent of the time required for bull markets. There are three phases: (1) abandonment of hopes upon which stocks were bought at inflated prices; (2) selling due to decreased business and earnings; (3) distress selling of sound securities regardless of value.

Secondary reaction. This is an important decline in a bull market or advance in a bear market, lasting from three weeks to three months and generally retracing one-third to two-thirds of the preceding primary price change. The size of a reaction is not a hard and fast rule, but rather only a guide.

Daily fluctuations. Daily movement is almost certain to mislead the trader except when lines are formed. Stocks must be charted because they develop patterns that have forecasting value.

Both averages must confirm. The industrial and railroad averages must be considered together. If one average does not confirm the other, the conclusions are certain to prove misleading.

Determining the trend. Rallies making new highs with declines that end above the previous low points are a bullish sign. Conversely, rallies that can't penetrate old highs, and make new lows, are a bearish indicator.

Lines. These are extended sideways movements for two or three weeks or longer where prices don't vary more than 5 percent. Such movement indicates accumulation or distribution. The former indicates an upside breakout, the latter a downside penetration.

The relation of volume to price movements. An overbought market becomes dull on rallies and active on declines. When a market is oversold it tends to be dull on declines and active on rallies. Bull markets terminate with a period of excessive activity and begin with light volume.

Double tops and double bottoms. These are of little value in forecasting price movements. They are deceptive most of the time. The reason for Rhea's conclusion is that the Dow averages rarely make simultaneous double tops or double bottoms. Hamilton used the double top theory in 1926 when he called a bear market incorrectly.

Individual stocks. Corporate stocks generally rally and decline with the averages. Individual stocks may reflect exclusive conditions and are not representative of any diversified list.

The clarity and precision of Rhea's guide to the Dow Theory are valuable for the speculator and the trader. The complete study and experience of the Dow triumvirate are contained here. The reader must be reminded that omniscience is an unattainable goal. The Dow Theory is not infallible, as its most devoted followers continue to remind us. It is, however, an effective way to determine the trend of the market, and that knowledge is an essential ingredient in our quest for investment success.

✓ **Russell, Richard**
  The Dow Theory Today. New York: Richard Russell Associates, 1960. 119 pp.

This study of the Dow Theory as presented in a series of articles in *Barron's* establishes Richard Russell as Charles H. Dow's foremost modern disciple. He is a worthy successor to William P. Hamilton and Robert Rhea. The author's conversion to the Dow occurred only after a thorough attempt to disprove its method. He is now a believer and is convinced that his duty to the mass of investors is to prove its validity. This book gives evidence that Russell knows his subject and can wear the mantle of responsibility with confidence.

The popularity of the Dow Jones Industrial Average is supreme, but the lay investor rarely knows enough to apply its lessons in his market operations. Talleyrand once said, "Everybody knows more than anybody." Russell claims that this maxim is the essence of the Dow Theory. The combined actions of all the people who are in the stock market determine the direction of prices. The theory maintains that stocks do not drift aimlessly but rise and fall in definite patterns. These movements are charted to determine when the market is in a bull or a bear phase. Dow concluded that there are three simultaneous movements in the market: the primary trend, the secondary reaction (the averages tend to retrace one-third to two-thirds of the primary move), and the final movement. The primary trend is most important for the investor, who should invest with this tide.

The term "Dow Theory" was coined in 1902 by S. A. Nelson in his book *The ABC of Stock Speculation.* The whole theory is contained in the articles Charles H. Dow wrote for the *Wall Street Journal* in 1901 and 1902. Dow never wrote a formal book on his theories, and it remained for William P. Hamilton to succeed him at the journal and expand on his ideas. Russell claims that William Hamilton called the turn in every bull and bear market from December 5, 1903 to December 10, 1929. His columns in *Barron's* and the *Wall Street Journal* are a matter of record. He made a mistake in 1926, announcing a bear market, but then reversed his decision. The Dow Theory is not infallible, but is considered by many market followers to be the most reliable barometer of stock trends and the economy. On October 25, 1929, Hamilton called the end of the bull market with a front page editorial titled "Turn of the Tide." It was followed by Robert Rhea who called the bottom of the bear market in 1932 within a few days. He announced the 1937 bear market, the 1938 bull market, and then died prematurely in 1938.

The Dow theorist does not question why. Rather, he leaves that to economists and statisticians. It is enough for him to know that the theory has been tested and that it works. Most investors don't follow the Dow Theory because of greed, laziness, lack of knowledge, and wishful thinking. "People tend to accumulate or distribute stocks within broad areas of undervaluation or overvaluation. These areas correspond to the formation of bear market bottoms and bull market tops."

Russell sums up the essence of the Dow Theory in his explanation of the formation of a bull market: "The three phases of a bull market are: the rebound from depressed conditions of the previous bear market as they return to known values. The second phase is the longest; when shares advance in recognition of a business improvement in an improving economy. The last phase is a period of prosperity and unbridled optimism. The public enters the market for the first time and buys low priced stocks of little value. Volume becomes excessive and the future looks bright."

It is imperative for the rail and industrial averages to confirm each other's movements as they penetrate earlier highs. The whole sequence of the bull market is repeated on the downside in a bear market, when a trend reversal shows a breakdown to new lows with the same confirmation by the rails. There are three phases of a bear market: (1) stocks selling minus hopes and expectations; (2) stocks reflecting deteriorating business conditions and lower corporate profits; (3) stocks selling at distress or liquidation prices regardless of earnings or value. Bear markets are shorter than bull markets. They last 60 percent of the time and usually retrace 50 percent of the preceding bull market.

The long term investor who has a vault full of IBM, Xerox, Bristol-Myers, or other proven growth stocks has no need of Russell's help. A great many stocks survive the most disastrous bear markets and continue to grow. It is rather for the trader who wants to play the trends successfully that this work should have enormous appeal. However, the universal importance of the Dow Theory and its popularity as an indicator of the market's trend make this book mandatory reading for all concerned investors.

Schultz, Harry D.
Bear Markets: How to Survive and Make Money in Them. Englewood Cliffs, N.J.: Prentice-Hall, 1964. 204 pp. $17.95

Bear markets strike fear into the hearts of investors. Most people close their eyes and ignore their existence, but not Harry Schultz. He tackles the problem with courage and know-how and lays a plan of action before the trader. That is only a small part of this comprehensive guide for stock market profits which provides an insight into the fabric of the market and works in all kinds of markets, bull and bear. But the fearless author, with the courage of his own convictions, concentrates on the bear cycles which, he claims, occur one-third of the time. He further states how important it is to operate in a falling market since prices fall more rapidly in a bear trend than they rise in a bull market.

Sandwiched among the chapters that explain the structure of bear markets and money-making tactics are explanations of the Dow Theory with direct quotations from the disciples of Charles Dow—William P. Hamilton, Robert Rhea, and today's follower, Richard Russell. Their comments sharpen the focus of the discussion of market trends, reactions, etc. Schultz believes that the Dow

Theory is as "old fashioned as a moon rocket," a sarcastic harpoon that elevates the Dow in importance as contrasted with those observers who feel it has outlived its usefulness as a gauge of market action.

A chapter on the advisory service industry actually proves how difficult prediction can be by quoting a number of services before the 1962 crash. Schultz then provides a list of market letters which he feels are worthwhile. Throughout the book he maintains that the investor must do his own work and make his own decisions. An excellent chapter discusses the tactics of short selling which is vital to an aggressive bear market effort. Although it sounds almost easy to win with Schultz's suggested procedures, any trader with actual experience knows how difficult it can be.

The importance of charts is made clear early in the book, and a master index consisting of 220 stock market indexes covers the spectrum of market measurement. There are explanations of a junior master index that contains eighteen relatively dependable indicators. Among the most popular are advance-decline line, odd-lot short sales index, Barron's Confidence Index, short interest, short interest ratio, volume, resistance index, debit balance index, and American Stock Exchange indexes.

An important segment of market knowledge, the psychological aspect of stock market behavior, has a great deal to do with the fear and doubt that bear markets breed. Men are basically optimists and find it impossible to sell short. The crowd is usually wrong, and it remains for the few contrary thinkers to apply the lessons in this book to increase their capital in bear markets, recessions, and depressions.

A product of the author's open-minded attitude toward the stock market reveals itself in his preparedness for bear market periods. It also develops in his discussion of the American economy, which he thinks is in trouble. The confluence of these attitudes results in Schultz's prediction that the United States is headed for the worst crash in its history—one that will dwarf 1929. Somehow, though, the reader has been prepared for the bombshell and will not quake with fear. On the contrary, with the instruction of a master analyst like Schultz, with his index of technical indicators, and his short selling techniques, a crash in stock prices could prove a major opportunity to make a fortune.

Smilen, Kenneth B., and Safian, Kenneth
Investment Profits through Market Timing: A Professional Approach. New York: Smilen & Safian, 1961. 78 pp.

There can be no argument with the authors' thesis that market timing is a valuable element in the search for investment success. It is just as important to know when to buy as it is to select the right stock. This book is concerned with the technical theories that help the trader select the proper market environment for his purchases and sales. The basic theories discussed are the Dow Theory, the Odd-Lot Theory, Barron's Confidence Index, and the Dual Market Principle.

The authors contend that the Dow Theory is no longer valid as a market barometer because its followers did not update it and express it in terms of current events. Dow's disciples apologize for the unrepresentative state of the current average, which is still used almost universally to represent the strength or weakness of the market. The industrial average still represents a majority of the dollar assets of all listed New York Stock Exchange corporations, and as such must have some validity. It still maintains its popularity as a market indicator in all the media.

The Odd-Lot Theory states that the small investor who buys less than one hundred shares of any stock is emotionally motivated, and therefore buys at the top and sells at the bottom. While this may be true, the authors correctly point out that the odd-lotter is right as often as he is wrong. The exception is at long-term tops and bottoms. Charles Dow said that these people buy during the final phase of a primary bull market and sell at the bottom of a primary downtrend. The distinction that Smilen and Safian make is that the market is made up of many kinds of stocks, and it is important to know the reaction in all of these areas.

Just as the odd-lotter is an indicator of what not to do, because he is a non-professional, Barron's Confidence Index helps the investor know what to do by watching the professionals. The advocates of Barron's Confidence Index claim that the sentiment of important investors and institutions forecasts the stock market two to four months in advance. When the yield spread between high grade bonds and those of lower quality begins to narrow, it is a clue that confidence is returning. The stock market will ultimately reflect that confidence. As the yield on bonds declines there is a shift into stocks by those investors who seek to capitalize on a renewal of the bullish sentiment. The authors again stress the fact that the market is a many-faceted area that cannot be approached in a simple way. They have tried to pave the way for the introduction of their own Dual Market Principle.

The Smilen and Safian Dual Market Principle assumes the existence of more than one stock market. The two groups of stocks are classified as cyclical and defensive or growth. The authors claim that these two main bodies of securities act independently of each other. They do, however, move together for long periods of time. The cyclical average is made up of twenty-three companies that are governed by economic conditions. The defensive-growth average has twenty-six quality growth stocks which are termed defensive since time can correct a mistake in timing.

This theory cannot be perfect, by the authors' own admission, because its avowed purpose is to measure human behavior. It is obvious that you can't predict the unpredictable. They feel, however, that their concept provides a better insight into the equity market's behavior than any other method yet devised.

The fundamental analyst who believes that charts are witchcraft and that all that counts is value and earnings would summarily disregard the contribution of these authors. It is the old argument of fundamental versus technical, even though the core of the Dual Market Principle is based on fundamentals. Smilen and Safian believe charts tell nothing. Interpretation is all-important. They assume that a chart traces a trend which continues until it is broken. They must be applauded for the initiative they have shown in developing an accurate method of market prediction through a broad use of both types of analysis.

Staby, Ernest J.
Stock Market Trading: Point and Figure Investing Made Easy. New York: Cornerstone Library, 1970. Distributed by Simon & Schuster. 96 pp. paperback: $1.45

Originally published in 1947, this book proved to be one of the earliest works on the point and figure method of charting. This system has been achieving more popularity with each succeeding year and therefore deserves careful study along with subsequent books of a technical nature.

Staby's book has taken the mystery out of point and figure charting and made it understandable to the lay investor. It has become the classic on the "three-point reversal" method of point and figure charting. In addition to the lessons on the point and figure method and the display of many charts to point out the rules, there are many truths and tenets of market philosophy interspersed among the various chapters.

The author has given the student technician a springboard from which he may pursue a more detailed study of the subject of point and figure charting, a most valuable segment of the technical area of stock market behavior.

Tape, Rollo (Richard Demille Wyckoff)
Studies in Tape Reading: A 1910 Classic on Tape Reading and Stock Market Tactics. Original: New York: Traders Press, 1910. Reprint: Burlington, Vt.: Fraser Publishing Co. 177 pp. paperback: $7.00

It is a common belief that trading on a short-term basis is a lesson in futility. The vagaries of a tricky stock market invariably shatter the confidence of the shrewdest stock operator. Rollo Tape (Richard Demille Wyckoff) declares that the art of tape reading can lead to a successful accumulation of profits, and he proceeds to instruct the reader in the proper method of achieving this goal. His suggestions are based on personal experience, and many actual trades are displayed to prove the point under discussion. Of course, there are many requirements necessary for success in tape reading. The proper mental equipment includes the ability to take a loss, to define the trend, to drill yourself into the right mental attitude, to stifle such emotions as fear, anxiety, elation, and recklessness, and to train your mind to obey its one master—the tape.

At first glance it would appear that the qualifications for being a successful tape reader would rule out almost everybody, especially the average man. The author points out that the average man never makes a success of anything, and thus there is no reason to expect him to be successful as a trader. Success in this field results from years of painstaking effort and concentration. Tape reading is not an exact science, for the factors that influence the market are infinite. No formula is possible. However, it is possible to develop a rough outline for the novice.

What is tape reading? It is not:

1. Looking at the tape to see how prices are running.
2. Reading the news and then buying or selling if the stock acts right.
3. Trading on tips, opinion, or information.

4. Buying because stocks are going up or selling because they look weak.
5. Trading on chart indications or by other mechanical methods.
6. Buying on dips and selling on bulges.
7. A hundred other foolish things practiced by millions without method or calculation.

Tape reading is rather the science of determing from the tape the immediate trend of prices. It is rapid-fire horse sense which helps the tape reader to make deductions with every shift in the market. He makes a decision with coolness and precision and acts upon it with alacrity. Supply and demand must be gauged. The tape tells the news before the tickers and newspapers do, and before it becomes current gossip. Everything from a war to a famine is reflected on the tape. The tape reader plays it close with a stop-loss order to protect his profit and limit his loss. The pure tape player does not carry his stock overnight. He wants a clean slate for the next day and would not want news at night to affect his holding.

Wyckoff has several suggestions for the beginner. At the outset he says that if you are lazy, don't start—tape reading is hard work. If you need money, don't begin—start right or not at all. Start small, don't overtrade, and select a broker who can give you and your orders close attention. Orders should generally be given at the market. Trade in high-priced stocks since they range several points in a day. It is advisable to trade in one stock at a time. Stocks, like human beings, have distinct habits and characteristics. Their moods must be studied if you expect to make money. Protect your profit with stop orders which are two points below your purchase. Use a trailing stop as the price goes up in your favor. Close your trades when the tape tells you to close, when your stop is hit, when your position is not clear, and when you have a large or a satisfactory profit.

The principal forces that are constantly at work in the market are accumulation and distribution, demand and supply, and support and resistance. The more adept you become in detecting these elements the more successful you will be. You must switch your position and go with the trend. Don't hold stocks for both short and long term; a conflict will arise when you see a down market and feel like selling out all your holdings. The author feels that so many opportunities for a few points appear that it is more important to try for a multitude of trades. Tape reading is the only known method which gets you in at the start of a move, keeps you posted throughout, and gets you out when it is over. It has made a fortune for the few who have followed it. It is an art in which you can become highly expert and successful as experience refines your techniques and teaches you what to avoid.

The experience of many years in the stock market has taught many wise traders that short-term trades are fraught with danger. The fickle market can make the most confident trader numb with fear, an emotion Wyckoff tells you to avoid. It is easy to write the rules but quite difficult to carry them out. Today's market is complex, with less leverage for the quick trade because of higher commissions. While the lure of fast profits will always tempt the unwary, to a great extent the advice in this book—the use of stop orders, playing the trend, and all the rest—will serve to protect the trader. This classic work will always instill renewed confidence in the battalions of profit-seekers. The hard work is worth it; success nevers comes easy.

Warren, Ted
How to Make the Stock Market Make Money for You. Los Angeles: Sherbourne Press, 1966. 318 pp. $5.95

It is unwise to disregard the advice of a man who has successfully demonstrated a method of reaping the rewards the stock market has to offer. That he interrupted his formal education only serves to reinforce the author's conviction that you don't need a doctorate in business administration to make money in the stock market. Ted Warren's early retirement to a life of world travel, free of financial need, should whet the reader's appetite for the key to his winning method. It is simply the use of long-term charts.

The author demonstrates his stock selection with a profusion of charts. He states that when a stock has formed a long-term base, it should be purchased for the inevitable rise. You must be patient since it does not happen immediately and may take years. But doesn't it take years for you to save money in the bank after working hard? Following the breakout on the upside, the stock usually moves at a 45 degree angle. When it breaks the trendline on the down side, it is time to sell. He claims that you should make 200 percent or more in a couple of years.

To implement his theory of success, Warren shows charts of Doctor Pepper, Pepsi Cola, Bond Stores, and Belding Hemingway, among others. These served him well, and allowed him to live in leisure and to travel with his wife to such places as Alaska and Australia. His success is the prime example his book can offer the reader. Although the chapters which deal in a negative way with floor trading and mutual funds are redundant, his method is technically sound and deserves the consideration of all investors.

FUNDAMENTAL ANALYSIS

✓**Bellemore, Douglas**
The Strategic Investor. New York: Simmons-Boardman, 1963. 394 pp. $7.50

It is heartening to find a book which counters the common misconception that the average person can't build a sum large enough to make life easier at retirement by investing in the stock market. The author claims that a conservative investor, employing $500 a year for the first ten years from the age of thirty, can accumulate $100,000 by the time he retires. An aggressive investor, with more time and effort devoted to the management of his portfolio can build an equity of $200,000. To dramatize his prediction of possible investment success, Bellemore says that an aggressive individual who invests $1,000 a year from age thirty can build his holdings to $250,000.

The method which this book emphasizes is regular investing, regardless of stock market levels, combined with buy and hold techniques. It is not a book for a trader, since the vast majority of nonprofessional, in-and-out traders have a poor record of success over a long period of years.

After establishing the goal which he asserts is possible, the author proceeds to explain how to gain the knowledge necessary for starting this program. He sets different standards for the conservative and the aggressive individual. He explores financial history for clues to understanding inflation, human nature, price-earning ratios, earnings, dividends, and stock trends. A whole section is devoted to the risks and pitfalls which should be avoided. It is interesting to note that only a few millionaires have made their money by buying stock. Most of them inherited their wealth, made it through stock options, or were movie stars.

In rounding out his advice, Bellemore points out sources of information and includes a discussion of security analysis for the layman to prepare him for his dollar cost averaging program of equity accumulation. It seems odd that Bellemore does not mention mutual funds at any time during his discussion. It is clear that the only difference between the author's system and that offered by the investment trusts is that, with the latter, the investor's money is constantly managed by professionals who assume the burden of stock selection, portfolio surveillance, and management, consistent with the objective of the particular fund.

In spite of that oversight, this overall view of the investment potential of common stock, careful explanation of the do's and don'ts, the how's, and the why's, is intelligently compressed into a volume which arrogantly predicts the reality of building a substantial equity with only a modest annual contribution, an equity impossible without the compound growth which can be achieved through common stock investment.

Crane, Burton
The Sophisticated Investor: A Guide to Stock Market Profits. Revised and expanded by Sylvia Crane Eisenlohr. New York: Simon & Schuster, 1964. 249 pp. $4.95

The title of this work should give the reader a clue to its intended audience. There are many investors who flatter themselves into believing that they are sophisticated, but would be found wanting in a test of their market knowledge. Burton Crane, who covered Wall Street for the *New York Times* for many years, has gathered a wealth of investment information for the advanced market follower. A neophyte would find the bulk of Crane's suggestions difficult to fathom and should study the multitude of fundamentals which can be found in beginner books.

The substance of Crane's book can be a great help to an investor or trader, for it analyzes the experiences of many Wall Streeters and states a course of action that should be followed in a particular situation. What is most important is that time has not altered the validity of Crane's conclusions. Here are a few examples of the author's advice which show that contrary action would be more profitable than the popular course which the public usually follows:

Never buy on split or merger news. There are many thousands of people who wait for the split announcement or the merger to be effective before they buy a stock. The fact is that forces are at work long before the news is announced which adequately discount the benefits of a split or a merger. Records are shown that clearly prove there is no advantage to be gained by strictly buying splits and mergers. It is more profitable to buy on the rumor and sell on the news.

The *long-term trap*. Crane claims that almost 90 percent of the stockholders are in the 30 percent bracket or lower and shouldn't worry about short term gains. It is a sop to the vanity of the investor with a profit both to advertise it to his broker and friends and to flatter himself into thinking his tax bracket is so high that he must wait longer than six months to take his profit. In too many cases the profit vanishes and the pride with it.

Don't buy a stock that isn't moving. It is better to wait until somebody else starts; then hop aboard. You can't be sure how long you will have to wait for a stock to act well, so why tie your money up? Purchase stocks when they are making new highs, not when they are on the bottom. One maxim that all of Wall Street agrees is necessary to avoid large losses and maximize profits is to "cut your losses and let your profits run." Crane goes along with that and expands on it with a chapter on how to use charts for profit—the technical approach to the market.

Chapters that reveal the author's experience deal with growth stocks, leverage, margin, and treasury bonds. In each case the explanation forms a clear recommendation for a preferred method of trading or investing. The most valuable essay asserts that a person of moderate intelligence can forecast the four major periods of the stock market that will help improve his timing. Crane believes that there are three steps in market forecasting: (1) from economic development to the government's reaction; (2) from the government's reaction to the public's reaction; (3) from the public's reaction to the stock. It is made obvious that there are telltale signs which telegraph the direction of the market, and, in a controlled economic climate where the government and the Federal Reserve Board expand and contract the supply of money and interest rates, these make the investor's job of predicting the turns in the market less difficult.

The written record of a man's accomplishments can do no less than light the way for those who come after him in a complex field of endeavor. This book is not meant for the entertainment of some nor does it criticize the actions or proposals of others. It is an attempt to offer the sophisticated investor an opportunity to sharpen his techniques.

Davis, Benton W.
  Davis on Dow. Larchmont, N.Y.: American Research Council, 1964. 151 pp. $6.95

Benton Davis predicted Dow 1,000 when it was unpopular and is now on record for Dow 2,000. He has positive reasons for believing in the inevitable upward movement of the American economy and the resultant *exponential* growth in the Dow Jones industrial average. It was the author who coined that phrase to describe the dynamic surge in the stock market's most popular indicator. His enthusiasm extends the Newtonian law of motion to the movement of stocks.

He claims that a stock in motion tends to remain in motion. This also implies that the demand for stocks tends to create new demand.

Davis devotes several chapters to a discussion of the social and economic forces which influence the movement of stock prices. They include population growth, inflation, money and credit (the lubricant), labor, and automation. He concludes that they all play a part in his exponential growth theory. The stage is now set for the author's ideas on how to play the game.

Under the old market pattern of boom and bust you could buy the leaders after a bust period and expect a rise equal to the market. In 1951 Davis saw that only a few stocks broke badly, and others actually climbed against the trend. He then determined that the old technique was outmoded. That technique consisted of a stock-bond averaging method whereby you shifted out of stocks and into bonds as the market went higher. As the market dipped to new lows you sold the bonds and moved back into stocks. Davis feels that today's stock market is a market of stocks. While certain issues move inexorably higher, some stocks stand still, and a good number of others work lower. It must have been unpleasant to see your stocks rolled over into a bear market in bonds while the stocks you sold doubled, tripled, and split some more.

Davis' method no longer recognizes the need to trade stocks for bonds in critical periods. "The objective is to keep funds fully invested at all times in the best performing issues." These stocks can be found in the charts. The best groups of stocks usually change with the market's tendency to rotate into new leaders. As your stocks show signs of weakness they should be replaced by others which show stronger technical characteristics. This method helps the investor cut his losses and let his profits run. It is an attempt to buy only the best stocks and stay with them until they cease to perform.

The constructive nature of this book should appeal to the reader who avidly seeks an investment approach with a good chance of success. It proceeds from the basic assumption that the market is headed higher and offers the author's best plan for achieving trading profits. The aggressive investor might well copy the plan Davis suggests if he can adopt the optimistic attitude that is necessary for its execution.

√Fisher, Philip A.
Common Stocks and Uncommon Profits, rev. ed. New York: Harper & Row, 1958. 164 pp. $5.95

When a successful investment counselor takes the effort to detail the method he has used to make money for his clients, the reader should regard it as an important formula which should be emulated. Since the author's company was capable of serving only a handful of people, he felt it his duty to describe his methods for the many investors whose custom he was forced to turn down. This book does that job adequately and effectively. It deals with the basic principles of what stock to buy, when to buy it, and, most important, when to sell it. Patience and self-discipline are two qualities an investor must have to make this method work.

There are fifteen important criteria which Fisher uses to determine whether a stock is a worthwile buy. While this list does not discuss each one at length, it displays a concern for the qualitative factors that are the standard of company measurement. In the author's own words, here is the list:

1. Does the company have products or services with sufficient market potential to make possible a sizable increase in sales for at least several years?

2. Does management have a determination to continue to develop products or processes that will still further increase total sales potentials when growth potentials of currently attractive product lines have been largely exploited?

3. How effective are the company's research and development efforts in relation to its size?   o

4. Does the company have an above-average sales organization?

5. Does the company have a worthwhile profit margin?

6. What is the company doing to maintain or improve profit margins?

7. Does the company have outstanding labor and personnel relations?

8. Does the company have outstanding executive relations?

9. Does the company have depth of management?

10. How good are the company's cost analysis and accounting controls?

11. Are there other aspects of the business, somewhat peculiar to the industry involved, which will give the investor important clues as to how outstanding the company may be in relation to its competition?

12. Does the company have a short-range or long-range outlook in regard to profits?

13. In the foreseeable future will the growth of the company require sufficient equity financing so that the larger number of shares then outstanding will largely cancel the existing stockholders' benefit from this anticipated growth?

14. Does the management talk freely to investors about its affairs when things are going well but "clam up" when troubles or disappointments occur?

15. Does the company have a management of unquestionable integrity?

The comprehensive nature of the requirements Fisher demands for his investments make it almost a certainty that with patience the stock market will prove the value of his caution. The rewards of this thorough analysis can make quantum growth possible for anyone, or so he implies with the record of his own selections.

Along with the valuable list of things to do, the author has a list of ten don'ts that will save you money and pain. They are the following: (1) don't buy promotional companies; (2) don't ignore a good stock just because it is traded over the counter; (3) don't buy a stock just because you like the "tone" of its annual report; (4) don't assume that the high price at which a stock may be selling is necessarily an indication that further growth in those earnings has largely already been discounted in the price; (5) don't quibble over eighths and quarters; (6) don't overstress diversification; (7) don't be afraid of buying on a war scare; (8) don't forget Gilbert and Sullivan (the flowers that bloom in the spring, etc.); (9) don't fail to consider time as well as price in buying a true growth stock; (10) don't follow the crowd.

There is a strong thread of optimism evident in Fisher's view of the American economy. In fact he states that the next fifty years will be a golden age, offering even higher risks and rewards than the past one hundred. The investor can now unearth those companies that will share in that glorious future. He can win those uncommon profits that Fisher promises by a careful reading and a faithful application of the lessons to be learned from this book.

Graham, Benjamin
The Intelligent Investor, 3rd rev. ed. New York: Harper & Row, 1965. 332 pp. $5.95

The wisdom of over half a century of investment experience by the father of fundamental analysis is contained in this book for the lay investor. Graham reveals the formulas that have guided him through the good years and the bad. They have withstood the test of time and therefore deserve the reader's thoughtful consideration and earnest application. In developing his theories for the reader, the author makes known his reasons for dissatisfaction with other popular investment philosophies. His words and thoughts are the most potent weapons for disputing those who find fault with his defensive approach to investing.

Experience has taught Graham the valuable lessons which developed into his investment principles. In essence he advocates four main steps in the selection of a portfolio: (1) adequate diversification; (2) buy large, prominent, conservatively financed companies; (3) they should have a record of continous dividend payment; (4) they should have a reasonably low price earnings ratio. Allied to this program is his central concept of investing, a concept he calls "margin of safety." In the bond market, the margin of safety is the "enterprise value" over debt of the margin of earnings over charges. In the common stock area, the expected earning power considerably above the going rate for bonds is the margin of safety. Graham insists that to be successful you must know your business and run it yourself. Don't let yourself be guided by what is popular. Rather, do what is right. Do not enter an operation unless your calculation shows it has a fair chance of showing a reasonable profit. Have the courage of your knowledge and experience. Courage becomes the supreme virtue after adequate knowledge. Above all be guided by Graham's tenet that investments should be based on arithmetic, not optimism.

There are warnings throughout the book which grow out of Graham's obsession with value, intrinsic worth, assets, etc. He cautions the investor to avoid new issues. He bans the purchase of all stocks that sell over twenty-five times earnings. This effectively excludes all growth stocks. His stated opinion is "never buy a stock immediately after a substantial rise or sell one immediately after a substantial drop." This contradicts the technician's claim that it is those stocks which make new highs and are in established uptrends that are the most desirable to own. Graham claims that "true investment principle is the opposite of the technician's argument that a stock should be bought because it has advanced and should be sold because it has declined." He feels that value will out. The intelligent investor has no cause to berate the perversity of the stock market, for in this very perversity lie both his opportunities and his ultimate profits.

There are several areas of Wall Street that come in for Graham's criticism. He believes that traders lose money in the end. He is partial to closed-end funds since they can be bought at 80 percent of net asset value (a 20 percent discount) while open-end funds (mutual funds) cost 108 percent (8 percent sales charge). Graham does not mention no-load funds which have no sales charge or load. The prevalence of wide diversification is a pragmatic repudiation of the fetish of selectivity to which Wall Street constantly pays lip service. Graham brands all services, market letters, and research predictions for their "Delphic phrasing that adjusts itself successfully to whatever the future brings." It is worthy of note that Graham, who has observed the market since 1914, believes that the French proverb, "Plus ça change, plus c'est le meme chose," applies to Wall Street. It means that the more things change the more they remain the same.

The importance of the fundamental concepts which Graham is known for and espouses so fervently in this book cannot be overemphasized. It should be re-quired reading for every investor. However, few investors read books on their favorite subject or take their investments seriously enough. A more careful public would be gratified at the rewards that their efforts would bring. For, as Graham puts it, "to achieve satisfactory investment results is easier than most people realize; to achieve superior results is harder than it looks."

Kamm, Jacob O.
Making Profits in the Stock Market, 3rd rev. ed. Cleveland: World, 1966. 180 pp. $4.95

If the reasoned, intelligent plan that this book proposes were followed more often by the average investor, success in the stock market would be a common occurrence. The author draws on his experience as an economist and financial counselor to analyze the proper approach to the market. He is convinced that it is necessary to apply an overall theory or plan. The core of this book is an out-line of the essential information needed to initiate a sound investment program.

The book is composed of four major segments: (1) attributes for stock market success; (2) what to buy; (3) when to act; (4) points to remember. The most im-portant prerequisites Kamm cites for investment success would rule out the vast majority of stockholders. His list of attributes includes common sense, unselfish-ness, patience, and courage—formidable and almost impossible criteria for the average investor to meet.

The heart of the book is contained in the second section, which is concerned with what to buy. There is a thorough description of securities, an explanation of the advantages of stock ownership, and a review of the defensive and aggres-sive treatment of assets. The author then launches into his studied analysis of common stock values. He points out the necessity for a hedge against the depreciation of assets through diversification and warns against overdiversifica-tion, "too many eggs . . . may result in no eggs hatching." The fundamental things to look for in common stocks are growth, low labor cost, and good management.

Now that the investor has been warned and informed, Kamm lists several of the conditions that should exist before he commits his funds. Economic and political conditions must be favorable, and industry and company conditions should pass his strict analysis. He may then develop his investment plan. Kamm explains dollar averaging, formula plans, compounding, and how to set up a portfolio. The final chapter sums up the author's conviction that there are four methods of making a profit: income stocks, growth stocks, special situations, and cyclical stocks. He believes that the experts who forecast stock information are wrong. He does this to reinforce his belief that the investor should make his own decisions. When a decision to purchase a stock is based on the background requirements outlined in this book the investor can truly sleep at night. He can be confident that the value analysis he has given his purchase will assure him of productive results within the reasonable period that patience demands.

Knowlton, Winthrop
Growth Opportunities in Common Stocks. New York: Harper & Row, 1965. 176 pp. $4.95

Most investors lose money because their buy and sell decisions are based on the emotions of the crowd—greed, fear, and boredom. A rare study of the potential for gain in the stock market is outlined by the author, who uses his experience as an analyst to substantiate his claims. He develops a strategy for investment, tells how to structure a portfolio, and explains the elements that make for corporate success. It is inevitable that the author should list a group of stocks and examine their merits in light of his requirements. It all adds up to an important case for the purchase of growth stocks.

The rational approach discussed in this book excludes wild dreams of overnight success or the big killings that most speculators seek. Knowlton expects a common stock to provide an annual return of 8 percent (3 percent from dividends and 5 percent from growth). He lists several suggestions for the investor: (1) keep only half your money in common stocks; (2) don't try to guess the market; (3) don't buy too many stocks—five or six will be enough for a portfolio of $100,000; (4) don't be too income minded; (5) know your objective; (6) buy only those companies that are successful, those that have control over their destiny.

An important element in stock selection is an adequate appreciation of the elements of corporate success. All successful companies innovate new products and services cheaper and faster, and are more flexible than their competitors. Another characteristic of a successful company is that it creates its own market for its new products. This market is usually large and growing. It is generally difficult for newcomers to break into the business, and the company always has adequate financial resources. Management should be modest and not too anxious to boast about its good performance. The return on invested capital is the most important concern of a business. Earnings growth and rate of return is the statistical test a company must pass to be successful. If that criterion is met, the company has no need to trumpet its achievements; the market is aware of its performance almost before it happens.

Knowlton analyzes ten companies with a view toward making the reader a successful lay investor, not a professional securities analyst. He states that per share earnings growth is a function of (1) sales growth, (2) profit margins, and

(3) capitalization (number of shares outstanding). The tests are applied to Avon Products, Hershey, Magnavox, Bristol-Myers, Consolidated Cigar (now a division of Gulf & Western Industries), Xerox, IBM, Minnesota Mining and Manufacturing, Pitney Bowes, and Fairchild Camera. The author concludes that Xerox, Avon Products, IBM, Consolidated Cigar, and Pitney Bowes should be standouts in the years ahead.

Problem companies can be bought on an interim basis, but you must be careful to determine whether the problem is under control. There are two types of problem companies, environmental and internal. The former suffer from competition and the desire to hold or increase their share of the market. This results in a sharp burst of capital spending followed by overcapacity, price-cutting, and the inevitable profit margin deterioration. The internal disorders of a problem company are an old, high-cost plant, stingy research, a weak product line, a strained balance sheet, and, obviously, a sleepy management.

Before you buy a problem company you must define the problem:

1. Is it out of management's control or does it take a more aggressive approach?

2. Avoid a company with a serious problem. There are too many investment opportunities to bother struggling with these problems.

3. Find companies that are in good financial condition.

4. Check other companies in the same industry.

5. Don't buy too soon after a management change.

6. Limit your investment in problem companies to those with dividends so that you receive a return on your investment while you wait for the recovery.

The essence of Knowlton's well conceived thesis is that you can mine the wealth that Wall Street offers. An intelligent approach through study, application, and careful selection of growth stocks can lead you to a financially secure future. It can also provide you with the rare thrill and satisfaction of success in an arena that has struck down some of America's most astute financial minds.

Laurence, Michael

Playboy's Investment Guide. Chicago: Playboy Press, 1971. 276 pp. $7.95

A unique blend of research, experience, and literary style has enabled the author of this book to develop a useful investment guide. It covers five major areas—the stock market, mutual funds, the bond market, collector's items, and the commodities market. The subject areas originally appeared as articles in *Playboy* magazine from 1967–1970. Michael Laurence is the youngest senior editor of the magazine, and his articles on commodities won him the coveted Gerald M. Loeb award for investment writing in 1968.

The material on the stock market is not new or startlingly different from that of other books, but Laurence's prose delights the reader with its originality and seems to lend a glamour and fascination to the same tired, old investment information. The stock market's ability to make money for the investor is shown at the outset by the example of two men who became instant billionaires with the public sale of their companies' stock—H. Ross Perot and Edwin C. Whitehead. The names of their companies are Electronic Data Systems and Technicon. It is not as easy to make money in the ordinary way by selecting stocks from the thousands of companies on the exchanges and over the counter.

The techniques of selection offer the investor management of his own funds through the fundamental approach of analyzing a company's financial status, its earnings, current price, and other statistical data which determine the worth of a potential investment and whether a stock is underpriced or overvalued. The technical approach resorts to charts which determine the trends of stocks in such a way as to point out those which are about to move up to higher levels. Each approach is exclusive and should be used individually, although it is possible to find hybrid technicians who value fundamentals. Laurence feels "that the two techniques appeal to such different personalities that the investor would have to approach schizophrenia to master them simultaneously."

For the investor who hasn't the time, interest, or knowledge to make his own decisions, the guide develops a thorough and clear idea of how mutual funds can be your substitute decision makers. For their professional help you are asked to pay a hefty sales charge or load. Laurence launches into a statistical comparison of the load, no-load, and closed-end funds. It is comprehensive, important, and throws the harpoon of doubt into the whole question of how worthwhile some mutual funds really are. It achieves the desired effect if the reader is led to do some serious thinking and is forced to make the decision which his own know-how can provide. It will improve his chances for success.

The bond market, which has found a new popularity since the tight money market of 1969–1970 and with triple A bond yields of 9 percent, is dissected with surgeon-like precision by the pen of Laurence. He points out that the small investor or odd-lotter, who is accused of being wrong all the time by selling stocks at the bottom, has proved to be right by his buying of bonds in large quantities at a time when yields were the highest. The stock-bond yield spread made common stocks look like a poor investment by comparison. It was also a time of great fear, illiquidity, and unemployment. The safety of bonds and the high yields appealed to the scared little investor.

The two subjects that make up the balance of the book are collector's items and commodities. They don't pertain to the stock market and therefore are not important to our subject. The point made rather forcefully by the author is that despite the publicity of huge profits in objets d'art or stamps, the market for collector's items is treacherous. Buyers are not always available when you want to sell. The commodity section which won a prize for Laurence is a masterpiece and a revelation for the uninitiated. The most startling part is an explanation of the commodity tax straddle which permits you legally to put off a short-term profit from one year to the next, and thus avoid payment of high tax rates.

Laurence excites the reader with his treatment of an analytical subject that could be dull and soporific. He uses terms such as "investment calculus," "mathematical legerdemain," "free-enterprise firmament," "arithmetical alchemy," and "silky-smooth sexual hemispheres" to liven up his guide for the eager novice who is anxious to discover a way toward investment profit. It is obvious that he has succeeded. Laurence comments that "commodities provide action . . . the sort of mercurial price movement that dilates the speculative veins and lets the adrenalin gush through unobstructed." This excitement leads the tempted reader to further explore the avenues for investment that he has seen in this guide. It is tragic that the laws of probability show that only a handful of the 32 million shareholders now on record will ever set eyes on this worthy book.

Loeb, Gerald M.
The Battle for Investment Survival. New York: Simon & Schuster, 1965.
320 pp. paperback: $2.25; hardbound: $5.95

The years have amply rewarded Gerald M. Loeb. He has achieved a stature in Wall Street that few people in our country's history have attained. He is a legend in his own time. The reverence and esteem accorded him by millions of professional and lay investors give the lie to the impression that there are no heroes in Wall Street. Gerald M. Loeb comes very close to filling that role.

His more than fifty years of investment know-how are gathered together under the title of *The Battle For Investment Survival.* This book has stood the test of time, having been in print continuously since 1935. This success is a testament to the worth and value of its contents—the advice which a thirsting public has sought from "the Dean of Wall Street."

It would be impossible to cover everything that Loeb discusses in his many articles of interest, but there are major areas of stress in his cornucopia of market advice that bear mentioning.

The careful reader would find a repetition of the idea that concentration is better than diversification. "Put all your eggs in one basket and watch that basket." Find a stock you like and buy it. Buy it on the way up. If it goes down about 10 percent, sell it and cut your losses. Never put your stock away and forget about it. Buy the stocks that are making new highs and have the most volume.

In the galaxy of stock market personalities Gerald M. Loeb retains a place of honor, and always will. The fruits of his career have not been saved for the elite few, but are ready to be harvested by anyone who is ambitious enough to absorb the lessons of his book. In Loeb's view, "It is not enough to know the fundamentals of successful investing, it takes an extra something, experience, judgment, and flair." Unfortunately not too many people have those essentials. For those who do, Loeb's coaching will do the rest.

Loeb, Gerald M.
The Battle for Stock Market Profits. New York: Simon & Schuster, 1971.
352 pp. $7.95

"The Dean of Wall Street," Gerald M. Loeb, a veteran of more than fifty years and one who has won more than his share of battles in the quest for success in the stock market war, has distilled the accumulated wisdom of five decades and poured it liberally into the more than one hundred chapters of this book.

The Battle for Stock Market Profits follows his best-selling *The Battle for Investment Survival.* Loeb claims that it is truly a struggle to wrest the riches that

Wall Street offers, but it is not out of the reach of the average individual. Of course, one must be armed with the proper weapons, just as a soldier in battle. There is no magic formula for winning, but it helps to have "experience, contacts, and flair." Before gathering actual, day-to-day experience, this writer suggests absorbing the many lessons and ideas which the "Wizard of Wall Street" has set forth in this worthwhile book. It is fortunate for those who have an interest in the stock market now, and in years to come, that a person with Loeb's wisdom and experience has also had the ability and inclination to put his thoughts in written form. Many of the most brilliant people in the stock market's history have failed to record their ideas and therefore have deprived us of valuable insights which can help us find our way to financial gain.

The many chapters in Loeb's book offer the investor a fund of advice from which he can formulate an attitude best suited to his own personal and psychological approach to the market. Investing is a lonely job and one which each person has to work out for himself. Few people can concentrate a large portion of their investment in one or two stocks and sleep soundly at night. Loeb reminds us that those who do this successfully reap the largest rewards. The nuggets of this gold mine of market information read like commandments and deserve the attention and respect of all thinking investors. You must bear in mind that their author has been so successful for so long a time that he has become a Wall Street legend.

Markstein, David L.
Nine Roads to Wealth. New York: McGraw-Hill, 1970. 216 pp. $6.95

In *Nine Roads to Wealth,* author David Markstein points the way to riches in many different areas. In each one he has painstakingly outlined the method of using leverage to gain the necessary foothold for achieving success.

Stocks, bonds, mutual funds, real estate, commodities, franchising, and mergers all offer a fascinating potential for rapid profits, and Markstein offers examples of how to proceed in each area. He warns that the use of leverage cuts two ways and does not offer guaranteed success.

The roads are there. The methods are explained in a lucid, informed way. Those readers who dare to try have the blueprint for dynamic success and are half-way home. The rest is up to them and their courage, motivation, and intelligence.

✓**Tso, Lin**
The Investor's Guide to Stock Market Profits in Seasoned and Emerging Industries. New York: Frederick Fell, 1969. 494 pp. $14.95

The concentrated knowledge and experience of one of Wall Street's most respected analysts is presented in a readable book for all who invest in stocks. There are few comprehensive, analytical guides to America's major industries that offer a condensed, literate coverage that the average reader can understand. This work does not contain difficult and undecipherable equations, ratios, and other professional data; it is for everybody.

Tso departs from the conventional treatment which investment books usually give to utilities, basic and natural resource industries. He does cover them adequately in scope and depth of treatment while succeeding in his attempt at uniformity. In addition he extends his coverage to such new areas as consumer and service industries, science and technology companies, and other special groups.

The author cautions the reader to be alert to political, social, and economic trends that change investment opportunities. He also clearly implies that emerging industries offer more opportunity for rapid growth than mature industries. He doesn't think public utilities are particularly attractive for investment because their rates are subject to government regulation. If the long term trend is toward more control, these regulated industries should be avoided. This group includes electric, gas, and telephone companies.

Several facts not obvious to the average investor are explained by the author and make good investment sense. For example, Tso is not so bullish on the automobile stocks, but feels there is a more valid reason for growth in the auto replacement parts market. This industry's sales primarily depend on the number of vehicles in use rather than the number produced every year. It is not vulnerable to slowdowns in new car sales, strikes, etc. Aftermarket sales are always up since the number of cars increases every year. The same facts generally apply to the replacement tire market.

Informative lessons such as these enlighten the reader throughout the book. Appraising each industry, the author covers mainly industry characteristics, diversification, industry problems, competition, foreign markets, and summarizes with an appraisal of the industry as an investment. In the newly developing industries Tso covers pollution control, medical technology, cable television, oceanography, and electronics. He cautions that the rotation of interest in the stock market changes investor sentiment from growth to cyclical to exotic areas and that it is important to be alert to these changes.

The organization and analysis of America's industries is a boon for the investor, broker, and analyst as a stock selection guide. A clue to those industries which the author thinks are best can be found in the composition of his own publicly held LTC Corporation. It should be noted that he has concentrated his emphasis in pharamceuticals, biologicals, and chemicals.

MUTUAL FUNDS

Dacey, Norman F.
Dacey on Mutual Funds. New York: Crown, 1970. 272 pp. paperback: $4.95; hardbound: $6.95

It seems to me that everyone knows about mutual funds, and that another detailed book explaining it all over again is unnecessary. Dacey, who is most well known for his best-selling book, *How to Avoid Probate,* thought that it was important to bring the public up to date on the subject.

The value of funds is unquestioned here, and their long-term record of performance is proof of their value. Is it necessary for the author to impugn the honesty of registered representatives to prove his point? If research departments of brokerage houses use "tea leaves" to divine which stocks to recommend, can fund managers do more? Does a positive recommendation of funds need the oblique disparagement of insurance companies, the Securities and Exchange Commission, and the self-same money managers with whom Dacey asks you to entrust your money?

Yes, the author makes almost as valid a case against the people in a fiduciary capacity as he does for them. After insisting that registered representatives prey on the emotions of investors for the purpose of stampeding them in and out of stocks because of commission, Dacey discusses the mismanagement of all those funds that bought letter stock thus immobilizing large amounts of money. He continues by blasting the SEC's inefficiency and especially its delay in approving his own Dacey Composite Fund.

While the author makes a strong case against some fund managers, he nonetheless feels that there are many responsible people in the industry. In a short epilogue, he stresses the benefits that can be obtained from prudent selection of mutual funds. Here are some of his closing words:

"By disclosing the imperfections of the Mutual Fund Industry I did not intend to deter you from employing the valuable services of funds. My purpose was to give you facts which would enable you to make an informed judgment in selecting a fund. For those of you who want financial independence by retirement age, or who are now retired but want to preserve what you have accumulated and make it productive, I know of no better way of achieving your objective than by employing the professional investment management obtainable through Mutual Funds."

✓Frank, Robert
Successful Investing through Mutual Funds. New York: Hart, 1969. 222 pp. paperback: $2.45

Mutual funds are the fastest growing investment vehicle in the United States, and the millions of shareholders old and new are entitled to a book which is written by a disinterested person whose sole purpose is to inform the public. That is precisely what Robert Frank has done.

In particularly well written and easily understood prose the author covers the whole field of funds explaining what they are, reviewing their history, detailing their advantages and objectives, and pointing out their risks. In a brief chapter, the record of performance is surveyed, and a careful review of the prospectus is explored.

In quick succession the author discusses the acquisition charges, no-load funds, the go-go funds, types of plans, management fees, and the legal protections provided. In a final chapter he guides the reader in making a selection to suit his own particular situation.

Amid the continuing debate over the abuses of the mutual fund industry, asset growth has continued inexorably. While the SEC resolves the problems of high sales charges and excessive management fees, etc., the public will continue to entrust its money to the professionals who are competent to invest and manage it. In writing this book Robert Frank has performed a service for those many thousands of neophytes who are eager to have a comprehensive study of the mutual fund concept.

Investment Company Institute
The Money Managers. New York: McGraw-Hill, 1967. 135 pp. paperback: $1.95

The Investment Company Institute is firmly convinced that the record of mutual fund growth and performance taken together is ample proof of the efficacy of that form of investment. Statistical evidence is amply supplied, and the geometrics of mutual fund growth stagger the imagination. It is not outside the realm of possibility, for example, that within a reasonable period of time institutional trading may become 80 or 90 percent of all stock trading.

The institute claims that there is no substitute for the benefits of mutual fund investment despite the specter of its size and importance. Professional management, diversification, and liquidity are the trinity which offer the average investor something more than is possible with his meager sum if it were invested in one or two stocks.

You cannot argue with the record or the basic soundness of the mutual fund concept. Its record also proves the value of long-term growth and dollar-cost averaging as the most certain method of achieving investment success.

Kaplan, Gilbert Edmund, and Welles, Chris
The Money Managers. New York: Random House, 1969. 261 pp. $6.95

The *Institutional Investor* is an exclusive monthly magazine with a controlled circulation of some 21,000 institutional money managers who are charged with the management of security portfolios of mutual funds, pension funds, insurance companies, universities, and foundations. Gilbert Kaplan and Chris Welles have put together nineteen articles which appeared in their magazine, and the public now has the opportunity to look behind the scenes at some of the most exciting "stars" in Wall Street.

Each of the profiles presented carefully details the unique qualities which set these money managers apart from the crowd, and which are in essence responsible for their success. They are generally young, in their thirties and forties, and are men of talent, ability, and industry. They earn enormous salaries and are the envy of all their fellow managers in the collective quest for the prize to which they all aspire—number one in portfolio performance.

Their varied backgrounds, personalities, and styles are in contrast to a common thread which weaves itself through them all—an abiding fascination with the stock market, a willingness to be daring with large sums of money, and the uncanny knack of being right in their selections. This common denominator that unites them all in a fraternity of almost Olympian majesty is the key to their awesome success.

The debacle in 1969 and 1970 was a humbling experience for almost everyone, including funds. There have been intimations by many that the go-go funds are dead and that the new breed of performance oriented managers has been taught a well deserved lesson. One must read *The Money Managers* to find an answer to those questions. The age of static, defensive money management is dead forever. Performance is the goal of every money manager who wants to truly live up to the objective written in his fund's prospectus. It can't be any other way for those new, undiscovered stars which have yet to shine.

Lester, Joseph
How to Make More Money from Mutual Funds. New York: Exposition Press, 1965. 152 pp. $3.50

"Knowledge is power" says Joseph Lester in the introduction to his book, and he has attempted to give the reader the benefit of his many years of investing experience to provide that knowledge. One cannot help but be impressed by the record of mutual fund growth. The author tries to explain in a simple way how investing for the long term is beneficial to the average investor. The overwhelming indictment of the contractual plan is really the essence of this book, and the constant repetition of it almost amounts to an obsession.

It is important to point out that there are three types of mutual fund plans: (1) the no-load plan; (2) the voluntary plan; and (3) the contractual plan. In the no-load plan, 100 percent of an investment is exchanged for mutual fund shares. You can buy a set amount on a monthly basis, and can stop or resume payments as your money becomes available. In a voluntary plan you may invest a given amount monthly, from which an average 8 percent sales charge is deducted and the balance invested in shares of the particular fund. You may skip months without penalty when money is not available. The contractual plan is a program for investing stated amounts over a minimum period of ten years. This plan entails signing a binding contract to pay each month, with penalties for not fulfilling its conditions. The sales charge of approximately 8 percent for the whole ten-year period is deducted by taking 50 percent from the first year's payments and the balance over the remainder of the term.

It seems a futile undertaking for the author to indict the contractual plan since 93 percent of the mutual fund plans, at the writing of this book, are not of the contractual type. Of course the remaining 7 percent represents a large amount of money, and for that reason the mutual fund investor owes a debt of gratitude for the advice contained in this work.

Mayer, Martin
The New Breed on Wall Street. New York: Macmillan, 1969. 128 pp. $10.00

The men whose responsibility it is to manage close to $300 billion are profiled by author Martin Mayer. This new breed of young men who have their own style, method, or technique of making money grow during a rising market are constantly in a sudden death race for investment success. It can make or break their reputation, and during the 1969–1970 market panic the obituaries were quick in coming. However, the sharp rebound which started in May 1970 proved that the performance game was very much alive.

This book has shed further light on this group of men, which includes one woman, Muriel Siebert, who have awakened a sleepy and dull business, the money management of billions. From the static, defensive past, the business has been dramatically changed into an aggressive performance-minded business. It has prompted William Donaldson to characterize it by saying, "Underlying all our problems is something healthy. Now and for the future, sleeping assets in trust departments will no longer be allowed to sleep. We have put the nation's money to work." This quote succinctly sums up the task of the almost five dozen money managers who are examined in this book. Interwoven among the stories of these men are some excellent photographs of the subjects, Wall Street, and some of its most famous landmarks.

Smith, Ralph Lee
   The Grim Truth about Mutual Funds. New York: Putnam, 1963. 122 pp. $2.95

The mutual fund industry, which has grown to more than $50 billion in assets, is given some rough treatment in this book. The author's ostensible purpose is to educate the potential investor as to how his money is handled by the professional managers to whom it is entrusted. When Smith completes his charges against the industry, the most ardent mutual fund investor should have his faith severely shaken. There is no letup in the author's head-on attack. He doesn't have one kind word for the industry.

At the outset the author makes it clear that the selection of a management company to do research is almost always a case of the officers of the fund appointing themselves to be advisors to the fund. This problem stems from a congressional compromise in the Investment Company Act of 1940 to make the law acceptable to the industry. The act allows 60 percent of the board of directors of an investment company to be composed of persons affiliated with an investment advisory firm. The contract must be renewed each year. Since the advisory firm usually creates the fund, it is a captive client. Every year the board of directors of the fund elects itself to another year of accepting the enormous fees from the fund. These are based on a percentage of the assets managed and not on the amount of work done. As a consequence of their stranglehold on the management of funds, advisory companies have sold their stock to the public and capitalized on their position with many more millions of dollars. The asset of the management or advisory company is the contract with the fund or group of funds that control a constant fee regardless of the fund's performance. It is usually one half of one percent of the managed assets.

The next complaint that the author has is the excessive load which most mutual funds charge, and the contractual plan which causes so many people to lose money if they have to sell their fund in the first few years. A sales charge of 8½ percent is the usual load, and 50 percent is deducted during the first year of the plan. The author makes a case for the no-load fund and in a statistical display tries to prove that mutual funds under professional management have not done as well as unmanaged investments. He cites the Wharton School report to prove his point.

The aggressive methods of selling mutual funds come under attack. In addition, the author claims that the caliber of personnel who sell the funds is not professional. At the early stages of fund growth in the 1950s there were all manner of people selling funds as a sideline with no experience or knowledge of the stock market. This caused many people to buy funds which were not suited to their particular objective. These were sold to them in such a way as to obscure the risks and accentuate the possible rewards.

One chapter discusses the excessive turnover of certain funds that are the captive customer of brokerage houses, many times to the detriment of the stockholder. The managers trade actively just to pile up large commissions. The give-up business that split up millions of dollars in commissions is an abuse that has since been abolished. In fact, negotiated rates have created some element of competition in the institutional sector of the market and may eventually mean the end of fixed fees.

In his conclusion the author calls for an end to the abuses he has brought to light. He asks that the law be changed to prohibit a director of a mutual fund from serving with an investment advisory firm. The fund's shareholders would save large amounts of money if the officers of the fund did their job and did not seek outside help. In the Public Utility Act of 1935, Congress prohibited utilities from doing business with an affiliated advisory or management firm unless business was done at cost. It can work just as well with the funds. Contractual plan buyers should be made aware of the harm that can come to them if they have to drop out during the early years, and salesmen should clearly reveal the sales commission received for each purchase and the size of the front-end load. The law should reduce the size of the load to make the purchase of a fund less onerous for the investor.

Every crusader can see only one side of an issue—his side. There is obviously a great deal of merit in the author's remarks and suggested reforms. But it would be a distortion of the truth to suggest that the mutual fund industry is all bad and has misled the stockholders who have faithfully invested their hard-earned money. The truth is that millions of people have received the benefits of professional management through mutual fund investment. That does not detract from the ultimate value to be gained from adoption of the suggestions found in this daring book.

√Thomas, Conrad W.
Hedgemanship: How to Make Money in Bear Markets, Bull Markets and Chicken Markets While Confounding Professional Money Managers and Attracting a Better Class of Women. Homewood, Ill.: Dow Jones-Irwin, 1970. 163 pp. $8.50

Alfred Winslow Jones is recognized as the father of the hedge fund, and his record of success promptly started a wave of explosive growth in both public and private hedge funds. Although in recent years the hedge fund record has been disgraceful, Thomas claims that hedge fund techniques form the basis of sound trading practices and should lead to investment success.

The basic concept of a hedge fund is that the managers may go short of a stated percentage of assets and thereby offset the effects of a downtrend. With the panic and crash of 1969–1970, the myth of hedge fund superiority came to an unceremonious end. It seems that the hedge fund managers shorted the wrong stocks or just didn't go short at all, but kept a portion of their funds in cash. This is a hedger's nightmare, because, if he doesn't go short and resorts to cash, he is not running a hedge fund; he is merely running.

Thomas does not subscribe to John K. Galbraith's theory that "financial genius consists of a short memory and a rising market." He admits that the hedge fund concept suffered an almost fatal blow in the bear market of 1969–1970. He feels that the future of hedge fund growth will be characterized by smaller management fees (the original fund managers received 20 percent of the profit) and marked evidence of sustained, superior performance.

OPTIONS

✓Alverson, Lyle T.
How to Write Puts and Calls. New York: Exposition Press, 1968. 125 pp. $6.00

Alverson sheds some light on a relatively little known area of the stock market—stock option contract writing. The author lays the groundwork for an investor with substantial resources to enter the business of writing option contracts. He lists the rules, as he sees them, from his many years of successful experience. In the process, Alverson explains the value of puts and calls and why the business has grown so rapidly in the last several years. It promises to continue that growth as the level of investor comprehension increases and as a consequence of the sharp rise in the volume of stock market transactions.

The author advises the writer of options to use only stocks of good quality that he would normally buy and to write calls rather than puts and straddles. In that way he will have a healthy business. The rationale is that when a stock on which he has written a call has risen in value and is called away, the writer must buy in the stock to deliver to the option buyer. Since the writer is long on the stock, he will benefit from the rise in value and will also have the premium.

Alverson explains the rules he believes are necessary to operate successfully, and he cites the tax advantages of options. There are many references to an SEC study of options which is very useful in understanding the business, and there is also a list of other books on the subject.

This book was a forerunner of the many works that followed in this highly leveraged field. It is important reading, not only for those who are anxious to enter the option writing field, but for the many thousands of writers who would like to improve their operations.

✓Dadekian, Zaven
The Strategy of Puts and Calls. New York: Scribner, 1968. 142 pp. $5.95

The fast growing area of options is carefully examined for the neophyte in this clear and understandable book that takes the mystery out of puts and calls. The author develops a strategy for an option writing program that ostensibly can net an individual 20 to 30 percent on his investment. His own experiences are described in detail, with examples showing the techniques necessary for a successful program.

The advantages and risks are plainly unveiled by Dadekian, who believes that profits can be achieved year after year whether the stock market goes up or down or remains stable.

To implement his system the author describes a record keeping system that is thorough yet simple enough to maintain a constant watch on all contracts in force at a given time. The field of options has grown rapidly in recent years, and books such as this have no doubt contributed to the knowledge that has made this growth possible.

Sarnoff, Paul
Puts and Calls: The Complete Guide. New York: Hawthorne Books, 1968. 174 pp. $9.95

There are literally millions of investors who have never bought a put or a call, presumably because they don't want to try something new. The fact is that options are only new to those who shun their advantages. The business of options is as old as the tulipomania of sixteenth-century Holland, and was thriving long before there was a securities market in America. This thorough book on the subject of puts and calls enlightens the reader to the possibility of exciting profits and the certainty of limited losses in his stock exchange transactions. It is the product of Paul Sarnoff's decades of experience in the option business, which has prompted him to declare that the purchase of puts and calls is the only sensible way to play the market.

In the United States options grew up with the stock market itself. Brokers started to sell them in 1817 when the exchange moved indoors. Jacob Little and Daniel Drew, two stock market greats, issued and endorsed puts and calls. By the Civil War speculation in "papers" were an integral part of the Wall Street scene. The modern system of options was developed by Russell Sage, who invented the straddle and the spread. He made a fortune and honored all his paper. There were weaker dealers, however, who reneged on their contracts. This plagued the business until the Securities and Exchange Act of 1934. The Put and Call Brokers Association was formed to guarantee uniform contracts and endorsement by New York Stock Exchange members. There are now twenty-four active members.

There are several reasons why traders use options. The most important are: (1) speculation; (2) leverage; (3) to correct market errors; (4) for protection of principal and trading maneuvers; (5) to average up or down or to pyramid; (6) for short or long term capital gains. Sarnoff discusses the uses of puts and calls from both the buyer's and seller's point of view. His analysis deals with the buyer of calls, explains the many reasons for their existence, and demonstrates their versatility. The purchase of a put is the same as selling a stock short, and, therefore, the opposite answers apply.

The buyer of a call is the owner of one hundred shares of stock with no risk except the cost of the call. This cost is called the "premium." The buyer of a put is a short seller of one hundred shares with the same limited risk. If the stock rises the benefit accrues to the buyer of the call. If the stock falls the owner of the put has the potential profit. An option can be exercised at any time during its lifetime. Many traders make the mistake of holding their options until the last day. The important thing is to nail down a profit when it becomes available. With this simple exposition of the way options work, let us examine several situations to understand how calls are used.

High leverage. The primary reason that traders use options is the high leverage that they can achieve. The percentage of funds necessary is sometimes as little as 5 percent as opposed to the 55 percent needed in a margin account. If a trader expects a stock to move, instead of buying one hundred shares of stock he can buy short-term calls on as many shares as he desires. If the price of the stock soars he can sell his calls at a profit, can go short against his calls, or position the stock by exercising his options and placing the shares in his account. He does so only if he feels the rise will continue beyond the life of the options.

Protecting a profit. If you find yourself with a profit in a long position of 500 shares of a listed stock, you can take your profit and replace your holding with calls. If the stock rises you can recapture the shares by calling the options covered by your calls. The best way to protect your principal is to buy calls on the shares being sold out. Large speculators who want to control additional shares of a particular stock buy big blocks of calls. They can therefore control the desired amount of stock without disturbing the market. Proxy fighters resort to this strategy.

Protecting a short sale. Calls should be bought simultaneously with a short sale. If the market drops the profit is diminished only by the cost of the calls. If the market rises the short seller can exercise his calls and replace the borrowed shares. This limits his total loss to the cost of the calls no matter how high the market rises during the life of those calls.

Calls for caution. If a tip is tendered, buy the calls. If the tip turns sour you only lose the premium. If it works out you can cash in or position the stock. Limiting your loss is the most cautious approach to a new commitment.

Resale of calls. Calls can be resold at a handsome profit if the price of the stock is higher and the calls have several months to run.

Premiums. "The price depends on the person most anxious to do business." Special options are cheaper; they represent an inventory of the put and call dealers and do not depend on negotiation. Calls on over-the-counter stocks require higher premiums because the writer must put up 100 percent.

Conversion. There is a process of changing a call to a put and vice versa for a small charge. Many investors don't know that this conversion is possible and allow their options to run out unprofitably.

This introduction to the world of options is important because it may be the first time that you have been exposed to the subject. Many investors have heard about options but are not aware of their advantages. Sarnoff is convinced that options can be used to hedge market commitments, to offset errors, to speculate with limited risk in any kind of market, and to effect short and long term capital gains, among others. He has proved his case extremely well, and exploded the common misconception that options are highly speculative and dangerous. He has forcefully demonstrated that puts and calls can be employed to develop a most cautious approach to stock market operations.

PSYCHOLOGY

✓Appleman, Mark J.
The Winning Habit. New York: McCall, 1970. 214 pp. $6.95

The author explores the psychology of the investor with a serious view toward understanding why one wins or loses in the stock market. All we can hope to learn is why things happen the way they do. As the author describes the various types that inhabit the money arena, he reveals with clarity the reasons why personality traits prevent certain individuals from developing "the winning habit"— that elusive ability which enables an investor to hold the good stocks and sell the bad ones, to buy cheap and sell dear, and finally to use the marketplace for what it should be, an investment arena to increase capital and not a social battle-ground where you have to outdo your neighbors and friends just as you try to have a better home, lawn, automobile, or outdoor barbecue pit.

Appleman delineates the market types that we all know—"the market masochist," "the tagalong," "the plunger," "the sport," "the bargain hunter," "the can't loser," and "the hyperactive trader." Without mentioning a single company or showing the usual confusing numbers and statistics, the author develops the interesting theories which form the basis for an eye-opening book. Many people can see their own reflection in the types described here, and would rather avoid identification than laughingly admit that they are hopelessly in a losing rut.

Displaying the intelligence of a man who understands that some questions have no answers, Appleman tells his story and leaves it at that. His persistent claim throughout the book is that "it is not the investment that succeeds or fails, it's the investor." As long as the anxiety-ridden investor with all his worries, pressures, and personality traits is making the buy and sell decisions, the profits will grow smaller and the losses will grow larger. In sum, the worried investor usually ends up in a position where he is always trying to get even.

✓Bernstein, Peter L.
Economist on Wall Street: Notes on the Sanctity of Gold, the Value of Money, the Security of Investment, and Other Delusions. New York: Macmillan, 1970. 240 pp. $5.95

To apply economic theory to the practical realities of the stock market is a tall order for anyone. For many years economists sat in their ivory towers, shielded from the unpredictable marketplace which exploded their theories with increasing regularity as the psychological condition of the people who made up the stock market reversed the logical order of supply and demand.

Peter Bernstein is not in an ivory tower, nor does he stay aloof from the stock market's lifeblood expression of economic thought. Indeed, he has interpreted that thought in a manner which gives new insight to the students of market behavior. He is considered a maverick or an iconoclast by many observers of the scene, whereas, in fact, he is creating a new school of thought in the areas where he has questioned the commonly held theories. His comments on inflation, gold, balance of payments, and his revealing facts concerning fixed income securities versus common stocks display intelligence, perception, and an almost prophetic wisdom. Two of his most astonishing revelations are that common stocks have not been a good hedge against inflation and that the economy has not had any inflationary tendencies during peacetime.

All of these judgments and more are to be discovered in this collection of essays written during the past twelve years for the service over which he presides, Bernstein-Macauley, Inc., which is now owned by CBWL-Hayden Stone. As a money manager, Bernstein claims that he is irritated by the repeated questioning of prospective clients who would like to know what they can expect from their investments in the future. "They refuse to believe that the future is unknown to us. Yet, the art of successful investing begins with the humility of facing up to the unknown."

In the search for investment success, it is important to deny the approach that declares enthusiastically that a stock should be bought when good news predominates. Prices then are usually at or near their highs. It pays to be contrary and run against the crowd. According to Bernstein, "The investor who follows majority opinion and standard forecasts usually ends up in the ditch." It becomes obvious to the reader of this book that clear, independent thinking will avoid the inevitable fall and lead instead toward that investment success for which we all strive.

Haas, Albert, Jr., and Jackson, Don D.
Bulls, Bears, and Dr. Freud: Why You Win or Lose on the Stock Market.
Cleveland and New York: World, 1967. 179 pp. $4.95

The stock market is a fertile area for psychoanalysis, and this joint effort by a stockbroker and a psychiatrist to plumb the secrets of human behavior under the stress of financial decision is a natural. Dr. Jackson has excellent credentials for his task with a former book titled *The Etiology of Schizophrenia.* It becomes apparent immediately with the authors' remarks that too much attention has been paid to statistics and not enough has been written about people, their hopes and fears, and the emotions, namely greed and vanity, which force them into their market decisions. The background of the bull market of the 1950s, which set the stage for the "pyramided optimism" that led to the 1962 crash, is an excellent laboratory in which to study the actions of investors. They turn out to be the same creatures of emotion that caused all other panics throughout our financial history. Humphrey B. Neill recently said in a letter to this writer, "We get so carried away with the questions of the moment that we forget that it all happened before." Case histories are provided to show how man develops unbridled optimism and surrenders reason to emotion. He can't believe stocks will go down. When he finally loses that feeling, it is too late.

The narrative continues to explore the areas of the market where psychology plays a major role. One chapter, "Sex and the Stock Market," attempts to show that even the vocabulary of the boardroom has overtones of sex. Such expressions as "selling climax," "puts," "breakthroughs," "straddles," and "violated the lows" are displayed as sexual symbols.

Haas and Jackson also examine the interaction of broker and client and obviously bring their experience into play. They provide an inside look at the motivations, abilities, and at times the unwarranted greed of some stockbrokers. Honesty should be in their own self interest since the clients' rewards coincide with their own.

The bear mentality is explored, and it is determined that even when the short seller is a winner he is somehow not happy. Nobody likes a bear—he is avoided like a plague. Americans are an optimistic people who thrive on happiness and bullishness. The essence of that attitude is treated at length in two chapters titled "Faith," describing the part which that attitude plays in the mind of the public and how it affects the stock market. Faith is reinforced by the hero worship that American investors display for the celebrities who are often seen and quoted in the media, and those who write regular columns on the stock market.

The final chapters allow the reader to gain some insight into the personalities of these heroes through brief interviews with leading market figures. The philosophies of Gerald M. Loeb, the late Armand Erpf, Anthony Tabell, Samuel L. Stedman, Kenneth Ward, and Lucien Hooper are discussed, and an analysis of the public reaction to their columns or predictions is offered.

The field covered by this book is obviously enormous and the authors have just opened the door. The subjects are essential to an understanding of several major aspects of stock market behavior. Expert, broker, client, bear, and bull are all components of this psychological review, and every reader can learn some valuable lessons when he sees himself in these pages.

Kelly, Fred C., and Burgess, Sullivan
How Shrewd Speculators Win: A Guide to Behavior When the Market Rises.
Original: Sears, 1932. Reprint: Burlington, Vt.: Fraser, 1964. 143 pp. $2.95

In their attempt to probe the mystery of the stock market's movements, the authors investigate the psychological weaknesses that hamper the investor's chances for success. They state categorically that "human nature is the one constant factor in the stock market. All other factors are variables." Therefore, it would be helpful for the speculator to be a practical psychologist.

The several chapters of this short book prove the maxim that good things come in small packages. There are hints throughout each section which reprove the speculator for behaving like an amateur. Why is it that a speculator never feels the same disappointment over a stock that goes down twenty points from his purchase price as he does if it goes five points above where he sells? Can the reader think of one case where the purchase of a stock is based solely on his own analysis? Or does he always rely on the recommendations of others so that he can absolve himself of the blame when the stock doesn't perform?

What makes speculation an art rather than a science is the uncertainty of the market's reaction to a news event. You can't be sure if the publicity has been thoroughly discounted until the release of the announcement is acted upon by investors. Kelly and Burgess claim that market analysts can use the same information to prove two diametrically opposite opinions. He cites a case which occurred just before the crash in 1929 where a young man declared that the bull market still had a long life because the increased use of machinery would enable manufacturers to produce goods so cheaply that they could find new markets among those who formerly could not afford to buy. Two years later, the same writer became convinced that the bear market was young because the machine had replaced millions of workers and reduced their buying power.

Kelly and Burgess have cut through to the heart of the matter in their development of market rules and in their comments on the nature of the psychology of market behavior. Here are some of their observations and conclusions:

"Fear is a greater prod than greed. A man may run for his life but he will walk to a restaurant to satisfy his hunger."

"Before forming an opinion ascertain the trend. *Weight trend* 70 percent *industry* 20 percent *stock* 10 percent."

"In a bear market nearly every stock goes down. In a bull market not all stocks advance."

"A stock is never too high to buy if conditions are right; and never too low to sell if affairs are turning from bad to worse."

The authors conclude their work with a group of rules. The most important are: (1) cut losses instantly, let profits run; (2) act on your own conviction, take a position, and don't just talk about it; (3) don't average down; (4) don't ever buy on margin; (5) never play a stagnant market; (6) when the market heads down, sell everything; (7) do not hedge; (8) it's always easier to buy than to sell; (9) never buy anything until the whole market has demonstrated its ability to ignore bad news.

Application of the experience, knowledge, and wisdom that this book contains should help the speculator and trader to win in the stock market. Unfortunately, the trader is often prey to doubt, which may cause him to ignore these truths and miss his goal. He must isolate the emotions that immobilize him in times of stress if he wants to follow the rules which lead to success.

√ **Magee, John**
The General Semantics of Wall Street. Springfield, Mass.: John Magee, 1958. 423 pp. $12.00

The importance of this book goes far beyond the borders of Wall Street. It delves deeply into the psychological self-deception that people use to avoid facing reality. They resort to semantics when they need to rationalize their behavior. Magee exposes this penchant for the abstract. He tries to enlighten the reader, by describing a clear course of action that will help him cope with things as they actually exist in the stock market and in life as a whole. Magee claims that we are taught to respect the maps and not the territory. He asserts that we should reject teaching when evidence does not support it. This applies to the great mass of wisdom which is available to those of us who have acquired the knowledge of written language. "Time-binding" is the concept of adding to the accumulated thoughts of all the masters which have been preserved by books.

If later discoveries prove their methods false we must reject their conclusions. Magee offers a well documented look at our value systems, psychological obedience to outmoded beliefs, and, in a pointed way, the precise reasons for our failure in the stock market.

In the market as in life we deal in high-order abstractions. What is a good, sound company? Will the market make new highs? People want clear-cut statements. These absolute directives demand a prediction. "If you buy now you will make fabulous profits!" You delude yourself when you treat the market as if it were a single real thing instead of a highly complex aggregation of individual cases. In every bear market some stocks go up and in all bull markets certain stocks go down. Self-regard is a most important reward in the stock market; in many cases it is more important than money. Boardroom habitues have a shelter from the problems of life and home. They pit themselves against the infinite forces of the market and have an audience for the victories they achieve. These denizens of what Magee calls "the chapels of commerce" seem to have definite ideas about the direction of the market. They second guess the action of certain stocks. They are in effect talking to themselves when they tell only the good things about their favorite company. There is no bad. There is no room in their set minds for facts that can disturb their preconceived judgments about a stock. They revel if news in the *Wall Street Journal* shows they are right, and quickly forget anything that challenges their faith. This dogged determination will often cause an investor to average his purchase at a lower price. He is not making a valid decision based on present facts, but rather is more interested in the obsolete opinion that caused the first purchase. He must prove that he was right or lose face. The loss suffered is not measured so much in money as in pride. Most investors can't afford to lose in the market, not because of the financial loss, but because of the humiliation they would suffer in the eyes of their fellow traders who watch their every move.

The same kind of problems come up over and over again, not only in the market, but in life as well. Magee says that we should ask the right questions. A question must be stated in terms that can be understood by both the inquirer and the one asked. The way to cope with the market is to look at the facts. Make sure the map gives you a true picture of the territory. This is difficult for us to do because throughout our life we have had certain directives pounded into us by parents, grandparents, school, and church. We are told to accept without looking at the facts. We do so with blind, unreasoning faith.

The author shows how good, sound stocks can change and make speculators out of investors. We refuse to see the changes that are taking place in the territory and cling to obsolete maps. The example of New Haven which was purchased at $250 a share and eventually was delisted and sold down to just sixteenths is given to point out the fact that investors are unwilling to look at the new face of things. They get further and further away from reality. The terms speculator and investor are high-order abstractions that deserve clarification. They have achieved moral implications in the minds of most people. The New Haven story and many others like it have served to blur the distinction between investor and speculator.

The income stock is the subject of a study by Magee. He examines a group of

1,000 stocks and shows that dividend stocks did not do as well as nondividend payers over a period of seven years. He feels that we must not make an either/or decision on income stocks; income is good, appreciation bad. It is more important to guard against the deterioration of capital. The word income blinds us to the facts. A related problem is the matter of inflation. The "put them away and forget about them" school seldom understands the erosion of buying power that results from holding stocks that don't appreciate in value.

Magee states that we must scale down our ideals to something within the range of possibility. Otherwise we will feel defeated, depressed, and discouraged. Once we have limited our goals, we will then be prepared to deal with the stock market and many other areas of life. We might think it a paradox, but Magee urges the reader to eschew common sense. It perpetuates obsolete ideas, false theories, superstitions, prejudices, and desires. It tells us never to trade on margin or sell stocks short. Common sense suggests that we buy stocks which have declined greatly and are at their lows. We must guard against prejudices and attitudes that are so ingrained in us that they distort our perception of facts.

This book does not offer any system, but it shows the reader how important it is to accept a new outlook which can cope with the unpredictable future. Instead of the big killing we settle for a great number of small gains. Small losses are taken in stride. Magee asks us to accentuate the negative. If we hedge and compromise we can narrow the gap between our aspirations and our performance. The stock market involves human intelligence competitively engaged in a contest of evaluation. The purpose of general semantics is to keep up-to-date maps to help in this difficult task. It is also important in life. "We must put away childish things and become men," says Magee. To do this it is necessary to break with the values that we have been taught to cherish. It calls for a drastic change with much of the tradition and custom of our environment. We must have a new point of view not only in the market, but in politics, law, religion, family life, social ambitions, and the goals we set in the world around us.

Neill, Humphrey Bancroft
  The Art of Contrary Thinking. Caldwell, Idaho: Caxton Printers, 1954. 201 pp. paperback: $3.00

Individuals throughout history have thought independently and taken a stand contrary to the prevailing mood of the crowd. It is the only way to avoid being swept along with the emotions of the mob. A flock of sheep must follow the will of its shepherd even if he leads them over a cliff. It is the same in the human arena.

Humphrey Neill does not claim to be the first to use contrary opinion, but throughout his life he has studied, researched, and refined all the recorded information on the subject and developed a theory of contrary opinion. He is known today as America's number one "contrarian," and is author of the *Neill Letters of Contrary Opinion.*

Let us examine some of the concepts which form this unique theory. In Neill's words, "When everyone thinks alike, everyone is likely to be wrong." If you want to avoid being wrong, learn to think contrarily. These thoughts in a concise way sum up the author's main argument. It is not easy for anyone to think, let alone throw his mind in unnatural directions. It is normal to think the same as the crowd, and when you go with the crowd you tend to leave the thinking to it. Since the crowd is usually wrong in the timing of events, you are subject to its failings. A crowd tends to think emotionally while an individual thinks with his brain.

Neill states that if one can get into the habit of thinking "opposite" to the crowd, he will be right more often than wrong. Sir Francis Bacon nearly 300 years ago admonished his students to "Doubt all before you believe anything! Watch your idols!"

If one relies on the theory of contrary opinion for accurate timing in the stock market, he will frequently be disappointed. This however does not invalidate the theory's usefulness in recognizing reversal areas. The author does not say that his theory is a surefire method for beating the stock market, but the wisdom of thinking things out and looking at both sides of a question will improve your average. It is a great advantage to be among the minority that does exercise its brain occasionally.

For a good part of the book Neill roams into a great many areas and quotes from a host of interesting books and authors to prove his theory. This book is an eye opener and a refreshing oasis in a desert of tedium and sameness. "The Vermont Ruminator" has a well deserved following, and it can now be said that the total has been increased by one.

✓Selden, George Charles
    The Psychology of the Stock Market. Original: New York: Ticker, 1912. Reprint: Burlington, Vt.: Fraser, 1965. 93 pp. paperback: $2.00

G. C. Selden's book is one of the early attempts to assess the effect of the psychological factors that weigh upon stock market decisions. It puts into clear perspective the importance of divining the mood of the crowd and, with robot-like detachment, of doing the opposite. It would be much easier to have computers make all the decisions and give all the orders. It seems that blood creates the emotion which causes all the mistakes in buying and selling securities.

There is excellent advice given in this well-written work, and it is just as important today as when it was written sixty years ago. Human nature is no different and the emotions which drive investors into their mistakes remain the same. Selden cautions against "inverted reasoning" which rationalizes our mistakes. He explores the "mental somersaults" that keep us locked into situations, and he counsels that we should "maintain a balanced mind and avoid abstruse deductions."

The author claims that the investor who owns a stock which is not performing for one reason or another develops a "peculiar sort of optimism" and cannot perform the important function of "decision without passion." He sums up the quandary of the investor in the following way: "In essence it is a story of human hopes and fears; of mental attitude, on the part of those interested, resulting from their own position in the market rather than from any deliberate judgment of conditions; of an unwarranted projection by the public imagination of a perceived present into an unknown though not wholly unknowable future."

It is almost eerie to read these lines which were written at the turn of the century and feel the light of their truths shining directly at you. There is hardly any trader or investor who cannot see himself on these probing pages, and there is no stock market buff who can't learn invaluable lessons from the psychological insights which Selden offers. He advises the trader how to win in the following terse manner: "To make the greatest success it is necessary for the trader to forget entirely his own position in the market, his profits or losses, the relation of present prices to the point where he bought or sold, and to fix his thoughts upon the position of the market. If the market is going down the trader must sell, no matter whether he has a profit or a loss, whether he bought a year ago or two minutes ago."

The value of all the advice in this short book should be obvious even to those who know it is impossible to follow. As one of the true stock market classics, *The Psychology of the Stock Market* belongs in every interested investor's library.

✓ **Wyckoff, Peter G.**
  The Psychology of Stock Market Timing. Englewood Cliffs, N.J.: Prentice-Hall, 1963. 224 pp. $9.95

Peter Wyckoff has put together an important book. It contains portions of a classic by Fred Charters Kelly, *Why You Win, or Lose.* There are so many lessons to be learned from the history of stock market behavior that it is difficult to draw up a truly representative list in a short evaluation such as this.

Let us say that the crowd is usually wrong, and it is important to try to act to the contrary. A successful trader in the market claimed that he held his fortune because he obliged the crowd. When they were raging bulls, buying everything in sight, he sold to them. When they were in panic, and selling everything they could at any price they could get, he obliged them by buying.

Another lesson to be learned is that of timing. The market moves in definite cycles of distribution, decline, accumulation, and advance. Jay Gould said, "The successful operator must know when to come in; more important, he must know when to stay out; and most important, he must know when to get out once he's in." This lesson is another ingredient in the all-important recipe for success in the stock market.

Another lesson the author points out is what he calls "the trader's trilogy"—vanity, hope, and greed. The greatest single enemy to stock market success is vanity. Next to vanity, the greatest foe of good judgment that must be guarded against is greed. Thirdly, our own "will to believe" or our hope that what we believe is true is the worst influence on our attempt to make a profit.

The lessons cited here are only a few of the valuable historical truths that Wyckoff has culled from former students of the market and from his own experiences in the market over the past twenty-five years. It is fascinating, eye opening, informative, instructive, and must reading for anyone who ventures into the no-man's-land of the stock market with its booby traps and well-intentioned friends who are amply supplied with sure things.

SPECULATION

Gibson, Thomas

The Facts About Speculation. Original: New York: Thomas Gibson, 1923.
Reprint: Burlington Vt.: Fraser, 1965. 109 pp. paperback: $2.75

There has been a great deal written about the evils of speculation and the importance of careful investment. Thomas Gibson has difficulty showing the difference between the two. He proves that the statements which claim speculation always results in losses are not true. His analytical tests show that only 80 percent of speculative ventures end in a loss. Speculation is an inherent attribute of humanity and is essential in the machinery of progress. Without it the railroads would not have been built nor our mines exploited. In fact, it was the means by which our country was discovered.

The author contends that the principal causes of loss in speculation are human error or intelligence. He cites the universal habit of buying after a prolonged rise at high prices. It is purely psychological. Anyone with average intelligence would admit that the time to purchase securities is when prices are depressed, not when they are inflated. He must also realize that there is a top to the market, and as prices advance they get nearer to the top and reduce the potential profits of a purchase. Finally, it is clear that the possible extent of a fall in price increases with each point of advance. It is as immutable as a law in physics.

To combat his problems the speculator must gain immunity from the influence of surface appearances through knowledge. Emotions cannot be allowed to play any part in his plans. Sudden wealth is a hopeless dream. Time is an important factor in the realization of success as in any other line of business. The knowledge gained in the study of security markets will be of value in every field of endeavor. The stock market is a visible record of the effects of economic, financial and political influences on values and prospects. The action of the market represents the composite opinion of the brightest minds in the world registered on the most delicate instrument in the world which in turn reflects probable future developments. It is barometric to a great degree. The market precedes business developments. A sustained rise or fall in stock prices foretells the future course of business.

Gibson outlines the principal causes of loss in speculation. They are an excellent guide to the trader and point out important clues which enhance his chances for success.

1. Buying at high prices after a major advance.
2. Operations on insufficient margins.
3. Dependence on tips and market appearances.
4. Dependence on charts or other mechanical forms of speculation.
5. The use of stop-loss orders.
6. Impatience and the inability to await results.
7. The psychological effects of greed and fear.

The last mentioned enter in some degree into all errors. Greed is responsible for overspeculation, for lack of discrimination in the selection of securities, and is a synonym for impatience. Fear causes people to sell when prices are low, and to refrain from buying when stocks are intrinsically cheap. Another important human error is the assumption that present conditions will continue to prevail indefinitely. The Romans said long ago—"omnia mutantur"— everything changes. Human nature does endure, and therefore this error will persist.

The author has little faith in the predictive ability of tape watchers and chartists. He claims that they have never produced a single authenticated fortune. His objection to the chartist is that he "confesses an ignorance of values and bases his operations on an attempt to detect what someone else is doing or has done instead of on what he should do himself." No business on earth can succeed on such a basis. The only reason to buy and hold stocks is because they are cheap. The scale order is the only logical method of a mechanical nature to be employed in speculative operations.

Gibson doesn't believe in stop-loss orders and decries the "quick turn syndrome" which is encouraged by advisors and market letters. The time element cannot be separated from speculation or any other business. The author exposes all the fallacies of speculation because he feels it necessary to "clear away the weeds before the field is planted, and Wall Street is full of the weeds of tradition, misunderstanding, and sophistry."

People will go to any length to secure wealth without work. Gibson concludes with a set of rules that should improve the speculator's chance for that elusive 20 percent:

1. Dismiss the thought of making money fast.
2. Eschew tips, mechanical methods, inside information, or market appearances. The 80 percent who lose use these methods.
3. Don't watch the market.
4. Large fortunes are gained by the exercise of foresight, courage, and patience.
5. Insufficient margins result in loss.
6. Ignorance of economic laws will lead to failure.
7. The higher the market goes the nearer it is to the top. The lower it goes the closer it is to the bottom. Reversing this logic is a common error.
8. Obtain all information regarding history, value, and status of securities dealt in.
9. Stop-loss orders should never be used.
10. Confine operations to listed securities.
11. Stay with the golden mean—the middle ground between ultraconservatism and rashness.
12. Buy securities that pay interest and dividends.

If these suggestions are adopted and carried out, the chances for profit are excellent. If they are ignored, losses are a foregone conclusion. The author repeats himself in his zeal to give the speculator a valid guide for winning in the market. The only problem is that the logic and reason contained in Gibson's advice are often overwhelmed by the triple handicap of greed, fear, and ignorance.

✓ **Harper, Henry Howard**
The Psychology of Speculation: The Human Element in Stock Market Transactions. Original: Boston: Henry Howard Harper, 1926. Reprint: Burlington, Vt.: Fraser, 1966. 106 pp. paperback: $3.00

In a rare dissertation on the difficulties of speculation, Henry Harper exposes man's penchant for rationalizing his stock market errors. He cuts away the foundation of the speculator's excuses and develops a basis for the belief in the following: (1) that you can't win in the stock market unless you have complete mastery over your emotions; (2) study of books, statistics, or instructions can't help you make profits in the market; (3) the stock exchange has a high degree of integrity and shouldn't be blamed for an individual's losses.

No other subject except love is of more vital concern to people. The reason investors and speculators can't win is that they beat themselves. All the resolve and theory that a person has when he enters the stock market flies out the window. He becomes subjective and is incapable of reason. He no longer controls the investment but is controlled by the currents around him. Books that proclaim how to make money in the stock market are wasted. It is not that the information is false or the reader is deficient, but that the application of a plan is almost impossible.

The author believes that tip sheets are false financial prophets that lead their followers astray. No amount of experience can help you act wisely under stock market conditions. You become disoriented like people in a forest and invariably go in the wrong direction. If you win for a period of time, your human impulses lead to optimism, rashness, and impatience. You rarely get away with the profit. The natural tendency for the winner is to continue to play until all the gain has been lost. The laws of psychology have been designed by nature for the discomfort of those who want to make a fortune.

The stock market is a fair and open game. Every man and woman who participates has an equal chance. There are many who gamble and guess, cliques which manipulate stocks up and down, but they are only a small part of the overall market. Supply and demand inevitably create stock prices. Investors buy stocks until prices get too high and then sell stocks until prices recede to the point at which they started. This process is as old as the market itself. When bullishness is epidemic, speculators are directed by sentiment rather than judgment. They act like a herd of cattle who rush blindly into a river or butt their brains out against stone walls. A witness to a panic in a theatre, an auditorium, or the stock market will learn that men are little saner than cattle.

Harper acts to dispel the popular misconception that the New York Stock Exchange is to blame for man's troubles. He firmly states that the exchange is a monument of integrity. It doesn't fix prices or create panics or depressions. It has no more control over the price of securities than the ocean has over its tides. There is no business where contracts that involve millions are ratified by a mere gesture. The quality of the brokers on the floor of the exchange is extremely high. Unethical practices are promptly detected and summarily dealt with. The investor can enter "the game" with his eyes wide open. Every fact about the company he wants to buy is available. If he deviates from sound principles, he can't blame anyone but himself.

The sum of Harper's comments serve to put the speculative ventures of man into their proper perspective. He lays the blame for failure where it belongs— with the speculator. The trader can get no sympathy from the author when he tries to shift the blame for his mistakes onto either his broker or the stock exchange. The enlightened speculator must enter the game with full knowledge that he brings with him the source of his own destruction. Financial suicide is almost impossible to avoid because of the psychological handicaps of man's own nature.

Hoyle

The Game in Wall Street: And How to Play it Successfully. Original: New York: J. S. Ogilvie, 1898. Reprint: Burlington, Vt.: Fraser, 1968. 80 pp. $7.00

The title of this book suggests that Wall Street is a game. Ninety-five percent of the trading is purely speculative and 5 percent is for investment. The best way to avoid a loss is to keep out of the game. But the omniscient Hoyle knows that he can't prevent the public from gambling in the stock market. He therefore tries to show the lambs some of the pitfalls and to teach them some rules of the game. This will hopefully keep the losses of these innocents at a minimum.

In 1898 there were only 130 stocks traded on the New York Stock Exchange. Two-thirds of the trading was confined to six or seven leading stocks. Hoyle believed that Wall Street was not a game of chance, but a game of skill directed by shrewd men who controlled millions of dollars. Seven big pools which had $60 million in cash were controlled by corporate insiders, banks, and insurance companies. The author contended that human intelligence decides the course and direction of the market. The actions of the pool generals were aided by publicity in every prominent newspaper in the country. Every year $100 million was taken out of the public's pocket.

The participants in this game included 7,000 bucket shops and 10,000–15,000 brokerage offices. They succeeded in taking not only money from the greedy public but their health and happiness as well. There is no business in the world that, win or lose, is so sure to wreck soul, mind, and body as Wall Street speculation.

Hoyle suggests that you confine your attention to seven or eight stocks that constitute three-fourths of the transactions on the exchange. Sugar, Tobacco, St. Paul, Burlington and Rock Island, Manhattan, Chicago, or Peoples' Gas and Union Pacific preferred were the leaders of his day, and the issues in which the pools concentrated. Bull campaigns were started by the pool generals when prices were low. They accumulated stocks when times were bad and sold them when everything looked good. The bull campaign began in gloom and ended in glory. It began at the bottom and ended at the top. The key words that describe pool operations are accumulation and distribution.

The author claims that speculation is a scientific study. If it is too much trouble for you to study this subject you have no business in it. It requires study, time, and patience to be a success in a profession or a mercantile business. Why does the amateur think that he can rush into speculation without any knowledge of the subject and make a fortune? In this game you must get in when everybody thinks prices are going lower and get out when they think the market is going higher.

Human nature remains the same throughout history. That is the real reason for panics. It is part of the character of the American mind to carry prosperity to the extremes that lead to an inflationary boom. Then comes the inevitable collapse in the form of a panic. Hoyle predicted no small panics for several years and no major panics for fifteen or twenty years. The future proved him wrong with the sharp market panics of 1901, 1903, and 1907.

The author's preference for winning is a "simple scale system." This involves buying and selling a certain number of shares at every point or half point up or down as prices advance or recede, and then taking profits on every transaction when it shows. It is important to know the trend of the market and go with it. In the final chapter there are twenty-six hints for a course of action in the market.

The character of the stock market is markedly different today from the period the author writes about. More than seventy years have passed, and the complex nature of today's Wall Street does not lend itself to the simple solutions that are suggested here. But people are the same—human nature hasn't changed. If anything, there are many more lambs today than there were in 1898. It would serve them well to read Hoyle's advice. Perhaps they can reverse the natural order of things in Wall Street.

Kelly, Fred Charters
Why You Win or Lose: The Psychology of Speculation. Original: Fred C. Kelly, 1930. Reprint: Burlington, Vt.: Fraser, 1965. 177 pp. paperback: $3.00; hardcover: $4.00

In this diminutive book Fred Charters Kelly propounds a theory of market psychology that lays the foundation for the contrary opinion theory later developed by that great contrarian, Humphrey Bancroft Neill. His valuable insight into market behavior represents a giant step toward understanding crowd behavior and the essential reasons for the crowd's failure in its quest for stock market success.

Kelly's contribution is most clearly expressed in his chapters describing the four greatest enemies to market success, vanity, greed, logic, and the will to believe. Let us take each one in turn and explore the reasons why they cause us to fail. Vanity, says Kelly, is probably the greatest single enemy of the stock trader. It is vanity which leads us to take small profits but large losses. When our original judgment is wrong and stock we purchase goes down, instead of selling it and buying another one, we buy more at lower prices in a futile attempt to get even. Our vanity will not permit us to admit that we were wrong. We must prove that our original purchase was correct. How many people sell the good stocks and hold the poor ones? It is also vanity which makes a man carry stock on margin, since he can carry more stock than he can afford. The most obvious example of vanity is the millions of people who have been holding bad stocks for years with various amounts of losses. It is their vanity which prevents them from admitting their mistake.

"Next to vanity, greed is the worst foe to good judgment," says Kelly. Famous last words are these, "Oh, if I had only sold when. . . ." Our greed is usually the forerunner of these words. People refuse to listen to the warning of brokers or friends. They are so optimistic by nature that they are not easily scared. We are too optimistic for our own good. According to the author not every optimist is a sucker but most suckers seem to be optimistic.

The next enemy of success is the logical behavior of investors. They fail to realize that their chance for success is enhanced by doing what appears illogical. When markets are depressed and the mood distinctly bearish, the normal tendency is to sell all your stocks. Good market sense would have you invoke the contrary action theory and buy an oversold market for the inevitable recovery.

It is more than forty years since this book was written. Many things have changed, including the size and importance of the stock market. However, Kelly's truths and insights into the behavior of investors have not changed. They continue to guide the wise investor in avoiding the emotional pitfalls which prevent him from grabbing the stock market's brass ring.

√ Keyes, Franklin C.
Wall Street Speculation: Its Tricks and Its Tragedies. Original: Oneonta, N.Y.: Columbia, 1904. Reprint: Burlington, Vt.: Fraser, 1970. 77 pp. $9.00

The contents of this lecture are a veritable sermon on the evils of speculation. The author inveighs against Wall Street and the stacked deck which he claims it represents. He calls it a game of chance run by millionaires that relieves the avaricious public of $100 million a year. In a rare display of charity, Keyes admits that there is a legitimate side to Wall Street. Corporate finance and government debt are a great necessity, and the stock market serves that function. It is the heart of the financial life of the country.

You must understand the climate of the period to appreciate the objections of the author. The turn of the century witnessed an orgy of trust building, pool manipulation, and bank greediness that rivalled any previous period in history. The public eagerly rushed into the market in numbers that equalled the gold rush of 1849. Volume soared to records in 1906 that were not eclipsed until twenty-four years later. Two panics in 1901 and 1903 cleaned out thousands of novices and professionals.

The author observes that only one in ten makes anything in the market, and only one in ten of those keeps his profits. You therefore have only one chance in a hundred to beat the game. Jay Gould, the famous speculator, controlled his companies and did not gamble—he knew what was going to happen. The novice never gets the courage to buy until stocks are on top. He also sells out on the bottom. He would have a better chance to win if he did the opposite. Insiders create the forces and conditions that affect the market. Banks in Wall Street know the true condition of the money market and therefore are able to act with confidence.

Why does the public keep coming back for more? They see others go to ruin and yet they still think they can beat the game. There is an inexhaustible supply of suckers. Thus the game goes on, and Wall Street has a thriving business. Speculation is fatal to most people who engage in it. If you win at the start, it lures you on to lose not only your money, but your hope, courage, and your capacity for honest work.

Keyes cautions the reader to avoid the market entirely. It is not necessary to "put your head into a lion's mouth to see whether or not it gets snapped off." He especially warns against brokers, the press, manipulators, and tipsters. The last of these send daily letters to their customers for five to twenty dollars a month. They are often employed by pools to unload stocks. They use guarded language in their letters to prove anything they want. No matter which way the market goes they can pick out a sentence that is right.

Two sad cases that ended in tragedy are detailed. One distraught speculator lost forty years' savings and blew his brains out as a result. There are unkind words for the Standard Oil crowd which controlled the National City Bank and others. They created money panics that killed the market so that they could snap up stocks at bargain prices from the scared public. Keyes' analogy of a speculator and a moth sums up the dilemma of human greed as it applies to the stock market. He says, "to the inexperienced, Wall Street is an ever alluring light toward which men seem drawn by some peculiar light. Continually the moths keep flying into the flame until their wings are scorched off and their charred carcasses fall at the foot of the candle with swarms of other dead."

The value of Keyes' diatribe is timeless. Today's peril is not the same as that at the turn of the century, but there is still need for caution. Man's folly is contained in the evil trinity of hope, fear, and greed; they are a constant barrier to success in the difficult art of speculation.

McNeel, R. W.
Beating the Stock Market. Original: Boston: R. W. McNeel, 1921. Reprint: Burlington, Vt.: Fraser, 1963-1967. 155 pp. paperback: $3.00

In the preface Mr. McNeel humbly explains that he has prepared this little book in an effort to set forth the fundamentals of success in speculation. The pages that follow offer substantial proof of the author's modesty, for he has truly written an important book that will last as long as the stock market is made up of people. And in the certainty that the human element will always be present, McNeel's advice offers valuable aid to the would-be speculator.

In essence, the surest way to be successful "beating the market" is to "beat yourself" since the emotions which speculation arouses lead to the errors which cause personal ruin. McNeel writes his book from a solid background including a ten-year stint as financial editor of the *Boston Herald* from 1912 to 1922. Specific comments that stand out in importance are the following:

"Speculation has universal appeal and therefore one must eliminate risk as much as is humanly possible."

"Abnormal conditions are never permanent, it is important to have the character to think independently of the crowd and buy when the market is low and morale is ebbing."

"The faith that our country will survive should help you in that effort."

"Character and intelligence lead on to success, since the market is a contest be-tween those who know the game and those who do not."

"The 'They' whom everybody refers to is an aristocracy of intelligence and courage and not of power."

Overriding all other considerations, the real secret of success in speculation is a problem of self-mastery and self-discipline as much as one of finance. It is not the stock market which beats speculators. It is their own unreasoning instincts and inborn tendencies which they cannot master, and which given free rein lead on to ruin. The book McNeel has given us does not offer a guaranteed formula for speculative success, but it does provide valuable information for anyone who risks his money in the stock market.

HISTORY

Allen, Frederick Lewis
Only Yesterday: An Informed History of the Nineteen-Twenties. New York: Harper, 1931. 370 pp.

The history of the 1920s demonstrates how a nation can allow a period of uncontrolled prosperity to go to its head. Allen traces the dynamic growth of industry, the dramatic social change, and the gay abandon of that postwar decade. He covers every area with historical accuracy and precision. The events build up to a financial crescendo and culminate in the greatest economic collapse in American history. The background of that panic is found in this book. The author allows the reader to establish the causes in his own mind after a careful look at the evidence of the preceding ten years.

After the war, Woodrow Wilson was shattered by an isolationist Congress that would not ratify his fourteen points and join the League of Nations. The sick President went to the people against his doctor's advice. His left side was paralyzed by a stroke, and he returned to the White House. Three months after Harding beat Cox, the heartbroken Wilson died.

The country was in a recession in 1920 and 1921 and this gave rise to a period of hate. There was a threat of Bolshevism, the KKK grew strong, and anti-Negro, anti-Catholic, and anti-Semitic feeling flourished. In 1920, J. P. Morgan's was bombed, and thirty persons were killed outright and hundreds injured. The crime was never solved, but authorities assumed that a radical group was responsible.

As business picked up the threat of communism waned, and the country was absorbed in all the new discoveries that added to their comfort and pleasure. Radio brought sports events, political conventions, and other types of entertainment into the home. The automobile boom led to a breakdown in prewar morals as the closed car became a "house of prostitution on wheels." In Europe Freud, Adler, and Jung were starting the sexual revolution.

After the untimely death of President Warren G. Harding in 1923, Calvin Coolidge ushered in a period of seven years of unparalleled prosperity. This business boom was caused by new discoveries that in many cases started whole new industries—rayon, cigarettes, refrigerators, telephones, cosmetics, chemicals, and electrical devices. Chain stores grew in number—grocery, cigar stores, and five and tens. Movies prospered. Radio Corporation of America sales grew from $60 million in 1922 to $842½ million in 1929, a 1,400 percent increase. Passenger car statistics revealed the startling growth in that industry. In 1919 there were 6,777,000 cars; by 1929 there were 23,121,000.

Success was worshiped and business was regarded with new veneration. Part of the excitement of the 1920s, with the improved means of communication, was the preoccupation with trifles, fads and scandals—the Leopold-Loeb murder case, the Scopes trial, and Lindbergh's flight. In 1925 the Florida land boom assumed the proportions of a mania. It lasted until a hurricane in 1926 killed 400 and injured 6,300, and left 50,000 homeless. The land boom caused heartache to farmers who were forced to pay taxes on increased valuations.

The year 1927 belonged to Charles Lindbergh who flew the Atlantic solo for a $25,000 prize. He was the hero of the decade—a chivalric figure in a world that had debunked God and spirtiual values. No American since Lincoln had commanded such devotion. In 1928 Babe Ruth captured the headlines with his home run hitting. The stock market continued to climb. Professionals were cautious after so many years of growth, but the envious public, which had missed out on all those years, was now gripped with speculative fever. The irresistible force of their greed propelled them into the market in growing numbers. It was at about this time that Max Winkler said, "The market was discounting not only the future, but the hereafter."

In the spring of 1929 call money was 20 percent and in a confrontation with the Fed (Federal Reserve Board), Charles Mitchell of the First National City Bank offered $20 million to speculators at 15 percent and up. This helped continue the boom which the Fed had tried to slow down. Brokers loans were now $6 billion up from $3½ billion at the end of 1927. It was preposterous. In economics as in physics the higher they go the harder they fall. The public was asking for disaster. In all the excitement responsible officials completely ignored the wild speculation that was fostered by the banks. It was condoned by ex-Governor Stokes of New Jersey who proclaimed that Columbus, Washington, Franklin, and Edison were all speculators. John J. Raskob in the *Ladies Home Journal* wrote an article titled "Everybody Ought to be Rich." Investment trusts multiplied like locusts; 500 were sold to the public with $3 billion in capital.

In early October the market sold off; it was blamed on two events. The first was the collapse of the Hatry Financial Group in England which led to forced selling by foreign investors. The second was the refusal of the Massachusetts Department of Public Utilities to allow Boston Edison to split its stock. Prophecy is the most hazardous of occupations, but the experts must forecast as a matter of course. What were they saying at this time? Roger Babson was bearish as he had been for a long time. Poor's letter predicted "further liquidation in stocks." Paul Warburg was alive to the peril of the situation and warned of a forthcoming disaster. The Harvard Economic Society was not alarmed. It predicted that the Fed would ease money and check the downward movement. Leonard P. Ayres of the Cleveland Trust was not convinced that a serious recession was in the making. Professor Irving Fisher of Yale was optimistic and issued his famous declaration, "Stock prices have reached what looks like a permanently high plateau." R. W. McNeel, Arthur Cutten, and Charles E. Mitchell were all bullish.

The impending disaster was to prove as frightening to the richest and wisest of investors as to the most foolish and simple holder of a few shares of stock on margin. On October 24, "the gigantic edifice of prices was honeycombed with speculative credit and was now breaking under its own weight." The selling produced fear for the first time in years, and as the bulls disappeared the support for prices vanished. A $240 million fund was pledged by five bankers at a J. P. Morgan meeting. With thousands of people now destroyed, a communique from J. P. Morgan's partner, Thomas Lamont, stated nonchalantly, "There has been a little distress selling on the stock exchange." Herbert Hoover pointed out that "the fundamental business of the country is on a sound and prosperous basis."

On Tuesday, October 29, 1929, the panic reached the proportions of a tempest. Millionaires of a few weeks before were impoverished by the results. White Sewing Machine Company which had been 48 closed at $11\frac{1}{8}$ on October 28. A messenger boy put in an order to buy at 1, and in the absence of any other bids, he actually got the stock for $1 a share. It was chaos. Orders were lost and people were sold out by mistake. In all, 16,410,030 shares were exchanged—a record that was to stand for more than thirty years.

Prosperity is more than an economic condition. It is a state of mind. The panic was the climax of a cycle in mass emotion. Attitudes changed dramatically. Dreams of riches were shattered. Adjustments had to be made. The psychological climate was changing. The postwar decade, "the new era," had ended. The rally in 1930 was short lived and more than 1,000 banks failed including the largest in American financial history, the Bank of the United States. This financial orgy wrote the end of a chapter in American economic history that would never be repeated. Allen has faithfully recorded for posterity its story from the early years of elation to its sad, disillusioning climax.

Brandeis, Louis D.

Other People's Money, and How the Bankers Use It. Original: New York: Frederick A. Stokes, 1914. Reprint: New York: Harper & Row, 1967. 152 pp. paperback: $1.95

This book by a well-known Supreme Court justice attacked the arrogance of American business leadership and raised questions about corporate capitalism. The original series of articles appeared in *Harpers* magazine. Brandeis feared the concentration and centralized power of corporate bigness. He felt it would force the transfer of privilege in American social policy from innovative to vested interests. It was therefore a political and moral fear rather than an economic one. Whatever the reasons, Brandeis was committed to the dissolution of the big corporations and interlocking directorates regardless of the costs in efficiency. The book contains his arguments in support of his views.

At the outset Brandeis points out the flaws of consolidation:

1. They were too large to manage.
2. Bankers who dominated management responsibilities had a conflict of interest.
3. Reduced competition contributed to economic inefficiency.
4. Interlocking directorates led to misallocation of resources and maldistribution of income.

5. Monopolies suppressed competition. New entries into an industry were tied up because innovation jeopardized capital investments.

6. Concentration of money was conducive to discriminatory credit practices, and inflated cost of money to new capital investment.

The feature of this book is Brandeis' resentment over investment bankers achieving their wealth without risk. They used "other people's money." Their power and growth came from wielding the savings and capital of others. "The goose that lays golden eggs has been considered a most valuable possession. But more profitable is the privilege of taking golden eggs laid by somebody else's goose." The investment bankers had that privilege. They controlled people through the use of the people's own money.

The Pujo Committee investigated the evils which Brandeis had described, but the legislation that resulted from their findings did not go far enough. The Federal Reserve Act, the Federal Trade Commission, and the Clayton Anti-Trust Act fell short of what Justice Brandeis had wanted. They did little to reduce the concentration of control in the economy. In 1915, 1925, and 1935 Brandeis continued to advise curbing economic concentration, but nothing was done. Arsene Pujo's investigation determined that J. P. Morgan members and the directors of their controlled trust companies (the First National Bank and the National City Bank) held 341 directorships in 112 corporations with capitalizations of over $22 billion. The sphere of influence of the bankers led to many industrial evils:

1. Prices were determined by agreement and not competition.

2. The money trust extorted excessive profits by suppressing competition.

3. Industrial liberty was suppressed. The intimidation of financial power was extended to the small, independent business man, professional man, and others who needed credit and had to buy products from the corporations controlled by the money lords.

Interlocking directorates served to suppress competition. No man could serve two masters. It tended to inefficiency, removed incentive, and destroyed sound judgment. Brandeis cited the endless chain of control through which the financial oligarchy operated. United States Steel was the nexus of big business. The few men who controlled steel were directors of twenty-nine railroads and steamship companies, the largest steel customers. Brandeis stated that before American business could regain its freedom, interlocking directorates had to be prohibited.

The issues brought forth in this book are fresh and vital today. At various times they are headline news. Corporate size now dwarfs that of Brandeis' time. *Other People's Money* is valuable for detailing the antitrust movement of the progressive era. It is dated in some of its arguments, but even now, fifty years later, it has a startling relevance.

✓ **Brooks, John Nixon**
   Once in Golconda: A True Drama of Wall Street, 1920–1938. New York: Harper & Row, 1969. 307 pp. $6.95

Since the history of every era has its heroes and villains, the historian can move his audience at will depending on how he treats the events with his talented pen.

Once in Golconda is a true story of the period following World War I. It covers the great boom of the 1920s, the 1929 crash, and the long depression of the 1930s—truly eventful years in the American past. John Brooks has reached the peak of his writing finesse in relating the story of the men and events that straddled this awesome score of history-making years.

Starting with the bombing of the Morgan Bank in 1920, and the Stutz corner by Allan Ryan, the author weaves his way artfully through that happy period which promised to make everyone rich, the 1920s. With the brush of a master, he paints the most skillful portrait of the events which led to the debacle of 1929. We are made acutely aware of those who warned us of the coming storm, and the leaders who claimed it could never happen.

The climax of this story has to be the sad end of Richard Whitney, "The White Knight," whose popularity led him to the presidency of the New York Stock Exchange. In the maze of events that led to his downfall and imprisonment in Sing Sing, we are witness to another case of a brilliant career ending in ruin. It is told with an insight and skill that should command the attention of the reader right through to its tragic finale. John Brooks has truly brought to life those exciting and eventful years in a rare and masterful way.

Brooks, John Nixon
  The Seven Fat Years: Chronicles of Wall Street. New York: Harper & Row, 1958. 240 pp. $5.00

In an introductory chapter John Brooks explains that the subjects of the various stories which make up this book were "selected for their intrinsic interest rather than their representativeness." They are intended to present a general impression of the period which *The Seven Fat Years* is trying to describe. It is the boom of the 1950s. All of the material in the book, excluding the introductory chapter, originally appeared in the *New Yorker* magazine in slightly different form.

Taken individually the stories are profiles of the people and events which formed that postwar boom period. Two stories detail the marketing of two mammoth stock issues—the original Ford underwriting and a secondary issue of General Motors. One tale studies in depth the celebrated proxy fight for the New York Central by Robert Young. Hugh Bullock, who manages one of the largest and most well respected groups of mutual funds, is profiled in the author's unique way.

Among the other subjects are a specialist, David Jackson, and how he handled a climactic day of trading in a stock recommended by Walter Winchell. Another is a visit with John Magee, who is best known for his book, co-authored by Robert Edwards, entitled *Technical Analysis of Stock Trends.* The critical difference between a true chartist or technical analyst and a fundamentalist is that earnings, news, or other aspects about a company don't affect the chartist's decisions. The primary reason for buying a stock is the action as described in the chart patterns and formations. For that reason Magee sealed up the windows of his office with boards and putty so nothing could distract him. All he had was a table, a chair, a telephone, a ticker, and an air conditioner. In that way he was free to make his decisions based solely on his charts.

As a group of articles, *The Seven Fat Years* is interesting and deserves a niche in the literature of the 1950s. It is not, however, a comprehensive history of the period. It is hoped that the author will some day direct his attention to the decade and write his impressions of those postwar years of adjustment.

Bullock, Hugh
The Story of Investment Companies. New York: Columbia University Press, 1959. 305 pp. $9.00

It is indeed fortunate for the investment community that the rare circumstances which combined to produce this book have given us a classic volume that will stand unchallenged as a source for the history of the mutual fund. Hugh Bullock, son of the founder of the Calvin Bullock Fund, has capped a lifetime in the fund business by merging his unique authority, experience, and knowledge with four years of thorough research to produce this authoritative history.

Starting with a detailed analysis of the whole trust movement from its early years in England and Scotland, Mr. Bullock pays tribute to those great men who were responsible for its beginnings. The individual he singles out for special praise is Robert Fleming whom he call "the Father of Investment Trusts."

The history of the investment company in America began in earnest in the 1920s with a deluge of closed-end investment trusts such as Tri-Continental, Atlas, Lehman, Equity, and others. These companies and other pyramided management companies in 1929 totaled 30 percent of all corporate financing. After the panic, investment trusts were poison to the investing public, and during 1930 and 1931 the so-called fixed trusts saw their heyday because the public wanted no part of the management that had let them down during the crash.

The term "mutual fund" crept into the official language in the Revenue Act of 1936, which permitted mutual investment companies to be relieved of federal taxes on income distributed to their shareholders. In 1940, the Investment Company Act divided closed-end and open-end funds and began to refer to the open-end variety as mutual funds.

The Investment Company Act of 1940 cleared the atmosphere, and renewed confidence caused the public to return in growing numbers to the mutual fund. The spectacular growth that followed led to the development of hundreds of new funds of all types, and coupled with the capital appreciation has made the mutual fund one of the largest pools of investment capital in the stock market.

In summing up, the author treats the mutual fund to which he has devoted his life with objective wisdom. "It is not a cure-all" or a sure thing, but unlike the investment trust of forty years ago, the stockholder now has a share of a fund with usually one class of stock outstanding, which can be redeemed at will. The fund also has a broadly diversified portfolio carefully supervised by professionals. In effect, the mutual fund has developed through a long series of successes and failures into the best investment vehicle the average investor is likely to find anywhere.

Clews, Henry
Fifty Years in Wall Street: "Twenty-Eight Years in Wall Street," Revised and Enlarged by a Resume of the Past Twenty-Two Years Making a Record of Fifty Years in Wall Street. New York: Irving, 1908. 1062 pp.

This tome is a tribute to Wall Street and the many dynamic personalities who have achieved a position of prominence there. Clews apologizes for his omissions after more than one thousand pages of stock market history. This proves the difficulty of covering every facet of the street in one book. The author starts in 1857 and ends his story in 1907. It is obvious that the major concentration of Clews' effort is in the earlier years of the half century. There is only a casual mention of J. Pierpont Morgan and other dominant figures of the latter part of the nineteenth century. The areas that do stand out in importance are: (1) a history of the New York Stock Exchange; (2) a biography of the outstanding leaders of their time—Commodore Cornelius Vanderbilt, Daniel Drew, and Jay Gould; (3) a diary of events from 1816–1884; (4) a discussion of stock market panics and the attempted gold corner which culminated in Black Friday, September 24, 1869; and (5) a brief mention of scores of individuals in the financial and business world who made their mark in the development of their region and the country as a whole.

Cornelius Vanderbilt's most dramatic achievement was taking on the whole New York legislature in Albany. They had defeated a bill which would have merged his Hudson and Harlem Railroads and the Harlem stock slumped. The legislators had shorted the stock beforehand. With the aid of John Tobin and Leonard Jerome, Vanderbilt bought the stock as the price was forced down until he owned 27,000 more shares than existed. This is the essence of a corner. The legislators could not buy the stock needed to cover their short sales; they were in a trap. Vanderbilt asked $1,000 a share. But Tobin and Jerome prevailed upon him not to destroy the street. Jerome said, "If you should carry out your threat it would break every house on the street." He settled for $285. Those are the possibilities of speculation. It also demonstrates the one-man power that Vanderbilt wielded against the legislature, the governor, and an assortment of "crooked" lawyers.

Daniel Drew had a fabulous career that ended in bankruptcy and ruin. At one time he had more cash than anyone in either Wall Street or America—$13 million. His most brilliant maneuver was a trick learned from an earlier leader of the "bears" named Jacob Little. Drew had loaned money to the Erie and received in return 28,000 shares of common and $3.5 million in convertible bonds. In 1866 he was cornered in Erie and was squeezed to cover his shorts. Drew surprised his adversaries; he converted his bonds and threw 58,000 shares on the market. He fed the bulls, settled his contracts, and escaped the trap which would have broken him. He was a unique figure in Wall Street and was unbeatable until he met Jay Gould and Jim Fisk. He said of Gould, "His touch is death." In the book, Clews recalls a dinner when Drew was at his peak. All the speakers glorified him, but the author warned that avarice might work his ruin. Five years later Drew was finished and broke. His bankruptcy schedule included a watch and chain valued at $150, a sealskin coat, $150, wearing apparel, $100, and a bible and hymn books, etc., $130.

The story of Jay Gould is so fantastic that it exceeds the bounds of fiction. Born in upstate New York, the son of a grocer, Gould rose to prominence in the railroad business. His modus operandi was to buy two bad roads, merge them under a new name, and float bonds at a good price. He would then sell the new road to a purchaser at a large profit, and if the new owner could not make a profit after a year or two he'd buy back the road at greatly reduced prices. Gould made a fortune as the manager of the Erie Railroad. He led the attempt to corner the nation's gold supply and later controlled Western Union and the telegraph field. Shakespeare said, "The evil that men do lives after them, the good is oft interred with their bones." Clews felt that in Gould's case the adage was reversed. The evil he did would be forgotten, and his disposition to be a builder would enhance his memory in later years.

Clews' account of so many business and Wall Street celebrities, their achievements, and ultimately their philanthropic bequests are too numerous for inclusion in this short review. Several dominant stock market personalities are mentioned here because of their importance to the post-Civil War period:

James R. Keene—"the Silver Fox," whose brilliance led J. P. Morgan to select him to manage the $1.4 billion United States Steel underwriting;

William R. Travers—a famous bull;

Charles F. Woerishoffer—a famous bear;

Addison Cammack—another bear who was Woerishoffer's intimate friend;

Russell Sage—king of puts and calls who was reputed to have kept the largest hoard of cash on hand in Wall Street, $20 million;

J. Pierpont Morgan—the great banker;

Edward H. Harriman—the railroad genius;

Charles M. Schwab—the great steel magnate.

The financial leaders cited here are not dealt with at length in this book nor is their contribution to the greatness of America and Wall Street done justice by the brief coverage given them by the author. However, Clews has proved his point about Wall Street with the massive record of individual achievements his book describes. "In America," he says, "no one cares about ancestry. There are hundreds of sons who intellectually dishonor great fathers. Brains, intelligence, industry, energy, and pluck are the words that stand for success in America. America is the true field for the oppressed and down-trodden. Birth is nothing—the fittest survive—merit is supreme."

The value of this work is beyond question. It is one of the few chronicles of Wall Street written at first hand about the last half of the nineteenth century. The author was well known throughout the street, and his personal acquaintance with the characters he writes about lends an unequalled amount of authenticity to his work. The thoughtful and eager student of stock market history will find a wealth of information in this comprehensive volume. Clews was a dedicated man who believed in the greatness and importance of Wall Street based on his trust and vision in the future growth of America.

Collman, Charles Albert
Our Mysterious Panics: 1830–1930. Original: Charles Albert Collman. Reprint: Westport, Conn.: Greenwood Press, 1968. 310 pp. $12.75

In studying a century of stock market history, Collman probes the major panics that not only destroyed the stock markets of their time but ultimately reached the average citizen who lined up at his bank only to have the wicket shut in his face as it was forced to suspend. Major studies of the causes and effects of stock market crashes could hardly be more accurate in describing the causes of panics and the desperation of those beggared by the results.

Events set in motion by men ultimately led to destruction as monetary disorder, bank failures, and bankruptcies followed in an uncontrollable succession of disasters. In 1837, 1857, 1884, 1893, 1901, 1907, and 1929 America suffered financial catastrophes beyond imagination, and the author has faithfully revealed the story of the men and events that contributed to those panics. He arrived at this conclusion as a result of his study: "The explanation of panics must show some factor that is common to them all, and in those which we have contemplated in Wall Street's history, they have uniformly revealed themselves as the result of human schemes and human undertakings." As for 1929 Collman states "that real progress such as the development of utilities, air navigation, radio, and motor enterprises were obscured by sordid examples of deception and rascality; by the acts of super-optimists, typified in the organizers of imprudent investment trusts, bank affiliates, bank chains; by stock market quacks, etc. Men do not make panics deliberately; they are their unconscious agents."

It is important for the student of history to learn from the lessons of the past, since the past is a guide to the future. However much we have done to alter the operation of the stock market through regulation over the years, Collman warns that it is the actions of men that create the conditions of their own undoing. The excesses of the late 1950s were responsible for 1962 and the strong bull market of the late 1960s laid the groundwork for the 1969–1970 crash.

Can man's self-destructive tendencies be curtailed? It seems to be a hopeless cause. It would do well for the wise man to be on guard for the telltale signs of trouble and head for the storm cellar when the clouds gather.

Dies, Edward B.
Behind the Wall Street Curtain. Original: Washington, D.C.: Public Affairs Press and Edward Dies, 1952. Reprint: Freeport, N.Y.: Books for Libraries, 1969. 153 pp. $7.50

It is difficult to escape the impression that the author feels a profound sense of respect for the subject of his study, Wall Street. He portrays the history of the street and profiles some of its most famous tenants with a reverence that strongly endorses the stock market and its value to the country. He looks upon Wall Street as a symbol of our democracy. He has written this book to dispel the misconceptions that the public harbors which are more imagined than real; he draws back the curtain and sheds some light upon the financial system as he sees it.

The story begins with a capsule look at the early days of our country before Wall Street became its financial center. In a racy, terse narrative, Dies sets the stage for those players who dominated the scene for more than a century, as America was growing into the richest and most powerful nation in the world.

His method is a unique study of history through short, informative, biographical sketches of the characters that commanded the attention of their respective eras. The early years are seen through the careers of Daniel Drew and Cornelius Vanderbilt, who always seemed to be in hot competition, first in steamboats and then in railroads. Drew looked at railroads as a speculative vehicle, while Vanderbilt saw them as a means of transportation across the country. After joining with Jim Fisk and Jay Gould as treasurer of the Erie, "the Preacher," who was the scourge of Wall Street as a bear operator making money by "fishin' in troubled waters," lost out to his pupil Jay Gould after fighting two disastrous battles with Vanderbilt over Harlem railroad stock. The Commodore acquired a vast network of railroads and improved them with new rolling stock, steel rails, steel bridges, and sturdy stations. He helped the country expand. He was to leave an immense fortune to his son, William, who is best known for his quote as recorded by an irresponsible reporter, "The public be damned."

The story of Jay Gould is remarkable. He was a financial wizard called by Daniel Drew, "the touch of death." His daring exploits would fill a book, but none was more bold than his attempt to corner the gold supply of the country in 1869. Jim Fisk was his ally and the corner almost succeeded but for Ulysses S. Grant's decision to sell gold at a crucial moment. Gould did not get caught, however, since he sold out near the highest price. Fisk repudiated his purchases made above the market to support the quotations. It was inevitable that the flamboyant "Jubilee Jim" should meet a tragic end. After a lover's quarrel with Josie Mansfield, he hounded her new boy friend until he destroyed him. Ned Stokes, who was to be indicted for blackmail, fatally shot Fisk in the Grand Central Hotel.

The next era deals with three of America's industry builders, Andrew Carnegie in steel, John D. Rockefeller in oil, and the most powerful financial figure in the country, J. P. Morgan. Carnegie and Morgan met in a test of business acumen when Morgan was forming the United States Steel Corporation. He paid under $500 million for the Carnegie Steel Company. Years later when dining on Morgan's yacht, Carnegie casually said, "I think I sold my company too cheaply; I should have asked for $100 million more!" "You would have gotten it," replied Morgan. This remained a source of irritation to Carnegie until the end of his days. It wasn't the money; it was the principle. Andrew Carnegie, true to his conviction that "he who dies rich, dies disgraced," gave away some $350 million to various philanthropies, leaving only $25 million to his family.

Commodities, money, politics, investment trusts, and the small investor are the amalgam that bring us up to date as Dies proclaims in glowing terms what's right with America. Outside of an intolerable tax burden, which he deplores, there is nothing basically wrong. He sums up with patriotic fervor, "Our magnificent financial system—our banks, insurance companies, our excellent stock and commodity exchanges—stand as a mighty rock in a sea of world disorder. Mistakes of the past have been admitted, corrective measures have been taken, and Wall Street, as a symbol of free trade by free men, will endure in the changing pattern of America's bold onward drive to a broader and greater destiny."

Eames, Francis L.
The New York Stock Exchange. Original: New York: Thomas G. Hall, 1894. Reprint: Westport, Conn.: Greenwood Press, 1968. 139 pp. $9.25

More than one hundred years after the Buttonwood Tree agreement of 1792 a thoroughly detailed account of the New York Stock Exchange was constructed by Francis Eames, its president in 1894. His admission that he undertook the task of compiling the history with reluctance underscores the reality that his descriptions consist of facts and that he could not possibly give the color and feeling of those early days as well as could one of the original members. Historians can be grateful to Eames, for his endeavor has faithfully recorded the scenes and conditions which are historically interesting, and will always stand as a factual record of the humble beginnings of the New York Stock Exchange.

Editors of *Fortune*
   The Conglomerate Commotion. New York: Viking Press, 1970. 180 pp. $4.95

One of the most phenomenal growth stories of the soaring sixties was the domination of the corporate scene by a group of companies called "conglomerates." Contrary to some widely held assumptions, the movement was not new. In the past there were giant consolidations in several industries led by powerful financiers, who built up their trusts to the point where government was forced to pass legislation preventing those mergers which tended to limit or restrict competition. These trusts were concentrated in one industry, however, and differed from the multi-industry giants of the 1960s which avoided government interference by spreading influence into unallied areas as they continued to grow in size and importance.

As in years past, the companies were led by fearless and astute financial generals who resorted to corporate magic with paper deals featuring preferred stock, convertibles, warrants, and other combinations of debt that made use of their high price earning ratios to acquire better-financed, but less aggressively managed, companies. The paper which was used became known as "Chinese money" since its value was totally dependent on the continued success of the mother company's common stock. In many cases the acquiring conglomerator hoped to defray the cost of his purchase with the earnings of the acquired company. This method was successfully used by many brilliant Wall Street personalities.

The conglomerate movement grew and flourished during the era of excitement in the mid-1960s, as the obliging institutions and the public pushed the prices of multi-market companies to new highs, and thereby made their acquisitions an easier task. They needed less shares of their own stock to make an acquisition when the market price of their stock was higher.

This book investigates the stories of a select few of the conglomerates, Litton Industries, Gulf and Western Industries, ATO Industries, in the wake of the severe recession of 1969–1970, and examines the reasons for the sharp setback in the fortunes of these former favorites. In doing so, the future of this form of corporate entity is debated by various authors of *Fortune* articles. The test of time is still the best way to find the answer to the ultimate success of many conglomerates, and 1969–1970 was the severest test any corporation could have undergone. Some companies have just barely survived and are limping through the 1971 recovery; others are healthy once again and are growing in all areas.

One thing is certain; the acquisitions have slowed down sharply, especially for those large billion dollar giants who have to consolidate their gains and learn how to stimulate internal growth. They have passed the point where an acquisition, unless it is huge, can possibly have any material effect on their earnings, and the antitrust division of the Justice Department is on record as being opposed to king-size mergers.

Fowler, William Worthington

Twenty years of Inside Life in Wall Street: or Revelations of the Personal Experience of a Speculator. Original: Orange Judd, 1880. Reprint: Greenwich, Conn.: Greenwood Press, 1968. 476 pp. $25.00

The turbulent years that are covered in this book reveal the triumphs and failures of some of Wall Street's most fabled characters. In his account of the delights and dangers of speculation, William Worthington Fowler traces the excitement of the years 1860 through 1880. His first hand knowledge of the people and events that shaped the bull and bear markets of that time make this book read like an intimate diary. Fowler's personal adventures in the market must take second place to the memorable battles of the giants that are only shadowy memories in the second hand accounts of contemporary authors.

The counterpoint of two great Wall Street heroes is told and retold throughout the early chapters—Cornelius "Commodore" Vanderbilt and "Uncle" Daniel Drew. Vanderbilt was a builder who believed in the future of America. When he bought a company he improved it and helped it grow with the aid of his enormous resources. Some of his favorite maxims give the reader an insight into his bullish nature—"I bide my time," "Never sell short." The result of his success is embodied in this one, "Never tell anyone what you are going to do until you've done it."

Daniel Drew was the legitimate successor to Jacob Little. He was an engineer of panics. This king of the bears died penniless and brokenhearted in the arms of one of his few remaining friends. But in his prime, as treasurer of the Erie, he amassed the most cash of anyone in his time—$13 million. Drew and Vanderbilt were the magnets which drew the metal out of the pockets of lesser operators. In the end, "the Preacher," as Drew was sometimes called, gave way to his pupils Jay Gould and James Fisk, Jr.

There is a succession of short profiles of the operators of the period. Addison Jerome, who was "Napoleon of the Public Board" for nine months, was dethroned in 1863 by Henry Keep. The latter started with no money at all and died with $4 million at an early age. John M. Tobin found one stock, learned all he could about it, and helped it rise. He sold it at a large profit. In 1864 he had $5 million. A short time later he was impoverished. Leonard W. Jerome, brother of Addison, believed in intrinsic value. He was generally a bull and felt that "fancies" in the long run would bring losses. Fancies were the growth stocks of that period. William Travers and Anthony Morse had their day in the sun. The former was a bear and the latter led pools in Rock Island, Pittsburgh, Erie, and Fort Wayne.

A highlight of that period was the attempted gold corner in 1869 by Jay Gould and Jim Fisk. In the most daring display of financial acumen, Gould and Fisk forced the price of gold to new highs in an effort to corner the shorts. Their only hope lay in the government's holding off sales from the treasury. They were assured of this by Abel Corbin, President Grant's brother-in-law. At the last moment the corner was broken when Grant released gold for sale. It was one of the most dramatic moments in the history of speculation. Black Friday was September 24, 1869.

Interspersed among the history that he unfolds, Fowler dispenses a large supply of wisdom culled from the experience of years of speculation. They are the maxims that famous speculators lived by in their quest for the riches the market had to offer. In a brilliant summation, Fowler warns the reader that speculation is no easy road to riches. He says, "From riches to penury and from penury to riches is but a step; darkness follows light and light darkness swiftly as day dawns or night falls in the tropics. This swinging to and fro between 'fierce extremes', these fitful pulses of trade beating off hour by hour and day by day the record of values, are the evidence and effect of purely human sentiment in action: of hope and fear, the greed of gain, the spirit of emulation, or the apprehension of loss. Speculators feel, see, and act with electric rapidity, and he whose feeling, perception, and action are at once the most correct and the most rapid wins the prize."

Fowler proved the difficulty of speculation in an account of his own trades. He started out with $500 and built his equity up to $100,000 at one time. Eight years later he was down to his original $500. Many times he tried to put the money in the bank and go off to the country, far away from the game. After boredom set in he invariably went back to try "one more flyer." The history of all those bold operators who made millions only to die in poverty can lead the reader to only one conclusion: if you speculate, be prepared to lose.

✓**Galbraith, John Kenneth**
The Great Crash, 1929. Boston: Houghton Mifflin, 1961. 212 pp. $3.50

Humphrey Neill has said, "Many a healthy reaction has proved fatal." The year 1929 is an extreme example of that truism. John Kenneth Galbraith provides a chronicle of that year with an in-depth review of the economic, political, and psychological events that contributed to the collapse of the stock market. It is perhaps important to add that the first shock wave in October and November of 1929 caught hundreds of thousands of stockholders by surprise. They thought it was a new era. Professor Fisher of Yale University said, "Stock prices are on a permanently high plateau."

The tragedy of the greatest crash in American financial history was that almost nobody escaped. Those who missed 1929 were lured in by the precipitous decline and the rally of 1930, only to lose their money in a yet worse decline through 1931 and 1932. On July 8, 1932 the Dow Jones industrials sank to an all time low of 42. This calamity caused a mass guilt that has commentators, economists, and analysts to this day searching for an answer to the questions, why did it happen, who was to blame, and can it happen again? Galbraith develops the answers in his study of the crash.

Although the background of the 1920s is not given detailed attention, there are indications that it was a period of boom. New industries such as airplane, automobile, radio, and electric utilities increased the demand for workers and supplied products for the eager buyer. Money became plentiful, and an era that had prohibition, Babe Ruth, and Lindbergh did not lack excitement. In 1925 there was a land boom in Florida that rivaled the tulipomania in Holland. It lasted until a severe hurricane in 1926 killed hundreds of people and destroyed thousands of houses. This cooled things off. But it was not too long before the easy money policy adopted by the Federal Reserve Board caused a speculative orgy to develop in 1928. Galbraith says, "It was an escape from reality with make believe and fantasy." Margin purchases swelled with call loans costing 12 percent. Corporations began financing speculation with their surplus funds instead of trying to produce goods. Banks were having a picnic borrowing from the Fed at 5 percent and lending in the market at 12 percent. It was, says the author, "the most profitable arbitrage operation of all time."

When times are good and everyone is prosperous it is difficult to expect those in power to complain. Ted Lewis would have found an affirmative answer to his perennial question, "Is everybody happy?" President Coolidge did not fear any trouble; he left office in 1929 saying that stocks were cheap. Secretary of the Treasury Mellon was an advocate of inaction. The Federal Reserve Board was incompetent and was described by President Herbert Hoover as mediocre. Benjamin Strong, head of the New York Federal Reserve Bank, took the lead in the easy money policy of 1927 in an effort to help the Europeans who sent a trio of delegates to ask for such action to help their economy.

In March 1929 Charles E. Mitchell of the National City Bank, who was a director of the New York Federal Reserve Bank, opted for easy credit when call money had reached 20 percent. The public fervor for stocks had reached the point where interference was greeted with disdain. Arthur Brisbane opined that "if buying and selling stocks is wrong the government should close the stock exchange; if not the Federal Reserve should mind its own business." The tragic truth is that the Fed's business is the stock market, the money market, and speculation. If it had watched the store, the boom could have been defused years before. But that was not meant to be. People were caught up in the frenzy and bought Seaboard Airline Railroad because they thought it was an airline. Holding companies were pyramided until the utilities were one maze of interdependent corporate regional giants. Galbraith calls their development "fiscal incest." Investment trusts were in high gear and $3 billion worth were marketed in 1929, 265 in that year alone. Investment bankers assured themselves of an adequate supply of business, and made additional millions by selling shares to the public at a premium over the offering price which they held and sold to insiders and friends. It was madness of heroic proportions, and nobody wanted it to stop.

There were those unpopular people who ventured predictions of doom, but they were ridiculed and disregarded. Roger Babson was on record for years predicting an end to the mania. His old refrain was meaningless because it was repeated too often. *New York Times* financial editor Alexander Dana Noyes plainly expected a day of reckoning. Paul Warburg called for a strong Federal Reserve policy and warned that the orgy of speculation would lead to a disastrous collapse.

The doubters and doomsayers had their day, and it was a panic of monumental size. The climax on Black Tuesday, October 29, 1929, came on a huge volume of over 16 million shares. It stunned the nation and beggared $1\frac{1}{2}$ million stockholders. It didn't matter if they were on margin or owned stocks outright. The avalanche of selling was the start of a bear market that lasted for years. It was a miracle that during the first week of the crash not one member firm of the New York Stock Exchange went bankrupt.

This book succeeds in helping the reader understand the causes and results of the boom and subsequent bust. Galbraith's conclusion sheds light on his hopes for the future. He claims that only misfortune awaits those who believe they can see the future, as 1929 plainly showed. Despite the SEC, a vigilant Federal Reserve Board, and new measures to control speculation and set margin requirements, the chances for a recurrence of a speculative binge are good. The reality of riches that a boom market can bring entices millions of people to enter. There are too many reasons, mostly political, which prevent the administration in power from using their controls to brake the boom. These may be to avoid unemployment and depression, and to escape the stigma of being identified as the "executioner of the prosperity." It is therefore easy for human folly to win out once again, and the individual must take an unpopular stand in the face of mass emotion. With the lessons of this history fresh in his consciousness, it should be the reader's task to recognize the signals early and avoid the painful consequences of another stock market crash.

✓ **Gould, Leslie**
The Manipulators. New York: McKay, 1966. 276 pp. $6.95

Bees will always be found near a honey pot. It is a natural thing. The same holds true for the scores of people who flock to the stock market to seek their financial destiny. They go where the money is. Leslie Gould's *The Manipulators* tells the story of those individuals in the 1940s and 1950s who made their fortunes without regard for right or wrong. They did so as a matter of will. They didn't care how many people were ruined by their actions. This was the big leagues, and it was every man for himself.

The first story involves Louis Wolfson, whom Gould calls "the raider." In retrospect, it appears that Wolfson was one of the early conglomerators, but his attempt at a major acquisition failed. He started with his father's junkyard in Jacksonville, Florida, worked out a shipyard deal after the war, and bought Capital Transit of Washington, D. C. He milked the company of its cash and sold it off at a handsome profit. He put together Merritt-Chapman and Scott, an accomplishment of great magnitude, and later failed in his attempt to oust Sewell Avery from control of Montgomery Ward. It is obvious that Wolfson was after Ward's large horde of cash. Had he succeeded things might have turned out differently. He also guessed wrong on American Motors and went short just before a major bull move started in consequence of George Romney's correct entry into the small car market.

Another raider is called an "Empire Builder" by Gould. He refers to Leopold Dias Silberstein who is known for his takeover of Penn-Texas and subsequent attempt to buy control of Fairbanks, Morse. His ultimate failure brought a successful lawyer, Alfons Landa, into the picture with the new Fairbanks, Whitney run by David Karr whom Landa installed to run the company. Today not one of the principals in this drama is around, and the company's name has been changed to Colt Industries.

The Pepsi Cola-Loft story concerns a man named Guth who used Loft as his personal project. The directors, who in most cases do not direct, allowed him to get away with it. Guth lost out on a fortune in Loft stock but got away with more than he deserved.

The salad oil scandal is the most fantastic story of all. It deals with "Tino" DeAngelis, who swindled American Express, the nation's biggest banks, the New York Stock Exchange, and others out of $200 million. The intricate details of how a butcher from the Bronx outsmarted some of the world's shrewdest speculators, traders, bankers, and brokers makes lively reading. The real story may never be known, but it is obvious that a large-scale fraud was perpetrated, one of the largest in history. "Tino" DeAngelis was sentenced to two consecutive terms of ten years each and concurrent terms of five and ten years, and a fine of $20,000.

The book continues with a record of the boiler room operators who swindled $42 million from the public in the Great Sweet Grass and the United Dye and Chemical capers. In the area of public relations it recalls the powerful force of Tex McCrary and Jerry Finkelstein in the strong bull moves of General Development and Universal Controls. Louis Chesler, the dynamic Canadian wheeler-dealer was a principal in those companies. U.S. Hoffman Machinery with Hyman Marcus and Harold Roth is also part of the public relations story, and of how the public gets taken in.

Gould has some harsh words for the "regulators" or the SEC. He cites the history of the commission and stresses the need for a strong policeman over the securities markets. Indeed the whole book is an indictment of the lack of proper supervision by the SEC. He ends that chapter with the question, "Who is to regulate the regulators?"

The author strongly opposes the Dow Theory chartists and argues that the thirty industrials are not representative of the large body of stocks. It is his contention that the Dow has given wrong bull and bear signals sixteen out of twenty-five times since 1930. Near the end of the book Gould discusses the 1929 crash in an essay titled "Emotion," and he theorizes on the possibility of another debacle. He concludes that even the managers who control vast funds are human and subject to their emotions. But there is one certainty that you can count on. There is always a top to a bull market and a bottom to a bear market. On a long term basis the investor who uses dollar averaging has the best chance for capital appreciation. This mechanical formula eliminates from investment the human element which has always been the bane of the trader.

The compound effect of the many stories Gould has brought together in this book should serve a valuable purpose. It cries out to the average man to exercise caution. It demands that he learn from the bitter experiences of those who blindly succumbed to their own limitless greed only to lose everything to the slick, hardened market operators. This book asks the SEC to do its job more efficiently so that the public is protected from these various manipulators. The lessons are here for the reader to learn, and the moral is obvious. The fact is that only an infinitesmal part of the more than 30 million stockholders will ever read this call for caution, nor will those who do heed its advice when their blood gets hot.

√**Hill, Frederick Trevor**
The Story of a Street. Original: New York: Harper & Bros., 1908. Reprint: Burlington, Vt.: Fraser, 1969. 171 pp. paperback: $8.00

This enlightening book is a comprehensive history of Wall Street from March 31, 1644, when a notice was posted locating the street, until its writing in 1908. If you can imagine the excitement of change, military, political, and financial, that marks the history of the thoroughfare which extends from Trinity Church to the East River, then you can appreciate the value of a detailed examination of the series of events marking Wall Street's progress through the years.

The catalog of famous names that dot the history includes Peter Stuyvesant, Captain Kidd, Peter Zenger, Alexander Hamilton, George Washington, Paul Revere, and others. Few streets in the world are entitled to equal fame. It was central to the founding of our nation and saw the inauguration of George Washington as the first president of the United States. Earlier in 1735 it saw the Peter Zenger trial in which an aging Andrew Hamilton rose to the occasion and delivered the most powerful plea for freedom of the press that America had ever heard, and won the hearts of the jury.

Wall Street's face continued changing as the years passed and its role kept pace. In 1792, its financial history formally began with the signing of the Buttonwood Tree Agreement. The political center of gravity shifted to Philadelphia and later to Washington, but Wall Street was the fashion center of the country. The banking system's establishment later added to its importance as the financial center of the country. It is difficult to estimate the importance of the events that laid the foundation for the great country that was to develop in the future. The tribute to Wall Street's importance was best expressed by the author Frederick Trevor Hill in these closing words: "The strip of land that had seen Stuyvesant's nine foot palisade rise to the gigantic walls of brick and stone which now enclose and shadow it, (little did he know how high those bricks and stone would eventually reach). The spot where Zenger's words were buried and the Declaration of Independence read . . . the route along which royal pageants passed and the ragged continentals made their triumphal march . . . the forum of the revolution and the birthplace of the nation . . . the haunt of fashion and the heart of business . . . the house of Hamilton (Alexander), the school of statesmen . . . the firing line of commerce . . . the battleground of politics and of money . . . the scene of financial masterstrokes and the speculative orgies of loud-tongued victories and wild-eyed panics . . . it is historic ground, of whose final destiny none dare prophesy."

Holbrook, Stewart H.
The Age of the Moguls. Garden City, N.Y.: Doubleday, 1953. 373 pp. $5.75

The history of America's economic growth is intimately tied to the events that marked the lives of many great men. Holbrook tells the dynamic story of those famous personages in capsule form so that they can all be included in one work.

He telescopes the drama of the builders, the rogues, the achievers, the dynasties, and the moneymakers. Although the quantity of capital was important to a point, the author observes that the drive which motivated these men came from the same source that moved Genghis Khan and Napoleon Bonaparte. They made America the richest and strongest nation in the world. Their urgent desire to span the plains with railroads, build the bridges, build the automobiles, and drill for the needed petroleum created new industries and millions of jobs. The fortunes that they accumulated were distributed among their heirs and in many cases were willed to foundations and trusts that remain today for worthy and philanthropic purposes. This is Holbrook's story, and he tells it with an awe and inspiration that mirrors the accomplishments of its subjects. It deals with the men whose leadership and dynamism made America great.

Cornelius "Commodore" Vanderbilt could have had a peaceful and happy life with the millions he amassed, but he was never more content than when he outdid "Uncle" Daniel Drew. Jay Gould and Jim Fisk tried to add to their Erie victories with a bold attempt to corner the complete gold supply of the country. The wily Gould was described by someone as "a person who did not get up early in the morning; he stayed up all night." The panic of 1873 caught many people off guard and wiped them out completely. It also provided a rare opportunity for astute men like John D. Rockefeller, Andrew Carnegie, and Henry Clay Frick, who used the bargain prices to buy out their competition. This put them into a favored position for the years of growth that lay ahead. Jay Cooke, the banker who sold bonds to finance the Union Army during the Civil War, went to the wall in the panic of 1873, and thirty-seven banks and brokerage houses went with him. Daniel Drew was caught with a load of stocks, and it marked his demise in Wall Street. He was $1 million in debt.

The great railroad builders, E. H. Harriman and James J. Hill, deserve credit for populating the west. Harriman would have dominated the railroads as J. Pierpont Morgan did the banks had he lived a while longer. The midwest was built by men like Swift, Aaron Montgomery Ward, Cyrus McCormick, Philip Armour, and Potter Palmer. George Pullman and Levi Leiter, Field's partner, also played a major role.

The far west had its share of heroes. Theodore Judah was the prophet and his four disciples were Collis Huntington, Leland Stanford, Mark Hopkins, and Charles Crocker. The west flowered under their leadership and their names are alive today in the institutions which they founded.

The rise of John D. Rockefeller and the Standard Oil trust was a phenomenon unmatched in American financial history, but one which proved that complete happiness is only a dream. Rockefeller is quoted as saying, "It is wrong to assume that men of immense wealth are always happy." Perhaps the feud and bitter rivalry between the houses of Morgan and Rockefeller caused them both uneasiness. They both had immense wealth and were haters. The Standard Oil Trust eclipsed J. P. Morgan's holdings when it controlled the National City Bank and had by far more assets than any bank in the country. The ambitious Morgan couldn't stand that, but his formation of United States Steel should have satisfied his giant ego.

The story of United States Steel was another case where the great Morgan was forced to extend himself to achieve his goal. A canny Scot, Andrew Carnegie, the best steel man in America was ready to retire, but he rallied his enormous resources to simulate a great expansion just as Morgan was about to buy him out. In the end it cost Morgan $492 million. Morgan got his money back and then some when he capitalized United States Steel at $1,402 million. The American reading public also shared in Carnegie's triumph since the $350 million he bequeathed to the country was used to build thousands of libraries. Carnegie gave away almost all of his fortune because he truly believed that "he who dies rich dies disgraced."

The lives of several industrial giants follow as Holbrook recounts in a terse manner the success stories of Henry Ford, Andrew Mellon, and Charlie Schwab. He also relates the sad story of America's biggest bust, Samuel Insull's $750 million collapse. The dynastic growth of the du Ponts, the Guggenheims, and the last mogul, William Randolph Hearst, round out this monumental recapitulation of American economic growth through the contributions of these men of heroic proportions. Hearst's affluence can best be measured by Holbrook's statement that he left $400 million despite the fact that he spent $15 million every year and lived until the age of eighty-eight.

The story which Holbrook tells in this book should be an inspiration to every American. The achievements of the moguls are unique to the American way of life and remain so today. The fire which burned in the minds and hearts of these heroes, their quest for money, power, and status did not die with them. It lives on in the new generations that have followed. While the accomplishments of the new moguls are too close for us to appreciate, time will give the historians of the future the perspective to see today's heroes as Holbrook saw those of the past.

Jackson, Frederick
A Week in Wall Street: By One Who Knows. Original: New York: Frederick Jackson, 1841. Reprint: Burlington, Vt.: Fraser, 1968. 152 pp. flexible cover: $6.00

The passage of more than a century has not dimmed the importance or the pertinence of Jackson's *A Week in Wall Street.* It is obvious that people have not changed since those early days, nor does it appear that they ever will. Once they start with stocks, they are faced with temptation which in turn leads to the inevitable greed.

Writing in 1841, when there were only a handful who trafficked in the stock market, the author shows how a stock rig was set up in the Morrison Kennel caper. The book is replete with insider collaboration and all the human response and counter-response that are as immutable as the laws of nature. The writing is difficult to read and absorb because of differences of syntax and the long, wordy sentences characteristic of the early nineteenth century. The book nonetheless contains a great deal of worthwhile advice and satirical wit. It is the author's way of showing his readers the Wall Street of his day. Jackson's sarcasm is not only directed at the brokers and the bankers who ran the street, but was aimed at the "flunkys" or the sheep who were forever being shorn. Since the author admits that he was "flunked," he is also poking fun at himself.

Among the chapters that add importance to this short treatise on Wall Street's early days is the one which describes what a panic is, how it starts, and what its consequences are. Since this book was written right after the panic of 1837, the effects of that catastrophe must have been fresh in the author's mind as he described the utter despair and havoc that a money panic can wreak on the population. In reflecting on the aftermath of this devastation, Jackson ends with a ray of hope for those who are struck down in a panic. He says, "It is better to laugh than to cry. Experience is sometimes a very hard, but always an efficient teacher, and those who have suffered will have the satisfaction to know better hereafter, who to trust and what to trust, and taught to rely more on themselves."

It becomes clear to the reader that the early experiences of people in Wall Street are as relevant to us as things that happened only yesterday. The titles and names may be changed, but the goals of the people remain the same: "caveat emptor."

√Kearny, John Watts
Sketch of American Finances, 1789–1835. Original: New York: Putnam, 1887. Reprint: Westport, Conn.: Greenwood Press, 1968. 160 pp. $9.75

In this carefully detailed history of young America's first forty-six years, Kearny has taken a mass of dry statistics, congressional laws, and other financial data, and molded them into an interesting, readable story of dedicated men who dealt with the problems of a huge domestic debt. Their goal was to redeem this public debt. The public demanded it, and Congress was responsive to their wishes. With prudent economy in public expenditures and without the aid of a tax on income, the government in 1835 was not only free of debt, but had a balance in the treasury of about $19 million.

It is refreshing to see what can be done by a government that feels the burden of high interest charges and burgeoning debt. It also brings to mind a vital question: how long can present-day America allow its national debt to balloon into such huge proportions—hundreds of billions of dollars of debt, $15 billion in interest every year? It defies reason how administration after administration continues to ignore this mountain that promises one day to envelop us all. The only reference to the national debt that is made every year is the president's request to raise the ceiling.

There can be no comparing of today's trillion dollar Gross National Product with the meager beginnings of our country when Washington was inaugurated in 1789, but the question raised by the substance of this book cries out for an answer.

Lawson, Thomas W.
Frenzied Finance: Vol. 1. The Crime of Amalgamated. Original: Ridgway-Thayer, 1905. Reprint: Westport, Conn.: Greenwood Press, 1968. 559 pp. $22.25

In 1899, Amalgamated Copper was born. It was to rob the public of over $100 million in five years. Its stock was sold to the public at $115 a share, and in 1903 it dropped to $33 a share. Thomas Lawson was the originator of the plan to build a copper trust, and with the help of Henry H. Rogers and William Rockefeller of Standard Oil he put his ideas into effect. This book is Lawson's story of how the public was taken in by the "system" and how he was unwittingly made the instrument of this enormous loss. In writing this book he obviously wanted to be acquitted of any intentional wrongdoing and placed the blame on the system. The latter was a process for the "incubation" of the wealth of people's savings in banks, trusts, and insurance companies. It was also the vast corporate consolidation which set a handful of men apart from the public and allowed them to disregard morality as they captured billions of dollars with impunity. The urgency of Lawson's story was underlined by his conviction that this system had grown more powerful than the government which was supposed to represent all the people's interests.

It was during the Boston Gas War, when Thomas Lawson helped J. Edward Addicks, the Boston Gas King, that he became acquainted with Henry H. Rogers. The brilliant Rogers was the big brain and master of Standard Oil at 26 Broadway. He formed opinions on all new deals and went upstairs for William Rockefeller's approval. Rogers laughed when Lawson first asked him to look into copper. Lawson felt that everyone would make money—the trust, the people, and himself. He knew that the price of copper would rise when its value was realized. It became an obsession with him. He sincerely felt that it would remedy the system because it would make money for the long-suffering public. Yet to execute the project he allied himself with the Standard Oil crowd, the very embodiment of the system. In his own defense, Lawson states that he always made public the truth about what was going on. His plans were advertised and explained fully in various interviews.

Lawson bought control of Butte and Boston Copper at $12\frac{1}{4}$ and advertised that it would sell at 50. Clarence W. Barron, an antagonist of Lawson and head of the Boston News Bureau, informed his readers that Lawson was a liar and that he would close up his business if Lawson were right. Later, when Butte and Boston sold for $130, Barron, acting for Standard Oil, urged his readers to switch to Amalgamated. Butte and Boston was to be part of the first section of Amalgamated, but Rogers pulled his first change on Lawson. Rogers had finally listened to Lawson's story and was impressed. He immediately contacted William Rockefeller, and an agreement was made whereby Standard Oil would furnish the capital and have 75 percent of the profit and Lawson 25 percent. Rogers bought Anaconda, Utah Consolidated, and United Metals Selling. Lawson tells of Rogers' dealings with Marcus Daly, Samuel Untermeyer, and the Lewisohns to impress the reader with the character of the man with whom he was now involved, a leader of financial genius. He exposes Rogers for what he really was, a confidence man who won by means of marked cards, crooked wheels, and bribed umpires. He perverted justice, undermined competition, and resorted to intrigue and graft. At the same time Lawson admits that he bowed discreetly to Rogers' demands. He secretly enjoyed being a part of this all-powerful system. His conscience and honesty took second place to the "jingling music of golden shekels." Great fortunes are seldom achieved without the sacrifice of morals or pride.

Lawson openly boasted in newspaper ads that Amalgamated stock was worth

30 to 60 percent more than the subscription price, that it was earning 12 to 16 percent a year and would always pay 8 percent dividends annually. In other words, Lawson guaranteed every subscriber a large profit. He became enraged when he learned that Rogers had increased the allotment to the public. He became aware of a plot to suck the little people in, force the price of the stock down under the weight of heavy sales and then buy in at rock bottom prices. Lawson's worst fears were realized. He was further demoralized when Rogers cheated him out of his legitimate share of the profits. The author accepted only $5 million when $9 million was to have been his proper remuneration. It was scarcely enough for him to protect the lines of stock he and his friends had pledged. Rogers and Rockefeller sold their stock to prepare for the next section, but Lawson gamely tried to hold the line. His guarantee to the public that Amalgamated would be 140 to 160 came back to haunt him. It did more than that; it ruined him.

The appeal to the public which Lawson made in this book was a sensible and reasonable one. It didn't explain either his greed or his alliance with the very forces he chose to condemn. Events in the many decades since the Amalgamated tragedy have proved that there is no remedy for the system, known today as "investment banking." The rules are different now with full disclosure and the Securities and Exchange Commission policing the issuers of securities. The public is still here, however, eager to line up for the El Dorado or Golconda of the hour. There can be no advertising that guarantees the rewards promised by Lawson with Amalgamated, but that does not seem to deter the greedy public.

Lefevre, Edwin
Wall Street Stories. Original: McLure, Phillips, 1901. Reprint: Westport, Conn.: Greenwood Press, 1969. 224 pp. $9.50

In 1901, Edwin Lefevre wrote several interesting stories about Wall Street. They don't run the gamut of stock market experiences but provide an entertaining and informative look at the complex social vortex where emotions such as greed and fear blend with psychological intensity.

Included is a serio-comic vignette about "The Woman and Her Bonds." It depicts the tragedy of being uninformed about financial matters, a situation in which many women find themselves after the death of their husbands. In this era of women's liberation there would be violent disapproval of the treatment accorded this widow in the purchase of bonds from her late husband's financial advisor. He was polite and helpful, but she was human, ignorant of the market, and afraid to lose her money. It is only one of a variety of incidents that happen every day in the life of a beleaguered stock broker.

"Pike's Peak or Bust" is a success story that ends in tragedy. The author traces the career of a young man as he quickly makes his way up the ladder of financial success and reaches the zenith of achievement as a partner in a New York Stock Exchange member firm. His ego and pride cannot accept the possibility that his success can be reversed. The vagaries of a falling market intrude upon his grandiose dreams, and he is plunged into bankruptcy.

"The Break in Turpentine" takes the reader inside the manipulations of a pool as Samuel Wimbleton Sharpe, one of the best pool operators in Wall Street, plans to rally the price of the American Turpentine Co. The interplay of emotions among the members of the pool clearly demonstrates what can happen behind the scenes, and how it actually does happen. Certain members of the pool decide to sell their shares on the open market in direct violation of their agreement. It does not escape the notice of Sharpe. Without making it known to his partners, he sells the stock short and drives the price down to a level which assures him a large profit in addition to his percentage for leading the pool. The guilty members accept their shame in silence as Sharpe explains why the profits were small Their faith in him as a pool operator reaches a new high.

Several other stories round out the lot and hold up a mirror for the reader in which are reflected those episodes which are part of Wall Street. They are timeless. This is a book about people and how the love of money makes them act.

Levien, J. R.

Anatomy of a Crash. Reprint: New York: Traders Press, 1966. Distributor: Burlington, Vt.: Fraser. 121 pp. paperback: $3.50

This book describes the events of 1929 which gave graphic evidence of the growing storm which finally broke in October. There are two chapters from Barnie Winkelman's book, *Ten Years of Wall Street.* One describes the record of General Motor's growth through the decade of the 1920s. The other describes pool operations. Other chapters contain charts of the blue chips, a speech by Richard Whitney reviewing the crash, and a chronology of the financial events of 1929 from the *New York Times.* The author offers no opinions or editorial comment.

The value of this work is contained in the various articles faithfully describing all the facts and news which transpired during that fateful year. Its tragic lesson is that, despite the confidence of leading economists, bankers, and public officials, a panic of confidence led to a massive, traumatic crash.

It would be helpful in understanding the most tragic period in American economic history if some commentary were provided by the leaders and writers of that era. It is unfortunate that not enough has been written about the catastrophic year that marked the end of a decade of prosperity and led to a long period of depression.

√Mackay, Charles

Extraordinary Popular Delusions and the Madness of Crowds. Original: London: Richard Bentley, 1841. Reprint: Boston: L. C. Page, 1932. Distributor: Burlington, Vt.: Fraser. 724 pp. $7.00

By the author's own admission, popular delusions began so early and have lasted so long that fifty volumes would not be enough to detail their history. But Mackay's classic work effectively depicts the folly of crowd behavior in a series of well-documented chapters whose subjects have their origins at the beginning of recorded history.

The first three chapters deal most directly with the stock market. John Law and the Mississippi Scheme, the South Sea Bubble, and the tulipomania serve as vivid examples of the overpowering confusion that seizes man in his quest for monetary gain. His loss of reason overcomes him only when he becomes part of the crowd; as an individual he can think and make rational judgments

In "The Alchymists," "Modern Prophecies," "Fortune Telling," "Magnetisers," "The Crusades," and "The Witch Mania," Mackay gives eloquent testimony to the endless folly that has held sway throughout the ages. He relates how millions of innocent people were killed, raped, tortured, and imprisoned without cause. Other chapters detail the continuing nonsense that becomes the fashion of the time. In "The Slow Poisoners," he tells how murder by poison became popular in Italy and gradually found its way into France and other European countries. Another chapter explores the duel as a means of settling quarrels, proceeds to strip the glory and courage which man attached to the contenders, and reduces it to the ridicule it deserves. The package might have been neatly wrapped if Mackay had included a chapter describing man's ultimate folly, war.

But even without such a discussion, *Extraordinary Popular Delusions and the Madness of Crowds* remains to this day a vital source book of man's folly and his inhumanity to man. In the stock market you must constantly apply the method described by Bernard Baruch, who writes in the foreword that you must continuously repeat "two and two still makes four" to avoid the many problems of a runaway market. And when you wonder if a decline will ever halt, the appropriate abracadabra may be, "They always did."

This philosophy expressed by one of Wall Street's most famous and successful speculators highlights the outstanding value of this book. It will remain forever as man's island of understanding in a sea of unrestrained desire and confusion.

Medbery, James K.
Men and Mysteries of Wall Street. Original: Boston: Fields, Osgood, 1870. Reprint: Westport, Conn.: Greenwood Press, 1968. 344 pp. $14.50

In a remarkably well written book, James K. Medbery captured the mood of the market one hundred years ago. He related the activities of the men who dominated that era, and in masterful prose tried to plumb the mysteries of the street. All he could do was stand back in awe as those "great operators" made the historic moves that distinguished them from the crowd.

We learn with unmistakable clarity how the Erie, Harlem, Morris Canal, and Hudson corners were effected and wonder why it took so long before this practice was outlawed. The author captured the speculative flavor and excitement of the era while dwelling at length on the defalcation and the sheep who went astray. The financial irregularities caused by unsuccessful stock speculation were a sad part of the history of that period. Medbery summed up that somber chapter of our financial history in a paragraph which says it all: "Until society gives the lie to that obsolete truism which declares poverty to be no disgrace, such labor would be only a fresh injustice; to penetrate the walls of state prisons, and the veiled secrets of the cemetery, in order to unearth the misdeeds of forgers, the malfeasance of bank presidents, at whose funerals clergymen by the dozen lent the testimony of their presence, and the unsuspecting frankincense of impassioned eulogy—of men who committed suicide of the body rather than endure the penalty of social suicide which their foolishness had wrought—of individuals dead, or dying under feigned names in foreign lands with the misery of a blighted past haunting them to the last breath. This is to add crime to crime as long as the public insists upon the worship of success, and measures its honors by length of purse."

Medbery described one average speculator and his misfortune in this way: "One man, just married, whose capital of $30,000 had been risked and lost in a single venture, sat in his dealer's room, unmindful of the busy stir around him, his teeth set as if in death, his eyes transfixed, his face like a winding sheet, and nothing to indicate that his heart continued to beat save the cold beads of perspiration on his pallid forehead."

In spite of the sad stories that weave their way through others of fortune builders and dynamic speculators, it is obvious that there is a strong undertone of hope and enthusiasm. The author made it clear that the time would come when New York and Wall Street would assume "the pivotal position it demands and allows, the paramount financial centre of the globe."

✓**Moody, John**
The Masters of Capital: A Chronicle of Wall Street. New Haven: Yale University Press, 1919. 234 pp.

The growth of industrial America from the Civil War to the end of World War I was an outstanding phenomenon. The great financial progress that gave birth to this rise of capital is the story of those titans of industry whom Moody calls "Masters of Capital." Their story is America's story. It covers the fields of banking, railroads, steel, and oil; the awe which the author displays for his subjects is obvious. Morgan, Harriman, Carnegie, Frick, and Rockefeller are the principal subjects of this book. Their power, concentration of wealth, and feuds drove them on to great feats of industrial success. The United States was the ultimate beneficiary of their dynamic lives, for the end of World War I found America a creditor nation to all of Europe—the greatest industrial power in the world.

The House of Morgan soared into prominence after Jay Cooke's failure in 1873. Morgan had a wide open field for financial operations. He refunded $750 million of government debt and restored American prestige. By 1879 the war debt was behind them, and bankers were able to turn to a new field of activity. The railroads had made a fortune for Gould and Vanderbilt, but a great period of overexpansion and speculation has pumped $4 billion into railroad capitalizations. By 1884 the gigantic structure of inflated railroads crashed. Rates toppled, dividends were cut, and it became imperative that constructive steps be taken to avoid chaos. Morgan moved in to reorganize several railroad systems into solvency: the Baltimore and Ohio, Chesapeake and Ohio, Philadelphia and Reading, Pennsylvania Railroad, and the Southern Railway System. Before the panic of 1893, Drexel, Morgan, and Co. were known as financiers and organizers of mismanaged rail properties. J. P. Morgan was a giant figure in railroads and banking. He had largely reorganized the entire railroad system of America. At the turn of the century he stood slone, healthy, vigorous, and prominent in his field. All his partners had died.

Andrew Carnegie was an ambitious Scot who rose from obscurity to become a giant in the steel industry. At a time when railroad construction was booming, Carnegie bought into the Iron City Forge Company. He had financial help from several railroad officials who gave him all the business he could handle. He gained control of Iron City during the bad times after the Civil War. He had made millions before the 1873 panic. Carnegie founded the forerunner of Carnegie Steel to use the Bessemer steel process and shrewdly called the new plant the Edgar Thomson Works after the president of the Pennsylvania Railroad. The reason for that was no secret. One of Carnegie's best customers was that huge railroad with its unlimited need for steel rails and other products.

The limitations of space prevent a more detailed account of the masters of capital. It is also the reason why so many others are omitted by Moody. Henry Clay Frick had the characteristic audacity of a successful man. He sent a letter to Andrew Mellon asking for $20,000. Mellon liked the tone of the letter and investigated. He was shocked to find a youth working for a few dollars a week. Mellon was impressed with this honest, bright lad and with his sincerity and intelligence. Mellon had also worked himself up from poverty. Frick got the money. H. C. Frick Coal and Coke merged with Carnegie, the ore fields of the Mesaba area were acquired, and a gigantic steel industry grew from a humble start.

John D. Rockefeller had a policy of keeping cash in the company. When hard times came and other refiners were in trouble, his Standard Oil was able to buy up his competition. This ability to save cash during the decade of 1860–1870 enabled Rockefeller to form the Standard Oil Company of Ohio in 1870 with $1 million of cash capital. It was the one great business corporation in America with no debt or banking affiliations. By 1881 the company had accumulated $45 million and had bought out most of its competitors. In 1882, the Standard Oil Trust was a bank within an industry. It financed the industry against all competition and loaned vast sums to needy borrowers just as other banks did. In time the Rockefellers became affiliated with the National City Bank and used their cash assets which grew to over $150 million by 1895 in railroad and other ventures. This Rockefeller bank overshadowed every other institution in the country, and Morgan's star was joined by that of John D. Rockefeller.

The powerful financial figures that Moody discusses in this book were the most important men of their day. Of course there were lesser lights that shone brightly for a time and made their contribution to the growth of our country. This look at a few key money managers is only a slice of the rich story of America's dynamic years of progress. It is enough, however, to whet the reader's appetite for the full story that is available to those who wish to pursue it with curiosity and initiative.

Munn, Glenn G.

Meeting The Bear Market: How to Prepare for the Coming Bull Market. New York: Harper, 1930. 276 pp.

It took a business boom of unheralded proportions to convince the public that the protestations of noted economists were true. Before 1928, the stock market was the province of professionals, corporate executives, and sophisticated traders. "The new era" rode in on the crest of new industrial expansion in steel, automobiles, aeronautics, radio, chemistry, and electrical utilities. The eager public rushed in to make up for lost time and tried to soak up the riches that the stock market promised. This period was examined by Glenn Munn in the aftermath of the crash that followed. In a thorough analysis, he explained why the panic happened and how the wise investor could prepare for the boom which he thought was inevitable. He was premature in his bullish prediction for 1930, but the years ahead ultimately vindicated his enthusiasm for America's growth potential.

The new era school of the late 1920s was reminiscent of the search for the fountain of youth, the promised land, and other utopias. The public was convinced that business cycles were obsolete and that the prosperity curve would move only in one direction, upward. Investors thought that stocks would have only technical, not major, reactions. Quality stocks could be bought regardless of yield, and prereserve-type panics were unthinkable. They argued that investment trusts, insurance companies, banks, and other institutions were a bulwark against a sharp decline in the stock market. In fact, they were largely responsible for the financial slaughter of 1929.

A correction was expected by professionals, but even the most pessimistic prophet of doom did not dream that catastrophe was around the corner. History repeated itself, however, and panic did occur. The unrestrained enthusiasm was transformed into despair and collapse with amazing rapidity. From September 3 to November 13, 1929, the Dow industrials plunged 47.8 percent. In ten weeks, two years of price gains were wiped out. The crash was characterized by its vehemence and the decline of values. These things stood out: the velocity of the decline, the number of casualties (people and stocks), and the record trading volume. October 28 and 29 accounted for 38.3 and 30.57 points in the Dow, or a combined total of 68.90 points in two days, representing 40 percent of the drop to the nadir. The margin myth was exploded by Munn when he revealed that those with slender margins fared better; they were sold out in the early phase of the decline. Outright owners of stock thought they could ride out the storm and were sold out at lower levels.

The author listed fifteen causes of the 1929 stock market crisis: (1) overspeculation on borrowed money; (2) impaired technical position; (3) rise in world money rates; (4) rise in rediscount rates, August 8, 1929; (5) disregard of fundamentals; (6) some groups having already sold off early in 1929; (7) business trend turning downward; (8) undigested securities; (9) concerted corporate financing; (10) foreign selling; (11) an unfavorable utility decision disallowing the split of Boston Edison; (12) investment trusts; (13) capital tax on securities; (14) new era psychology; and (15) tariff discussions. Munn was wrong in his assessment of the outcome of the crash. He did not think it would result in an extended period of business recession. The depression of the 1930s proved that the sell-off in the market had a painful and prolonged aftermath.

Munn displayed a large measure of courage in the wake of 1929's market slump. He poked his head out of the storm cellar to detect signs of an end to the bear market. He was early with his optimism, but saw enough indicators to encourage his bullish stance. Credit was deflated, production was below normal, and retail trade was down. Unemployment was high. Security offerings had decreased because the public was psychologically not disposed to buy stocks. Volume of trading was diminished, and dire predictions were advanced by many people. Dividends were passed, and some companies failed. When the "lunatic fringe" turned short-seller, it was a sign that the bear market was over.

The author looked adversity in the eye and called it opportunity. He said, "When stocks are despised and rejected of men; when confidence turns to fright; when the exuberant populace of a few months previous jettisons stock at a sacrifice; when the mob abandons faith in America's enterprises; when pessimists howl calamity; when the stock market is writhing in mortal anguish: That is the heydey for the patient bargain hunter." Munn's optimism in the long-term future of America and the opportunities that would develop a new bull market was based on population growth, a strong desire to raise the standard of living, and the growth of leisure involved in the shorter workweek. He further advanced his thesis of recovery on the economic, political, and technological factors that he believed would develop in the ensuing years. On the economic front, Munn looked for more mergers, improved marketing, and aggressive development of foreign markets. Politically, he saw government aid (cooperation and subsidization) and stabilization of nations in underdeveloped areas. In the technological area, the author looked for large growth in the development of electricity in homes, railroads, rapid transit, modern housing, television, and many other areas.

The prescience of Glenn Munn was most remarkable since his optimism developed when the prevalent mood of the country was desparate. He dramatized the important lessons of the contrary opinion theories of Humphrey B. Neill, which maintain that you must think and act opposite to the emotions of the multitude. The author was a widely followed technical security analyst, and his choice thoughts and post mortems on the 1929 crash are a valuable addition to the literature of that vital period in America's financial history.

Neill, Humphrey Bancroft
   The Inside Story of the Stock Exchange. New York: B. C. Forbes, 1950.
   345 pp.

Recurrent periods of confidence and fear sum up the human equation of the stock market. Boom and bust are the result of man's inconstant moods, his passionate greed, and utter despair. Through it all, the stock exchange, with an assist from the banks, creates the capital that lubricates our financial system and builds the new industries that make our country prosper. Neill traces the history of the New York Stock Exchange which is inextricably tied in with the political, psychological, and economic story of the United States. He binds the hopes and fears of millions with the rise and fall of the market. He does not condemn or defend the exchange as many writers do; he just presents the facts. They tell the true story of a marketplace that has seen the frantic crowds rush from one mania to another, making money now and losing it later. All the while the New York Stock Exchange remains at its old stand, ready to do the business that is necessary for the good of the country.

The first part of the book deals with the story of the exchange from the Buttonwood Tree Agreement in 1792 until the end of the nineteenth century. The author recalls the contributions of the founders of our country, such as Alexander Hamilton who established the United States Bank. The heritage of America was linked undeniably to money and profits. Capital and labor made business. The Stock and Exchange Board, as it was then called, facilitated the creation of capital to finance the railroads in the 1830s, 1840s, and 1850s. Andrew Jackson killed the second United States Bank in a battle with Nicolas Biddle and started state banks turning out bank notes for everyone to use. This led to the crash of 1837.

The dynamic genius of Jay Cooke promoted the sale of bonds to finance the Civil War. The stock exchange was enlarged and equipped with a stock ticker. It was fast becoming the largest securities exchange in the world. Overexpansion and Jay Cooke's failure led to a crash in 1873. The exchange closed for ten days. A depression dragged on for five years through 1878. The exploits of the "four horsemen," Commodore Vanderbilt, Daniel Drew, Jim Fisk, and Jay Gould, lent glamor and excitement to a lively period in our financial history. Two more panics, one in 1884 and the other in 1893, proved once again that economic psychology was basically human nature in action—faith, confidence, hope, fear, and greed. Money and men were stimulated by confidence, and fear tore down what confidence built up.

The era of the trusts at the turn of the century began with the formation of United States Steel and the Amalgamated Copper Trust. The first third of the new century was unequalled in our history. Many of today's giant companies were born in those prolific years of corporate formation. The panics of 1901 (the Northern Pacific corner) and the "rich man's panic" of 1903 followed in quick succession, but they failed to stop the forward rush of corporate growth. Even the decline of 1907, which followed the 1906 earthquake and fire in San Francisco, could only put a temporary halt to economic progress. The effects of the 1907 "banker's panic" brought a cry for reform which lasted until the First World War and brought about investigations of the stock market by the Hughes Commission in 1909 and the Pujo Committee in 1913. The latter tried to ascertain the capital concentration of the Morgan-Baker-Stillman group, a money trust with interlocking directorates. Exposure of this cabal led to the creation of the Federal Reserve System.

In order to accomplish a cure, a patient must first be sick. A healthy person doesn't go to a doctor. Neither does a prosperous nation adopt reform measures. When profits stop, change becomes inevitable, just as bragging about losses follows a depression. The public should not throw stones at Wall Street. If the get-rich-quick crowd did not send their dollars to the stock market, the operators would have no customers to whom they could sell.

Neill concentrates his postwar spotlight on William C. Durant, a giant of the auto industry who twice controlled General Motors only to lose out in 1920. The decade of the 1920s was a textbook lesson on how the market builds up an overinflated head of steam and then falls of its own weight. The author feels that the causes of 1929 were (1) easy credit, (2) pools and syndicates, (3) investment trusts and holding companies.

The depression of the 1930s was the same repetition of confidence followed by fear. Depressions knocked the props out from under pyramided orders, inflated ideas, and flimsy credit structures. Dreams were shattered. The mania of speculation bred its own destruction. This time it was complete. The Roosevelt years brought new reforms. The Securities and Exchange Commission and full disclosure are the result of the securities acts of 1933 and 1934. But in the depths of the depression, money was pumped into the prostrate economy by the billions, and the seeds of the next cycle were being sown.

Neill has made his point well. America's love of speculation will always return again. Human nature always reacts as it did during the tulipomania in Holland. The New York Stock Exchange, however, will continue to serve as the heart of our financial system. It will pump a steady stream of capital through the arteries of our business world and help maintain the growth necessary for the economic health and welfare of all Americans.

Nelson, S. A.

The ABC of Stock Speculation. Original: S. A. Nelson, 1903. Reprint: Burlington, Vt.: Fraser, 1964. 232 pp. $5.95

As one of the early admirers of Charles Dow, the author tried to persuade him to write a book incorporating his ideas and writings. For some reason, Dow refused and never did put his thoughts together into a comprehensive framework. Nelson did the next best thing, however, and was able to get permission to reprint several of Dow's editorials from the *Wall Street Journal.* These essays form the basis of what Nelson termed the Dow Theory. Although the editorials are the heart of this book of advice for speculators and are actually the basis of modern technical analysis, they don't represent all of his work.

In addition to the Dow editorials, this book contains the advice and work of other crafty speculators, excellent explanations of the short-selling process, pool operations, and other information on stock manipulation.

It hardly seems possible that a book written in 1903 can be so meaningful to the present-day reader. In all but a few cases this is so. It is also important for the student speculator to absorb the wisdom of those who spent their lives on the scene, observing and writing about the events that shaped the financial world of their time. In essence, *The ABC of Stock Speculation* is one of the early gems of Wall Street's written history.

Noyes, Alexander Dana

The Market Place: Reminisences of a Financial Editor. Original: Boston: Little, Brown, 1938. Reprint: Westport, Conn.: Greenwood Press, 1969. 384 pp. $13.75

The Market Place reviews fifty years of American History, encompassing both the political and financial areas, as the author traces his growth in the journalistic profession.

Throughout the book there are personal experiences of the author that are authentic, eyewitness accounts and are not found in any other histories. They only serve to enhance the value of this book which details the presidential conventions, subsequent campaign issues, and how the country divided its vote.

The reader has a ringside seat as William Jennings Bryan, the silver-tongued orator famous for his "Cross of Gold" speech, addresses New Yorkers at Madison Square Garden. Noyes wades through the Spanish-American War, the trust-building period of the early 1900s, and the trust-busting efforts of Teddy Roosevelt who suceeded McKinley after his assassination.

Careful attention is given to the years that followed, including Wilson's election, the European War, and the failure of Wilson to convince Congress of the importance of joining the League of Nations. The exciting period of the 1920s with the fantastic growth of all the new industries are detailed by Noyes. The crash is given a thorough inquest which includes the thoughts and statements of important people of the day.

The sequel to the panic is dissected so well that it is possible actually to experience the events that caused many sharp traders, who correctly foresaw the September–November 1929 drop, to lose with a vengeance during the 1930–1932 plunge to the bottom.

The author concludes his reminiscences with the start of the F.D.R. years. There is a fascination in walking through history and sharing the experiences vicariously with someone who was writing it first hand. Treat yourself to this kaleidoscope of five American decades brought to you by a professional writer of great stature.

Pecora, Ferdinand
Wall Street under Oath: The Story of Our Modern Money Changers. Original: New York: Simon & Schuster, 1939. Reprint: New York: Augustus M. Kelley, 1968. 311 pp. $9.50

In the aftermath of the great crash of 1929 and the depression that followed, no more brilliant effort at bringing the abuses of the period under the glare of public scrutiny was attempted than the Pecora Investigation, the subject of this excellent book.

Justice Pecora was counsel for the Senate Committee on Banking and Currency, and, for a period of seventeen months starting in January 1933, he subpoenaed some of the richest men in the country and asked them, under oath, how they accumulated their fortunes. As it turned out, the clever counsel proved conclusively that the establishment had been using its influence and position to the detriment of the helpless public who had lost billions of dollars during the stock market crash.

Among the witnesses whom Pecora questioned were Albert H. Wiggin, head of the Chase National Bank, whose testimony brought out the fact that he had made millions of dollars during the crash by selling short his own stock. Others included Charles E. Mitchell, chairman of the First National City Bank, Otto Kahn of Kuhn, Loeb, and J. P. Morgan, son of Morgan the elder, the most powerful figure in the history of American finance. Richard Whitney was president of the New York Stock Exchange during the investigation and tried to carry its banner high. His personal tragedy was in keeping with the sad aftermath of the crash and the mood of the country during the depression. "The White Knight" misused his clients' funds and, because of some bad speculations, sent his firm to the wall. He ended up in Sing Sing Prison.

The value of the hearings became apparent almost immediately. The Roosevelt administration passed the Securities Act of 1933, the Truth in Securities bill, and the Securities Exchange Act of 1934, providing among other things for the Securities and Exchange Commission to act as a policeman over the industry. There is no doubt that the abuses of the past led to the reforms of the New Deal, nor can there be any hope that the stock market will ever be completely free of those who would use it to their own advantage without regard for the law.

Pound, Arthur, and Moore, Samuel Taylor
They Told Barron: Conversations and Revelations of an American Pepys in Wall Street. New York: Harper, 1930. 372 pp.

A diary which contains conversations and revelations about Wall Street would have little value unless the author could lend authority and authenticity to its contents. It is therefore important to know that Clarence Walker Barron was the father of financial journalism. He strode through the decades of his productive life as a powerful and important figure, an intimate of most of the greatest names in the financial life of the country.

Barron started a newspaper in Boston called the Transcript, which sold for 1¢. In 1887 he founded the Boston News Bureau, and in 1902 he bought the *Wall Street Journal.* His forty years of financial life restored honesty and integrity to financial journalism. His position of prominence in the stock market brought him into contact with the famous and infamous people of those exciting decades. His early years as a court reporter proved invaluable to his method of making shorthand notes of all the conversations he had with the great figures of the time. The diary was to be the basis for an autobiography which Barron planned to write. He never got around to writing it before he died. The editors have sorted the multitude of notes and diaries into a semblance of order.

There are conversations with the key railroad magnates, Edward H. Harriman and James J. Hill. Charles Schwab of United States Steel ruminates about his successful methods of getting the most out of his men. There was no union then, and he didn't want to be put in a position where labor dictated to management. He was a powerful and persuasive salesman. Andrew Carnegie put Schwab in charge of Carnegie Steel and said, "You can make as many mistakes as you want, but don't make the same one twice!" Schwab arranged for J. P. Morgan to meet with Carnegie. Out of that contact came United States Steel.

There are insights about the famous builders of the automobile industry. One of the greats was William C. Durant. It was stated in Barron's notes that Durant would have been worth $500 million and would have retained control of General Motors had he not speculated. He owed $27 million; three banks and twenty-seven brokerage houses were involved. If nothing had been done, the banks and several brokers would have failed. The du Ponts and Morgans came in and took over his General Motors holdings. There are other conversations with Henry Ford, Buick, Leland, Nash, and the Fisher brothers.

This diary has finally lifted the veil of secrecy that stood between the public and the people who made events. The reader should feel exclusive as he looks behind the scenes at the Teapot Dome scandal, or conversations between John

D. Rockefeller and J. P. Morgan. He must be overawed when he reads that Ogden Armour inherited $200 million from his father Philip Armour or that Andrew Mellon had one certificate for Gulf Oil that was valued at $350 million. It is also disclosed that Duke and Ryan were both worth $250 million. It must be a surprise to learn that J. P. Morgan left only $50 million. For those readers who become bored with the repetition of such large fortunes, a Mrs. Owen states that "the most important human quality is an insatiable intellectual curiosity." Since the reader is obviously possessed of that quality, he can leave the reading of this book enriched with the knowledge that the money of the wealthy is not the only sign of a successful life.

They Told Barron is a valuable record of the conversations of the people who made the news. This look behind the scenes providing an opportunity to learn how these famous people behaved when the spotlight was turned off is a truly great addition to the literature of the stock market. The thorough student should read this book for the unpublished events it details. The curious will certainly want to plumb the secrets and sensational facts that are revealed by the pen of the legendary Clarence Walker Barron.

Regan, Donald T.
   A View from the Street. New York: New American Library, 1972. Distributor: Norton. 220 pp. $7.95

There are only rare occasions in stock market history when leaders of the industry have the intellectual competence to describe and interpret the events of their time. This book marks one of those occasions. The events of the 1970 disaster in the stock market, the culmination of which was a nearly 370 point drop in the Dow Jones industrial average, are carefully surveyed by Donald T. Regan, chairman and chief executive officer of Merrill Lynch, Pierce, Fenner, and Smith, the largest retail brokerage house in Wall Street. He reviews the causes and consequences of this major market break and explains the reforms that have resulted. Regan suggests his own list of outspoken reforms which are in opposition to those of the majority of his colleagues on the street. Time will prove the merit of his proposals.

Three days in May 1970 were a critical period in which a decade caught up with itself. Fear fed on itself as the excesses of the 1960s were squeezed out of a panic-ridden market. The public and the institutions were selling equities of proven value at sacrifice prices. Emotion had taken hold, and cool reason was nowhere to be found. The situation instantly improved on May 27, 1970, when the market rode up 32.04 points in the Dow Jones industrial average—the largest single gain in history up until that time.

What were the causes of May 1970? Economics alone was not responsible, although that was certainly part of the problem. We live in a highly complex social-political-economic world, and in 1970 psychological and foreign events clashed with this domestic bag of trouble. In addition, on April 29, President Nixon launched an invasion into Cambodia, and in the aftermath the killings at Kent State University depressed the nation's mood and spirit. Zero growth in the money supply and a squeeze on corporate liquidity combined to cause trouble in the market.

Individual cases of corporate trouble such as the Penn Central bankruptcy, and the large deficits of Chrysler and Trans World Airlines jolted an already shaky Wall Street. Funds started to move into a cash position. That meant fewer buyers and more sellers. Regan delves into the infinite forces that weigh upon stock prices such as the money supply, interest rates, inflation, capital goods spending, etc. They were all working together to deflate market values.

The Vietnam War was a drain on the economy, and it poisoned the national mood. Inflation was rampant, consumers were saving at a record rate, wage increases were far in excess of productivity, and our balance of payments was in a deficit. To meet this situation, on August 15, 1971, President Nixon imposed a wage-price freeze, a suspension of redemption of dollars in gold, and an import surcharge on all dutiable products. Regan feels that forceful action was necessary, and so did Wall Street. It led to the largest day in history.

Regan foresees a central marketplace with a volume of 50 million shares daily by 1980. He feels that some modified form of institutional membership will exist, and he sounds the clarion for competitive rates even though he is aware that many small firms will inevitably fall by the wayside. Regan attempts to excuse the conflict of interest that exists within brokerage houses that carry on a commission business and manage money at the same time. He counters "a man cannot serve two masters" with "a man who cannot serve two is unlikely to be hired by either."

The stock certificate will be eliminated in the market of the future, and electronically delivered orders and research information will aid the specialist and the registered representative. These improvements will make purchases of stocks cheaper and help the investor with his decisions. Regan is convinced that constructive change will add vitality to an industry which must mature to survive. He realizes that relics of the past will remain, but feels that we must look to the future with courage and optimism.

Rogers, Donald I.
The Day the Market Crashed. New Rochelle, N.Y.: Arlington House, 1971. 316 pp. $8.95

This book tells the story of one day, Black Thursday, October 24, 1929, a day which saw an avalanche of sell orders that totaled more than 12 million shares—a record. It was to be followed by Black Tuesday, October 29, 1929, the largest volume day in stock market history up until that time. Sixteen million shares were traded, and a low point of just over 70 points in the Dow Jones industrial average was reached before a recovery set in. The author selects October 24 as the actual date of the crash, claiming that although the sharp drop caught everyone by surprise, Black Tuesday was not wholly unexpected.

Rogers reports the rapid shift from elation to despair among people caught up in the excitement of the rising stock prices. They had witnessed a decade of growth that saw new industries capture the imagination of the country. In fact, they were eager to believe the statement of a prominent economics professor that the country was in a new era when everyone could be rich. The success stories that the stock market was responsible for during that decade led the masses into stocks, many of them on small margin. It was this road that they had chosen to travel in making their fortune.

Their reverie was unceremoniously ended by the disaster of a market that plummeted sharply lower, with fear replacing confidence, and no possibility of absorbing the blocks of stock offered by frantic sellers. Late in the morning of October 24, leaders of the five largest banks had a meeting at J. P. Morgan's and hastily arranged to support key stocks with a fund which Rogers states amounted to $24 million (other sources place the figure as high as $240 million). In their attempt to shore up the sagging market, the banks designated Richard Whitney, Vice-President of the New York Stock Exchange, to place the orders. Rumors spread quickly all morning about the meeting at Morgan's, and it was a dramatic moment when Whitney stepped onto the floor of the exchange and shouted his order to buy 10,000 shares of U.S. Steel at 205. It was then selling at 193. He proceeded to other posts and placed similar orders for other key stocks. A rally ensued in many of the stocks Whitney ordered, but the majority of stocks found little support. The result was a mixed market that closed down over 12 points after a partial recovery in the afternoon—a prelude to Black Tuesday when $10 billion was lost, and millions of people were wiped out overnight.

The personal stories that Rogers details bring the disaster close to home. The reader can see the reaction of the various types of people who were part of that hectic market of 1929. A sidelight of that tragic day involved a couple who owned a block of 580 shares of Studebaker and who were sold out by mistake— an event that happened to thousands in the hysteria of the hour. The result was a credit balance of over $33,000 and an overjoyed couple, a rarity on that morning after.

The stock market crash in 1929 and the economic collapse that followed still live in the memory of millions. The depression is a specter that haunts the stock market and the authorities who guide our economic destiny. Can it happen again? Of course it can, despite all the safeguards, laws, and governmental controls. The stock market consists of people, and when they lose control they stop thinking and act like a mob. The crowd follows like sheep and can't act independently. We must have books like this to keep the memory of our folly alive. If we hold the mirror up to our eyes often enough, a repetition of the traumatic days of 1929 can be avoided.

Sobel, Robert

The Big Board: A History of the New York Stock Market. New York: Macmillan, 1965. 395 pp. paperback: $2.95; hardbound: $8.95

There are few financial writers today who have the intellectual audacity to attempt a project as vast as *The Big Board.* Wall Street should be grateful to Robert Sobel for the truly gargantuan feat of telescoping the complete record of the New York Stock Exchange into one readable volume.

For those people who want to learn about Wall Street's vital history, Sobel has pieced together the fabric of the past with a brilliant job of painstaking research that took years of work. It also required a thorough knowledge of the subject and a particular skill to be able to deftly insert the words of famous people into the proper context of his broad, dynamic story.

The author accurately documents the exciting years of the past. His grasp of the big picture, the total concept of each era, keeps the reader glued to the book, eager to learn about the interdependence of Wall Street and the country. The quality of this work and its importance as history is unquestionable. It is the first and only comprehensive account of stock market history since Edmund C. Stedman's *The New York Stock Exchange,* and although the pure magic of that tome is legend, it only covers the period up to the start of the twentieth century.

The Big Board takes the reader through another sixty critical years of growth and records their indelible events with an historical clarity and a style that will remain a standard for years to come. It is unlikely that anyone will attempt to duplicate Sobel's monumental work.

✓Sobel, Robert
The Curbstone Brokers: The Origins of the American Exchange. New York: Macmillan, 1970. 296 pp. $7.95

The Curbstone Brokers of the late nineteenth century gathered each day at Broad Street and Exchange Place. They came in any kind of weather, rain or shine, to carry on their business of trading in stocks. They wore bright hats and gay-colored jackets to distinguish themselves from the rest of the crowd. Their associates manned telephones and sat on the window ledges of nearby buildings. They used hand signals to communicate because it was impossible to hear anything above the din of the hundreds of shouting voices. Such was the scene at that crowded intersection, one that kept the police busy keeping the flow of traffic alive. These were the Curbstone Brokers whose colorful history Robert Sobel pieces together from the remnants of information he was able to obtain from survivors and written records. It takes the reader through 130 years until they finally moved indoors in 1921.

In the early years the Curbstone Brokers were those who could not make the Big Board. After the panic of 1837, trading ground to a halt. It wasn't until 1845 that the worst was over. Prosperity returned in 1847 with the Mexican War. The out-of-doors brokers tried to join the Board at this time, but most of them were black-balled. Reasons were never given, but few Jews or Irish Catholics were members. Expelled and blackballed members formed the Bourse which was larger than the Board but after several years was no longer mentioned. The members either joined the Board or returned to the outdoor market at Wall and Hanover.

At this time a pattern was established that lasted seventy years. The Stock and Exchange Board (forerunner of the New York Stock Exchange) was the dominant securities exchange. Its members also belonged to banks and insurance companies. They were the political and social aristocracy and belonged to the best clubs. The Board did not accept marginal business; it traded only in well-established companies. This left the field wide open for the Curbstone Brokers to exploit new industries and their securities. New issues were first

traded outdoors and then moved to the Board. The gold mining boom helped
the Curb's power and wealth grow faster than the Board's.

In the years that attended this boom, several rival exchanges developed to try
for the lucrative rewards of speculation. The Open Board, the Mining Exchange,
the Gold Exchange Room, and the Petroleum Board all were tenanted by Jews,
Irish Catholics, and other minority groups which had been excluded from membership on the Big Board. Their exchanges permitted continuous trading which
was tempting to members of the conservative Board which had only two
auctions a day. There was also Gallaher's Evening Exchange which allowed
trading all night at 5th Avenue and 43rd Street. The largest of the minor exchanges was formed in 1885. It was called the Consolidated Stock Exchange
and was an amalgam of several petroleum and mining exchanges. It handled
odd-lots, pipeline certificates, commodities, and mining shares. It posed the
biggest threat to the domination of the Big Board, and in 1907 the Little
Board paid $1.2 million for a new building at Broad and Beaver Streets.

The panic of 1907 led to cries for reform, and the attempt to break up Wall
Street resulted in the Stock Exchange becoming stronger than ever. The pressure
was concentrated on bucket shops and the more speculative operations of the
smaller exchanges. Legislation was passed while Charles Evans Hughes was
governor that made the operation of a bucket shop a felony. A broker could no
longer function as a bookmaker. In 1909, the Big Board began a crusade against
both the Little Board (Consolidated) and the Curb under the pretense of imple-
menting the Hughes Committee's recommendations. Under the leadership of
Frank Sturgis, chairman of the Stock Exchange, a campaign was launched to
rid the financial district of the bucket shops and the thieves that existed at the
Consolidated and the Curb. Sturgis hoped to have no less than a monopoly of
all securities trading in New York. The good relations which leaders of the exchange had with Emanual Mendels saved the outdoor market from extinction.

Mendels moved forward under the impetus of the Hughes Committee Report
to organize the outdoor market. He tried to pave the way for a move indoors
by cooperating with Sturgis of the Big Board. Such a move was costly because
of real estate prices and construction costs. Mendels agreed not to deal in securities listed on the Exchange, and the Board reacted by pirating mining stocks
and other Curb stocks and admitting them to trading at the Unlisted Department
of the Exchange at lower commissions. The Curb was forced to submit to this
theft because of the Big Board's greater strength.

In 1910, the Unlisted Department was eliminated with most industrials
going to the regular board and the mining issues to the Curb. This was suggested
by the Hughes Report, and it resulted in an expansion of the Curb's business.
For years the Unlisted Department had been the chief threat to the Curb. Now
it was gone. The gap between the Exchange and the outside brokers had
widened. The Exchange came to terms with the Curb and continued its fight
with the Consolidated. By 1912 the Big Board and Curb dominated all securities trading in New York, and the Consolidated was reduced to odd-lots and
nonexchange securities. The Big Board was also no longer opposed to a move
indoors for the Curb if it did not deal in Big Board stocks.

At this point, Edward McCormick assumed leadership of the Curb. He revived the idea of an indoor market which Mendels had put forth before the turn of the century. McCormick was more independent than Mendels. He did not consult the Exchange. He polled Curb members about the possibility of a move in 1914, but the start of World War I put an end to his plans. All exchanges closed down for 3½ months. After the war the Little Board lost strength. It had been a haven for small-time gamblers and odd-lotters. Their prosperity allowed them to transfer their operations to the Curb and the Big Board. In 1927, the Consolidated lost its building, its officers were in jail or disgraced, and it just faded out of existence without a formal obituary.

The Curbstone Brokers' prosperity in the five years following the war robbed them of their usual excuse that they lacked funds for a move indoors. A meeting was held at the Commodore Hotel in 1919 by Curb leaders Edward Mc-Cormick and Alfred B. Sturges. In attendance were such powerful figures as John McCormack, Franklin Leonard, Carl Pforzheimer, and Dudley Gray. It was at this meeting that Curb leaders decided on a move. Reporters learned that pledges of $500,000 had been made for a new building fund. Memberships originally costing $1,500 were to sell for $350,000 in 1969. On December 18, 1919, McCormick announced that a site had been purchased on Trinity Place just west of the Trinity Church graveyard. It became apparent that the reason a site closer to the Exchange was not selected was that McCormick wanted to escape the domination of the Big Board.

Groundbreaking took place on December 5, 1920, for a $1.2 million building. On June 27, 1921, the Curbstone Brokers met in their colorful attire, and led by Edward McCormick they walked to their new home at 86 Trinity Place. The New York Curb Market had finally moved indoors after 130 years at the mercy of the elements.

✓Sobel, Robert
   Panic on Wall Street: A History of America's Financial Disasters. New York: Macmillan, 1968. 469 pp. $8.95

A panic may be described as uncontrolled emotion superimposed upon a crisis. In the course of almost 200 years of American financial history there have been twelve disasters which fit that definition. Robert Sobel has selected these debacles because of the nature of their declines and the impact they had on the country. There were many crises that did not develop the proportions of a panic, and others where the decline was steep but was spread over a longer period of time.

As the story opens, "William Duer and the Wall Street Panic of 1792" is detailed. With the art of a reporter, Sobel recounts the giddy success of the master speculator. The break in prices that caused his downfall was the difference between unmatched wealth and jail. News of Duer's incarceration started the panic, and we learn immediately that panics start in periods of extreme optimism and end with a total lack of confidence.

The narrative develops the background of each period with its political and social events and cleverly injects the important financial figures who straddled those decades of early growth. Giants like Alexander Hamilton, Nicholas Biddle,

Commodore Cornelius Vanderbilt, and J. P. Morgan were in some cases more powerful than the president and his administration. Their financial power was enough to shore up the weakened banking system and to restore confidence to the country. This happened in 1792 when Hamilton shortened the panic, in 1893 during the Cleveland administration, in 1901 during the Northern Pacific corner, and in 1907 after the Knickerbocker Trust suspension when J. P. Morgan used his vast influence and great resources to prevent disaster. In the process he saved his own wealth from the ravages of a country in financial ruin.

Other panics were caused by speculation, overexpansion, and bank weaknesses as in the "Western Blizzard of 1857," and as in 1869, when Jay Gould and Jim Fisk almost cornered America's gold supply. The story develops an intensity that seems almost unreal. Truth is stranger than fiction, especially in the emotion-packed gold room on Black Friday, September 24, 1869. "Grant's Last Panic" in 1884 was precipitated by Ulysses S. Grant's son, Buck, and his partner, Ferdinand Ward. The period was marked by numerous cases of embezzlement, overspeculation, and flights to Canada to escape imprisonment. Ward's genius was quickly reduced to shambles when Grant & Ward was forced to the wall with assets of $67,174 and liabilities of $16,792, 640. A pathetic ex-president was forced to write his memoirs in his waning years, while dying of cancer, to pay off the debts caused by his son's disaster.

The big crash of 1929 was preceded by the bull market of the 1920s. New industries grew to the sky overnight, and the country was on a plateau of prosperity where everybody would be rich. That was the scenario for the greatest panic of all. Over-expansion, speculation, and excessive margin are cited as some of the major causes of the crash. Sobel maintains that it is a myth which remains to this day that 1929 led to the depression of the 1930s. To prove his contention, the author cites the fact that there was not a single major bank failure as a result of the October panic. Sobel claims that the first quarter of 1930 was a period of lost opportunities. If the Federal Reserve had continued to shore up the economy as it did in November and December 1929, the 1930–1933 bank failures might have been prevented, and the depression that followed might not have occurred.

In response to his own question, "Can panics be prevented," the author poses another, "Can wars be prevented?" He leaves it to the reader to decide whether maturity and wisdom can overcome fear and strip humanity of its worst disasters. His conclusion contains prophetic words which explain how major modern panics can be avoided, "The price to be paid may well be an expansion of state and federal powers and a loss of economic freedom." The current state of our economy reflects the fears of that statement with price and wage control boards selected by the government to oversee management and labor settlements.

Sobel leaves the reader with a worrisome list of causes for a possible future panic, one that may be worse than 1929: (1) an atomic confrontation between Russia, China, and the United States; (2) loss of confidence in our government; (3) weakness in institutional buyers (mutual funds, pension funds, and insurance companies) brought on by uniform pessimism; and (4) a blow to the political leadership of the United States. Obviously, the author and his readers abhor the thought of another plague of fear and a financial debacle, but if the lessons of history can be a deterrent, this book has shown us how to keep our future confident and financially sound.

✓Sobel, Robert
The Great Bull Market: Wall Street in the 1920s. New York: Norton, 1968.
175 pp. paperback: $1.65; hardbound: $5.00

The stock market crash of 1929 marked the end of an era of great prosperity. John Kenneth Galbraith, author of *The Great Crash,* deplores the fact that his book was the only one dealing with the subject. While it is true that his is the most famous book about the 1929 panic, there are others. The mythology that grew out of the crash has distorted and grossly exaggerated the facts, and it is regrettable that an event of such monumental proportions, and an economic turning point in the history of our country, should not have attracted the interest of more historians and financial writers in the 1930s and 1940s. To bring things into their proper perspective, Robert Sobel has written a definitive and well documented history of "the roaring twenties." The whole decade is examined with emphasis on the events that took place during the prosperous years and that led up to and were responsible for the debacle in October 1929.

The growth of new industries during the 1920s was in large measure the cause of an exciting stock market. The auto, motion picture, electrical equipment, radio, and steel industries combined to excite the imagination of the stock buying public. After the great war, with Europe's economy shattered, it was natural for American business to look overseas for eager customers. Added to this was a great domestic demand for new products. "Consumerism," a burgeoning demand for products on credit, was fed by a healthy young advertising industry. This led to the purchase of stocks on margin, which security salesmen claimed was no different than buying a radio on time. In fact, it made more sense buying stock on margin since its value could appreciate, while the radio depreciated. This attitude could hold sway only when business continued to boom, earnings increased, and stock prices soared. The consequences of a slowdown in demand or an outright drop in business was almost unheard of in that era of prosperity and easy money. The Federal Reserve Board did little to curb the enthusiasm that was engendered by booming business and a sharply rising stock market. Added to this euphoria were Prohibition, Babe Ruth, and Charles Lindbergh.

It was almost too good to be true. "The age of excess" had reached the stage about which Bernard Baruch would later write, "When beggars and shoeshine boys, barbers and beauticians can tell you how to get rich it is time to remind yourself that there is no more dangerous illusion than the belief that one can get something for nothing."

The market crashed and brought the whole house of cards tumbling down, with margin calls and billions of dollars of paper value which had taken years to build up being wiped out in short order. Fear had overcome a stubborn confidence and a greed which seemed to be everlasting. As the author points out, the market panic was not followed by an economic collapse. In fact, the solvency of the banks attested to the possibility of a recovery. The market did rally for six months into 1930, but the government and business did nothing of importance to prevent the slump which followed. Therefore, Sobel maintains that the depression could not be blamed on Wall Street. *The Great Bull Market* is a unique book, and it contributes greatly to a clear understanding of the events that led up to the debacle of 1929 and the period of deep despair which followed.

Stedman, Edmund Clarence

The New York Stock Exchange. Original: Stock Exchange Historical Co., 1905. Reprint: Westport, Conn.: Greenwood Press, 1969. 518 pp. $25.00

More than a century of American history is ably and meticulously described by the author with the New York Stock Exchange at the heart of the narrative. Impressed with the importance of his task and imbued with the spirit of his dedication, Stedman delivers an awe-inspiring panorama of the men and events that shaped our country's past. The book starts with the latter part of the eighteenth century and ends with the start of the twentieth century. The author leaves no doubt that the growth and importance of Wall Street has led the United States into a position of preeminence in the world.

The subject matter is so vast and its record so important for future generations that the work has remained a source book for all who are interested in the history of the stock market and the country. Throughout the years encompassed by this book, panics and bull markets shaped the destiny of the men whose careers created a legend. They also include many who rose to fame and are now forgotten in the rush of new and more earth-shattering events.

Jacob Little, Daniel Drew, Commodore Vanderbilt, Jay Gould, and others illuminated the scene with their daring and then receded into historical limbo. Their exploits are recounted with precision, and the reader need only read through these pages to be transported into those fantastic, formative years that saw the pendulum swing from banks to canals to railroads and then to industrial development. While all this was happening, our country was growing in population, wealth, and prestige.

There is no doubt that central to this growth and achievement was a marketplace that raised the funds to build the canals, railroads, and industries and that was a source of capital for a government that had to borrow to finance wars, build its defenses, and pay its debts. This vital hub at the center of America's wheel of progress was, and still is today, the New York Stock Exchange. Edmund Stedman has given us a vital history from which we can truly draw inspiration. It is a monumental task which he has accomplished with precision and style.

Thomas, Dana L.

The Plungers and the Peacocks: 150 Years of Wall Street. New York: Putnam, 1967. 314 pp. $6.95

To write a history of the past 150 years looms as a formidable task for even the most talented writer. It is difficult to select the most important events and personalities that comprise the concentrated record of Wall Street through the years. Although there is not enough space for everything in one book, Thomas has done well to keep his work representative, accurate, and vital. It is true that a good part of the book concerns the decade of the 1920s, the 1929 crash, and the depression that followed. However, the importance of that period cannot be underestimated, and its thorough retelling is always valuable.

The story starts with a brief review of the early years of Wall Street and skips quickly to the Civil War period and Jay Cooke's audacious and aggressive sale of bonds to finance the Lincoln Administration's conduct of the war. The next episode retells the attempted gold corner by Jay Gould and Jim Fisk in 1869, the complicity of Abel Corbin, President Grant's brother-in-law, and the last minute sale of gold by the treasury to break the corner. This period ends with the unhappy events that culminated in the panic of 1884 in which Grant was the victim of Ferdinand Ward. Grant's son, Buck, and Ward formed a brokerage house that traded on the ex-president's name and reputation. Not only that, they used his money as well. James Fish, president of the Marine National Bank, got involved with Ward, and after a mountain of debt was piled up, a bad market forced Grant and Ward to the wall together with the Marine National Bank. Ulysses S. Grant, broken and ill, was forced to write his memoirs to pay off his debts.

The next chapter reviews a long line of bulls and bears. The industrial development of the country gave rise to the men who were destined to leave their mark on the history of period, Daniel Drew, Commodore Vanderbilt, Edward H. Harriman, James R. Keene (the Silver Fox), and J. P. Morgan, among others. With a fast look at the gaudy fashions of that period, Thomas sweeps into the twentieth century and briefly mentions Charles Dow, the founder of the *Wall Street Journal,* and his disciple William P. Hamilton who built a religion out of Dow's essays and developed the Dow Theory, later refined in the early 1930s by Robert Rhea.

The major concern of this book is reached with the bombing incident at J. P. Morgan's in 1920. The pock-marked foundation still stands as mute evidence of this dastardly act which took many lives and is still unsolved. The 1920s roared onto the scene featuring a postwar America eager to take advantage of the surge in new industrial growth in automobiles, radio, and utilities. It was also a time of Prohibition, Babe Ruth, and Charles Lindbergh. An orgy of growth and excitement fed by fiscal irresponsibility, professional pronouncements of a new era when everyone would be rich enticed the public into the stock market in record numbers. The 1920s gave rise to the giants of industry and the plungers who, like pied pipers, led the small investor into the market. Among the names that stand out are William C. Durant, founder of General Motors, the Fisher brothers, Henry Ford, Mike Meehan, the specialist in RCA, John Jacob Raskob, the du Pont secretary who advised them to buy their interest in General Motors, and Jesse L. Livermore, "the Boy Plunger" from Shrewsbury, Massachusetts. Out of this welter of men, money, and motion America entered the fall of 1929.

The pain that attended the mass wipeout of October 24 and 29, 1929, was suffered mutually by countless thousands of people who staggered in numb disbelief like a fallen boxer whose eyes can't focus on the referee's movement. He rises only to be struck down again by a more violent blow. It was a knockout from which it was impossible to recover. Those fortunates who were astute and unemotional enough to escape 1929 with their money, bought into the 1930 rally and lost it all when the market declined to its lowest point on July 8, 1932, a Dow reading of 42. One of those who lost everything was William C. Durant. His $100 million dwindled to practically nothing. Some reporter found him washing dishes in a diner in New Jersey, and it was later explained that he owned the place. Hardly a just end for one of the prime movers of the 1920s, the founder of General Motors.

The author sums up his Wall Street history with a look into the future. The technological explosion is surveyed carefully, and Thomas raises the paradox of a sharp rise in the rate of illiteracy while the increase in the body of knowledge is inundating the intelligent man of today. The computer is slowly taking the mystery out of stock market decisions. The technological inroads still cannot predict mass emotion and the resultant direction of stock prices when giant institutions and millions of individuals run for the exits at the same time. This fact makes the recurrence of panics almost a sure thing. Our only hope is to minimize their impact by intelligent control of the economic forces that cause extreme movements in the stock market.

Train, George Francis

Young America in Wall Street. Original: Derby and Jackson, 1857. Reprint: Westport, Conn.: Greenwood Press, 1968. 398 pp. $15.75

In a series of articles written in the capitals of Europe, Paris, London, Rome, and Vienna, Train gave spellbinding accounts of the Sepoy Rebellion in India and of a visit to the celebration of the Order of Maria Theresa (the Hapsburg Dynasty), an event that took place only once every one hundred years. He described with agonizing reality the Leghorn Holocaust which involved a panic in an Italian theatre that took forty lives and injured hundreds. Rarely is a written history told with such verve, animation, and wonder. It reads like fine poetry. But what has this to do with Wall Street?

This contemporary history brought together the events that shaped the world of that mid-nineteenth century period in all the capitals of Europe. England was supreme at that time and America was still suffering growing pains. Upon his return home, the author, faced with the panic of 1857, searched for the causes and bemoaned the bubble of inflation and western land speculation, which he believed caused the suspension of the great Ohio Life Insurance and Trust Company, the event which precipitated the crash. People living beyond their means did it, and Train sadly compared that madness to the Mississippi Land Scheme, the South Sea Bubble, and the tulipomania.

"Times are changing," he warned, as he lay bare his soul. Despair and frustration alternated with a challenge for the great future of America. His overwhelming sadness at the state of America's finances is easy to discern. His foreboding was prophetic, for it was only a few years before the war between the states was to tear the country apart. Times were changing then, and times are changing still. As the Romans said, "omnia mutantur"–everything changes.

Winkelman, Barnie F.

Ten Years of Wall Street. Philadelphia: John C. Winston, 1932. 381 pp.

The ten years referred to in the title of this book are the decade of the 1920s. There is no other era in American business that can compare with those years in excitement, except perhaps the formative years at the turn of the century which attended the industrialization of the country. Barnie Winkelman captures the flavor of that period through an analysis of the fabulous growth of such leading corporations as General Motors, Radio Corporation of America, and United States Steel. He also makes incisive comments about the stock market milieu, pools, and famous personalities as he traces the history of the panics that led to the greatest financial collapse in history.

There is a quick recital of the dark days of Wall Street's history. The collapse of the Joseph brothers in 1837 started the concatenation of events culminating in 1907 with J. P. Morgan's rescue of the country. The character of the incessant conflict that raged in the financial markets has changed with the years, but it cannot hide the fact that ethics do not exist. Behind the illusions, dignity of names, solemn corporate power is the fact that the street sells paper for money and at the highest price. The tragedy for the public is that it buys only when prices soar and are near their highs.

The story of General Motors' growth from its early years concerns William C. Durant who pyramided his private ventures and left himself vulnerable to a decline. In the sharp recession of 1921, Durant was forced to resign as General Motors slide to 8 1/8. Du Pont acquired a substantial interest, and in 1925 business doubled. In 1926 it doubled again. No achievement in industrial history has equaled the concentrated growth of General Motors. United States Steel fought for status with General Motors. Together they captured the imagination of the public and took turns as the most active stock. It was a neck-and-neck race that led the country to new levels of prosperity.

Professional opinion in 1928 was that the bull market was over. But front-page newspaper headlines caused the public to enter the speculative arena. They discarded all fear and dashed headlong into the hysterical, feverish market. In 1929, the great body of stocks was lower. Only a few leaders continued to advance. The trust managers were bidding against themselves, forcing prices higher. The year 1929 was a very difficult period for investors. Throughout the year the market became more irregular and feverish.

In the chapters that deal with tips, pools, and short selling, the author proves to have a wealth of stock market wisdom, wit, and experience. He spices his narrative with many maxims and clever observations. A group of samples follow: "The trader is simply a Don Quixote tilting at windmills;" "A chart is like an instrument that depends for its tune on the skill of the player;" "It can be said of investments as was said of bayonets: one cannot sit on them."

Winkelman finds little justification for investment trusts of any kind. The plea for diversification is without merit. You can buy shares in many companies or one large diversified company. He calls the trusts a snare for men of small means. Management fees are without foundation since there is little work for management. You can understand the author's view in the wake of the disaster of 1929 and the part that 500 trusts played in that debacle.

The author decries the evils of speculation and the perils that face an investor in Wall Street. He sums up the feeling of millions of stockholders, disillusioned or otherwise, in these words: "We hold no brief for the machinery of the exchange. We have not spared its shortcomings or abuses, and they are many. For Wall Street epitomizes the ethics and ideals of American business. At its best it reflects the romance of our industrial achievements; at its worst it mirrors the greed and callousness of the rank and file businessman and of financiers, high and low. However the greatest outcries against Wall Street emanate from those who enter the lists not for legitimate investment, but as a certain road to immediate wealth. The fury of a woman scorned is but a mild flurry compared to the snarling rage of the unscrupulous who have embarked on a neat plan to fleece the public only to find themselves fleeced by others."

This book, with its variety of subjects, captures the flavor and excitement of the 1920s and is a classic that will grow in importance through the years. It has preserved the records of the most exciting decade in our financial history. It makes the valid point that a more responsible banking community, one without "economic myopia," would have saved the country from the tragic consequences of its greed and folly.

Warshow, Robert Irving
The Story of Wall Street. New York: Greenberg, 1929. 362 pp.

The excitement of Wall Street history and the experiences of its most fabled personalities have served to overcome the sterile and colorless style of this book. As the story unfolds, Alexander Hamilton is laying the foundation of the young nation's financial structure. By the time he dies in 1804, the banking system which he fathered has made it possible to develop the country's industry, while the public stock exchange has launched other large financial ventures.

The establishment of a stock exchange made the industrialization of the United States possible since it took large sums of money to finance the railroads which provided the main source of transportation in settling the country. Years later, the oil industry was founded and dominated by John D. Rockefeller. Andrew Carnegie then became the main force behind a vibrant steel industry. The most brilliant mind in American finance, J. P. Morgan, straddled all important phases of America's growth with railroads, investment banking, and his greatest accomplishment, the formation of United States Steel. The last major industry discussed is the automobile industry with Henry Ford and Will Durant gaining the author's raves.

There are few detailed comments on the development of Wall Street as it grew to reflect the needs of the country. Rather, a parade of profiles of the great speculators and some of their greatest coups are presented. One fact which is brought home clearly is that in spite of the great fortunes that the famous traders amassed, they invariably died broke. The author probes the careers of such Wall Street greats as Jay Gould, Daniel Drew, Cornelius Vanderbilt, and Jim Fisk. His tales also involve such figures as E. H. Harriman, James J. Hill, Jacob Schiff, Charles M. Schwab, and John "Bet-a-Million" Gates.

It is admittedly difficult to compress so much history into one book, and on that basis one cannot expect too much depth. There is enough, however, to command the attention of the reader and to whet his appetite for the stock markets of the decades to come.

BIOGRAPHY

Baruch, Bernard M.
Baruch, My Own Story. New York: Henry Holt, 1957. 337 pp. $5.00

The autobiography of Bernard Baruch affords the reader a unique opportunity to relive an exciting period of stock market history. Of particular interest is Baruch's account of the Northern Pacific corner that precipitated the panic of 1901. It is a first-hand report, all too rare in history, by a man who saw it happen.

Bernard Baruch started his career as a broker with A. A. Houseman and Co. and, after years of trial and error, developed a method of speculating that ultimately made him a wealthy man. Eventually he left his position at A. A. Houseman and bought a seat on the stock exchange so that he could speculate on his own and not be responsible for the interests of any customers. His reputation grew in importance until "Barney" Baruch became an elder statesman and an advisor to many presidents.

In readable prose, Baruch threads his way through the pages of political, social, and economic history while describing his dealings with some of the greatest names of the day. Among the galaxy of Baruch's circle were J. P. Morgan, whom he describes as the greatest financial mind in American history, "Diamond Jim" Brady, John "Bet-a-Million" Gates, E. H. Harriman, and others.

Although Baruch's fortune was made before the 1929 crash, the subsequent formation of the SEC, and the securities laws of 1933 and 1934, his philosophy of speculation outlined in this book deserves a careful reading. Since it has evolved from a lifetime of successful experience on the firing line, it can guide an investor even in today's complex stock market.

Borkin, Joseph
Robert R. Young: The Populist of Wall Street. New York: Harper & Row, 1969. 236 pp. $6.95

More than a century after the great railroad men had passed from the scene, a Texan named Robert R. Young rose from obscurity to challenge the powerful Morgan and Guaranty Trust banking establishment for control of the New York Central Railroad. The events that led up to this confrontation form the substance of Borkin's book.

Young's rise to prominence in the financial world started with his purchase of the Alleghany Corporation from George Ball of glass-jar fame. Ball had taken control when the Van Sweringen brothers went bankrupt during the depression. Young's partner in the venture was Allan P. Kirby, heir to a chain-store fortune. Alleghany was a holding company having a $3 billion book value and 23,000 miles of track. The key to this vast enterprise was the rich, coal-carrying Chesapeake & Ohio Railway. Alleghany was a financial nightmare. It was $80 million in debt, a debt costing $4 million a year in interest. In addition there was $22 million in arrearages on the preferred.

If that wasn't enough, a bad market in 1937 caused huge losses in Alleghany, and Robert Young's health failed. He was placed in a Newport, R.I., rest home under a psychiatrist's care. His illness didn't last long, however, and in 1938 Young was well enough to wage a successful proxy fight for control of the C&O. He started a campaign to win over the small stockholders with advertising techniques that he developed and used effectively in the future. His provocative ad, "A hog can cross the country without changing trains, but you can't," is the most widely remembered public relations tool Young used.

Young battled those forces who used their power and control in their own self-interest and not for the public good. He fought a successful crusade for competitive bidding in securities which reshaped the future of investment banking. At the end of his career the "battle of the century" was joined in the proxy fight for control of the New York Central Railroad. Arrayed against Young were the powerful forces of the great banks with all their influence in the federal agencies such as the Interstate Commerce Commission, the Securities and Exchange Commission, and state and federal courts. Appeals to stockholders through the press created such keen interest that the vote took on the character of a national election.

Young's dramatic victory was the last in an active and stormy career. The people's warrior once more succumbed to the intensity of his business life. In 1958, with his pride shattered because of a reversal in New York Central's fortunes, Robert R. Young ended his life with a shotgun blast in the billiard room of his Palm Beach mansion. It is not known whether Young took his own life for business or personal reasons. He was still a multi-millionaire at the time of his suicide and carried a million dollar balance in his checking account. Whatever the reason for his tragedy, it is clear that Young has truly earned a place of honor in the history of American business.

Lefevre, Edwin
   Reminiscences of a Stock Operator. Original: New York: George H. Doran, 1923. Reprint: Larchmont, N.Y.: American Research Council, 1964. 308 pp. $5.00

This book is supposed to be a work of fiction, but it is an open secret that it is the biography of Jesse Lauriston Livermore. The dedication to "the Boy Plunger" is a clue to that truth. Further proof that it is Livermore's story comes from the text itself. Spending his early days as a youngster in the bucket shops, he won so often that the owners refused his business. Later as a successful trader on the

New York Stock Exchange, he made multimillion-dollar fortunes and had all the trappings that accompanied them, a home in Palm Beach, a yacht, and beautiful women. The good times were followed by periods when all was lost, and he had to make a fresh start.

This was Livermore with his glamorous, infamous forays as a bear, from a lucky coup on a Union Pacific short just before the San Francisco earthquake to a multimillion-dollar bonanza in the commodity market when he owned enough cotton to clothe the whole country. The narrative is racy and full of market wisdom and trading tips. The fact that the subject eventually was a beaten man who took his own life cannot tarnish the validity of his method.

This book, in fact, is almost an encyclopedia of trading advice from a master who lived through good times and bad, who learned from bitter experience why he lost, and who tried harder the next time around. Edwin Lefevre captures the excitement of Livermore's career and, at the same time, preserves much of Livermore's market wisdom for the investors of future generations. Times may change, but people still react the same as they did in that hectic, roaring bull market of the 1920's and the preceding two decades. The best way to understand Livermore is to read the list of maxims containing his market and trading philosophy. Here is a partial list of his tenets:

"Always sell what shows you a loss and keep what shows you a profit."

"Of all the speculative blunders there are few greater than trying to average a losing game."

"Stock market post mortems don't pay dividends."

"In bull markets bear items are ignored and bull news exaggerated, and vice-versa."

"A man may beat a stock or a group at a certain time, but no man living can beat the stock market."

"Stocks are never too high to buy or too low to sell."

"When you want to get out. . . .get out!"

"Never buy stocks cheap."

"The analysis of the week that has passed is less important than the forecast of the weeks that are to come."

"Be bullish in a bull market and bearish in a bear market."

"To be angry at the market is like getting angry at your lungs because you have pneumonia."

"Some time elapses between making a mistake and realizing it."

"A trader can only rise by knowledge; he falls by his own blunders."

"Courage in a speculator is merely confidence to act on the decision of his mind."

"History repeats itself all the time in Wall Street."

"Beware of a stock that refuses to follow the group leader."

"A man may know what to do and lose money if he doesn't do it quickly enough."

"Never try to sell at the top. Sell on a reaction if there is no rally."

"It was the kind of market in which not even a skunk could make a scent."

"The only way to sell . . . is to sell!"

"The most persuasive salesman of all is the tape."

"Don't argue with the tape . . . quit while the quitting is good . . . and cheap."
"Never meet a margin call; close out your account."
"Follow the leader."
"There are fashions in the market just as in women's gowns, hats, and jewelry."
It should be obvious to the reader of this review that there is value and substance in the knowledge that can be gained from a thorough look at Lefevre's tribute to a famous operator. Most important for the trader, the focus is on market procedure and not the personal life of Livermore. It remains to this day, almost fifty years after the original publication, the most complete and authoritative book on the stock market life of one of Wall Street's most celebrated speculators.

Martin, Ralph G.
The Wizard of Wall Street: The Story of Gerald M. Loeb. New York: William Morrow, 1965. 184 pp. $6.00

This is the story of Gerald M. Loeb, whose name is synonymous with success in the stock market. He is variously called the Wizard or the Dean of Wall Street. He has won a reputation for excellence with a record of over fifty years of experience and accumulated wisdom. This biography tells us very little about his personal life, but deals exclusively with Loeb's market philosophy. We do learn that he suffered from infantile paralysis when he was a young boy and was married to a woman named Rose sometime later in his illustrious career. But market knowledge was Loeb's trademark and is really the essence of this story of his life.

A few of Loeb's opinions are the following: "Never make an investment that does not appear after investigation to be an equally good speculation;" "Find the right man, not the right stock;" "Two lessons . . . deep, intensive research in a few stocks and flexibility of movement." He often said that unpopularity was his guidepost in the selection of stocks.

Loeb was not infallible although the legend of his success does not include many errors. He did make a mistake in New York Central. Instead of selling when a dividend was declared and the stock was at its peak, he hesitated and sold on the way down with big losses. Loeb told that story for a reason. "It is easy," he said, to sit and write an investment book and say "cut your losses" or "never let emotion outrule an investment principle," but that's easier said than done. "None of us are computing machines; we're human beings. We all make mistakes. The great trick is to keep these mistakes at a minimum."

There are three areas of decision where Loeb has independent thoughts that vary from those of many other analysts and investors. He doesn't believe in buying a split stock except in anticipation. Many times the peak is reached just at the time of the announcement. Loeb has mixed feelings about the value of charts. There are too many chartists now, and they cause the movement in a stock—a very poor kind of strength. He also believes there can be a great fallacy in a company's cash flow. It sounds better than it really is.

In Loeb's opinion, the key to investment success is to insure the safety of capital by cutting losses quickly in a stock that goes down 10 percent or more. Know your stock, concentrate your action, and put in or pull out before the breaking point. His thesis remains, "Put all your eggs in one basket and watch the basket." He doesn't mean one stock, but a handful.

Loeb has worked almost all his stock market years for E. F. Hutton and has been a partner for more than twenty-five years. He is in his office very early each morning, checks his charts, reads his mail, plans his day with an associate, and is prepared for the drama that will unfold on the tape before the average broker has even reached his desk. He believes in tape action more than in anything else. It tells the true story. His love for the stock market is undiminished after all the years he has devoted to it, writing his syndicated column and market letters, or just finding stocks to buy for his many discretionary accounts. In Loeb's opinion, Wall Street is a place where the curtain goes up every day on a new show, and he always sits in front row center.

There is a perpetual value in the concentrated wisdom to be found in this book. "The Wizard of Wall Street" has long since been inducted by his colleagues and millions of others into an imaginary stock market hall of fame. The years have been kind to him. He has made his contribution to an industry which claims him with pride, a contribution that will help millions of investors for many years to come.

Rheinstein, Sidney
Trade Whims: My Fifty Years on the New York Stock Exchange. New York: Ronald Press, 1960. 211 pp. privately printed

The thoughts and events detailed in this book are the pleasant memories of a man who knew more people and more stories than most members of the New York Stock Exchange. Sidney Rheinstein was a specialist for fifty-one years and traded in seventeen companies, among them, General Foods, Phillips Petroleum, Famous-Players Lasky (Paramount), Lehman Corporation, Studebaker, and Goodrich. In the course of his five decades on the exchange he made many friends and obviously enjoyed his life-style.

The specialist is only vaguely understood even by the most sophisticated stock market operator. It is Rheinstein's contention that the smooth flow of the market for all the years that it has been in existence is due in great measure to the excellent work of the specialist. He feels that the newspapers and other media malign him unfairly simply because it makes good copy for the uninformed mass of readers.

The circle of friends that the author brings into his commentary includes a great many of his classmates from Princeton. There is proof in these pages that Rheinstein harbored a love for that school which lasted all his life. This writer has learned from a personal friend of the author that he willed 150,000 shares of Canadian Pacific to Princeton. The value recently was approximately $12 million. Among the well known friends of Rheinstein were Bernard Gimbel, Gene Tunney, Al Smith, and Jim Farley.

Rheinstein's life was greatly regimented, eating in the same clubs every day for years on end. He also paid daily visits to a Turkish bath. It was a life style to which he had become accustomed and which he loved. He had his job, his friends, his wife, and they comprised his pleasureful life.

Throughout the book there are stories related to the stock market, anecdotes, market expressions, and the philosophy that guided the author through his memorable life. This visit with Rheinstein is an inside look at the years from 1909, including the "Big Wind" (Black Tuesday, October 29, 1929), to the present day. He believed that history repeated itself, especially in Wall Street. Panic is still possible when people lose faith in the value of the paper they own, and all decide to throw it on the market at the same time. The impression you get from this book is that you can make money in the market and enjoy the comforts it can buy. The way to do that is to take positions in good stocks for the long term. Traders make just enough to get by. Big money is made by holding stocks for their inevitable growth.

Sarnoff, Paul
Jesse Livermore: Speculator King. Palisades Park, N.J.: Investors Press, 1967. 136 pp. $3.95

Jesse Livermore, one of Wall Street's legendary speculators, is brought to life in an interesting biography that reveals enough to excite the reader as he rides the fortunes of "the Boy Wonder." J. L., as he liked to be called, was purely a speculator and made and lost four multimillion-dollar fortunes. He took his own life in the hat-check room of New York's Stork Club, deep in debt, with no hope of making another comeback. It is important to know how he lived his life to understand the ignominy that led to his final act.

The farm boy from Massachusetts was driven by ambition in a field which offered the ultimate for those who succeeded. He loved the good life, the trappings, the women, and the fame. His one failing was an inability to save any of the money which his fabled speculations were able to amass. He was a big spender and courted the press which played an important part in spreading his fame. Livermore made good copy.

In order to assess the sum total of a man's life, especially one whose exploits as a speculator will leave his name indelibly inscribed in the Wall Street hall of fame, it is necessary to read the facts as they are known. Because of the many failures during his career there were many people who had no faith in J. L. It was not pleasant to be making comebacks all your life. His personal life was unhappy with a succession of wives and a playboy's love for pretty women. At one time Livermore's name was linked with Lillian Russell, although "Diamond Jim" Brady was more prominently mentioned as her close friend. The exciting years that his wealth brought him provided the pleasure in his life. The happy interludes on his yachts or in Palm Beach rubbing elbows with the prominent people he tried to emulate were the times he relished the most. It may not be the measure of success for everybody, but it served to satisfy the ambition of this would-be plain dirt farmer from Shrewsbury, Massachusetts.

Wyckoff, Richard Demille
Wall Street Ventures and Adventures through Forty Years. Original: Richard D. Wyckoff, 1930. Reprint: Westport, Conn.: Greenwood Press, 1968. 313 pp. $15.50

The sum of this man's life could not have been more aptly described than it is in the title of this excellent book. Richard D. Wyckoff's Wall Street career was truly an adventure. It comes alive in its retelling. The reader is treated to a nostalgic trip through history as the author relives his past.

Not only was Wyckoff's forty years an adventure, but they were hard work and long hours. Although they aggravated, exhausted, and in the end almost killed him, no one could have loved them more. A career on Wall Street is probably the most demanding of professions, the world's greatest game, and the author was determined to learn how to play.

His ambition and desire to succeed was obvious from the time he took his first job for $3.00 a week as a Wall Street runner. The industry and determination which helped him achieve a position of importance in the field he loved was the hallmark of his success. His career spanned four of the most exciting decades in Wall Street history, and the men and events which made up those years form a good part of this book.

James Keene, Otto Kahn, and Jesse Livermore are a few of those who are mentioned by Wyckoff who met them personally and who, in this book, tries to recall their views and methods of trading. As a Wall Street celebrity in his own right, the author is probably most widely known as the publisher of *The Magazine of Wall Street*. He also had an advisory service based on the technical action of the market called *The Trend Letter* which made him a good part of his fortune.

In a retrospective look at his career, Wyckoff realizes that he had worked under high pressure for too many years and that that is what caused his health to fail. He sums up in these very important words with a warning to those who might be tempted to overwork: "Business organizations, advertising and selling campaigns, putting over deals, marketing securities, fighting competition, gaining prestige, making money, these are not all there is in life. But with most of us, it takes some sort of shock, it would seem, to waken us to the fact that we are not married to these things, that beyond a certain point they are not necessary in our lives. It is not until we extricate ourselves and gain distance, and time to consider, that we begin to see that they are only a few things out of the many that make life worthwhile."

Zeckendorf, William, with McCreary, Edward
The Autobiography of William Zeckendorf. New York: Holt, Rinehart, and Winston, 1970. 312 pp. $7.95

Reading this autobiography should only increase the admiration you have to feel for William Zeckendorf, whose real estate exploits are destined to earn him a place in history. After he learned the business, he proceeded to remake the face of America and Canada with a vision that often shook the ordinary real estater, and that is proving even to this day his foresight and innovative ability.

Throughout the narrative, you are impressed with Zeckendorf's daring as he develops areas of Washington, D. C., the U. N. Plaza, Denver, Montreal, Kips Bay Plaza, Lincoln Towers, and many others. The problems of Wall Street banking institutions were solved by this entrepreneur with hardly any reward but the consolation that he had saved Wall Street and New York's real estate values from a disastrous drop.

The history of Bill Zeckendorf is replete with stories of how others profited more than he did by holding on to the properties he developed. Zeckendorf was incessantly moving from one project to another, always looking for bigger and better things. It was to lead to his downfall in the end, when laboring under the burden of an enormous debt he was forced to sell under pressure to meet his commitments.

It is a real estate story which opens the door to some of the most exciting deals of the last three decades. You have an inside look at the man whose flair and talent for the promotion and development of property entitle him to the name "Mr. Real Estate."

BOOKS FOR
THE BEGINNER

Brunson, George S.
Intelligent Investing: Profit Making Moves in the Stock Market. Jericho, N.Y.:
Exposition Press, 1971. 191 pp. $7.50

If the neophyte investor lacks sufficient investment knowledge, his search for
the answers to all the important questions has ended. *Intelligent Investing,* an all-
embracing book of information on sixty-four different subjects, opens enough
doors and sheds enough light for even the most confused beginner to learn the
rudiments of the stock market. It is sufficient to start the newcomer on his way
and interest him in a more detailed study of the subjects covered in this book.

Under the three broad categories of "Orientation," "What to Buy," and
"Timing," the author selects and explains the most fundamental terms necessary
for a broad understanding of the stock market. Among them are margin, mutual
funds, new issues, bonds, charts, odd-lots, and leading indicators.

In a series of subjects that continue to probe other areas of importance, the author explains taxes, leverage, growth stocks, and the balance sheet. It is impossible to cover completely or adequately the myriad of subjects that make up the
stock market, but this book embraces all of the most important subjects that
give a clear understanding of how the stock market works. The novice or sophis-
ticate will come away from reading this work with a wider acquaintance with the
basic terms and vital topics that help the individual in his struggle for success in
Wall Street.

Cobleigh, Ira U.
All about Stocks: A Guide to Profitable Investing in the '70s. New York: Weybright and Talley, 1970. 243 pp. $6.95

Most investors enter the stock market woefully unprepared for the decisions
they are called upon to make. Their fantasies of success without effort, abundant riches, and other dreams are doomed to failure. The proper approach to the
potential of equities is a sound fundamental knowledge of the basic background
of stocks and the stock market. Ira Cobleigh succeeds in distilling a mass of facts

109

into this book, and the reader can come away a much wiser person. He can learn how the corporations are formed that create the capital which makes up the stock market. He will be informed about the varieties of corporate debt and the excitement of growth stocks, and enlightened with a study of the listed markets and the over-the-counter markets which originate thousands of new issues every year.

An industry review details the importance and the outlook for a host of major market areas, such as pollution control, petroleum, computers, franchising companies, leisure time, utilities, insurance, transportation, money, and service industries. Cobleigh urges the reader to look for newcomers in the fields of prefabricated housing, cassettes, pharmaceuticals, education, instant foods, golf and tennis, health building, and home mortgages. For those who feel that they are not capable of selecting their own portfolio, a complete chapter is devoted to the investment help which can be supplied by member firms of the New York Stock Exchange, banks, investment counselors, financial services, and mutual funds.

But the author's avowed purpose in writing this book is to educate you to invest on your own. He traces the fashions in investment from the pre-World War II period up to the 1970s. He feels that growth in the decade of the 1970s will not be explosive. Nonetheless, the Gross National Product will increase from $1 trillion to $2 trillion by 1980. Bond yields of $7\frac{1}{2}$ to $8\frac{1}{2}$ percent will not frighten management because bond interest is deducted before taxes, and the rate of inflation will mean payment with cheaper dollars. Research will be vital in the future since change dictates that new favorites will replace today's heroes.

Natural tendencies will keep speculation alive. The author observes that 7 million out of the 30 million stockholders will continue to take king-size risks for giant gains. He advises the speculator to follow several rules:

1. Do not engage in daily or short-term in-and-out trading.
2. Profitable speculation takes six months to three years.
3. Cut your losses and let your profits run.
4. "Stock prices are the slaves of earning power."
5. "Discern a trend and then invest, and aim to sell before its crest."

Richard Demille Wyckoff was once asked which books to study to supplement his *Tape Reading Studies.* He replied, "Read everything you can get hold of. If you find a single idea in a publication it is well worth the time and money spent in procuring and studying it." The point is not only obvious, but almost painfully clear. The lessons are in this book for those who sorely need them. Ira Cobleigh has indeed come close to giving the investor a treatise that tells him "all about stocks."

Engel, Louis
How To Buy Stocks, 5th rev. ed. Boston: Little Brown, 1971. 339 pp. $5.95

It is Louis Engel's conviction that stocks will go up over the long term simply because they always have. He also flatly states that we are a nation of financial illiterates. With over 30 million stockholders at the latest count, there are many people who have entered no-man's-land without any armor.

In his attempt to educate this army of uninformed investors and the many others who are now looking to enter the market, Engel does a thorough job of explaining a multitude of subjects in the field. These fundamentals should be drilled into the minds of all investors so that they may intelligently face the important task of selecting those stocks that will send them on their way to financial security.

In all of the many chapters concerning stocks, bonds, how to pick a broker, how to buy and sell over-the-counter stocks, and how much it costs to buy stocks, etc., the author maintains an objectivity that enhances the value of his advice and lends an air of professionalism and authority to his work. A glaring exception to that objectivity is Engel's obvious dislike for investment trusts or mutual funds. His expressed opinion is that the fantastic growth of the funds is due solely to the sales incentive created by high sales charges. Is it possible that the performance of the many excellent growth funds caused an influx of public money into the fund area? The example of Gerald Tsai, Fred Carr, and Fred Mates, who attracted many millions of eager investors to their performance banners, is positive proof that the fund medium gained popularity through its excellent performance and not necessarily as a consequence of aggressive and highly motivated salesmen.

The value of this book is attested to by the fact that 3 million copies have already been sold. In disseminating authoritative information to an eager public Engel has performed a vital service. He is helping in his own way to educate that massive army of financial illiterates, and to start them on that journey which leads to a mature knowledge of the stock market and the possibility of a successful future.

Finley, Harold M.
Everybody's Guide to the Stock Market, 4th ed. rev. Chicago: Henry Regnery, 1968. 256 pp. $4.95

This all purpose guide for the stock market beginner ranks high in that category of books which aim at educating the tyro investor. It contains the answers to many of the questions that the complicated subject of Wall Street poses to the uninitiated.

In following the progress of a mythical company from its inauspicious incorporation until it becomes a public company, the author answers many of the questions which the newcomer usually asks. Although as the book progresses, the subjects become more involved and sophisticated, the reader becomes increasingly educated and equal to the task of comprehension.

An explanation of the Dow Theory introduces the subject of market indicators. It serves to enlighten the reader and interest him in the area of technical market indicators, volume indications, panics, and other areas which Finley adds to his coverage. A discussion of credit and taxes gives breadth and substance to the exposition.

Three excellent chapters conclude this book, "Your Professional Assistants,"

"How to Improve Yourself as an Investor," and "What to Expect." Finley's prose is clear and honest. It promises nothing specific, but does lead the reader to believe that the knowledge gained from reading this book can add just the right amount of confidence to tip the scale in his favor in the quest for profits in the stock market.

Jarvis, N. Leonard
A Woman's Guide to Wall Street. Englewood Cliffs, N.J.: Prentice-Hall, 1969. 195 pp. $6.95

There is no dearth of books intended to help the woman in her quest for financial success. Leonard Jarvis has used his investment know-how to develop a useful book for anyone who needs help in the stock market. It is a useful guide to the intricacies of Wall Street.

The usual amount of attention is devoted to the various odds and ends that are necessary to an understanding of the functions and structure of the stock market. A careful look at the career opportunities for women is one of the vital elements of this work that adds to its value and importance.

Another outstanding characteristic of this book is the attitude which pervades the author's comments on the promise of stocks. His background as an analyst lends stature to his discussion of the companies that he lists in the chapter,"The Growth Stocks of the Future."

Leonard Jarvis' *A Woman's Guide to Wall Street* is not merely a boring reiteration of the necessary fundamentals, but contains a combination of facts and a fascination with the potential for financial gain through common stock investment.

Kahn, Harry, Jr.
A Primer For Profit in the Stock Market: A Manual for the Small Investor. Garden City, N.Y.: Doubleday, 1960

The small investor can take heart from the affirmative attitude expressed in this book. It states that you can make a profit in the stock market, although there are the usual risks. What is more important, the author develops a program that encourages, warns, and then coaches the reader in a studied attempt to gain the rewards to be found in the stock market.

The basic needs of the investor must be met before he can think of stocks. A bank account with enough savings to get by in an emergency, adequate life insurance coverage, and a steady job should be the prerequisites for any investor. All surplus funds can then be used to invest for profit in the stock market. Kahn sums up a method which can be successful. He urges you to choose intelligently, but slowly and carefully, hang on unemotionally, and sell only for a good reason—a tall order. It calls for a man without blood. Buy only for the long pull, find an industry or firm you have faith in, and concentrate geographically in the areas of greatest growth (Florida and California). Do your homework—determine the attractiveness of a stock by its yield and price/earnings ratio.

Kahn follows immediately with a thorough survey of key industries and his assessment of their importance and desirability. He discusses railroads, oils, utilities, electronics, banks, chemicals, drugs, aircraft, and construction. His opinions are dated, but his insight and observations are timeless. He is afraid of the well-known growth stocks and would rather find a small growth company at the threshold of a dramatic breakthrough. His definition of a growth stock is that it (1) sells at a high multiple, (2) has small dividends, (3) has earnings which rise each year, (4) has many periods of sharp rises, and (5) develops and markets new products reflecting excellent research and sound forward-looking management.

Since this book is a primer for beginners, Kahn explains the jargon of Wall Street. He suggests that the investor should read the *Wall Street Journal,* the *New York Times, Fortune, Barron's,* etc. There are short definitions of bonds, preferred stocks, rights, warrants, margins, short-selling, averaging, and tax selling. This fundamental information is accompanied by a description of the stock exchanges, a brief explanation of the Dow averages, and a lesson on how to read the financial pages.

Mutual funds are suggested for those investors who have no time to do the careful study necessary to prepare for their own investment program. They are also recommended for the beginner in the market. Gains may be slower because of the wide diversification that increases the safety of fund investment. Dilution of a possible sharp gain is the result. The conclusion is clearly in favor of funds; they are attractive to investors of all types.

Kahn reiterates his suggestions to the reader who is eager to win in Wall Street. He offers this list of advice:

1. Stick to the long range view.
2. Don't feel restless when you have idle capital.
3. Don't wait too long to buy a stock that looks good.
4. Don't hold on to a stock too long.

This valuable treatise is a lesson in the art of investment that will maintain its validity forever. It doesn't offer an easy road to riches, but holds out the reward of satisfactory profits to the person with patience. Do your homework, study such relevant factors as earnings, yields, management, etc., and then make your decision. Avoid emotion, rumor, instinct, and tips. Follow these rules and they will bring you solid profits.

Kahn, Lotte
Women and Wall Street. New York: MacFadden-Bartell, 1963. 160 pp.

This appeal to the women of America, who comprise more than half of the corporate stockholders, is a familiar one. It starts out with a definition of how important the stock market can be to the widow, the wife, and the single girl. It evolves into a guide for an investor of either sex and explores the whole gamut of the Wall Street scene. There is a brief history of the New York Stock Exchange, its operation, the specialist's function, and the broker's importance in the market. Before too long a complete, though perfunctory coverage of dozens of subjects helps the novice appreciate the value and importance of a basic stock market education.

To the widow, Lotte Kahn offers an inflation-proof income for life. It is imperative that she be careful to choose safe issues that allow her to sleep soundly. The temptation to try the "sparklers" that promise quick profits must be resisted.

The wife is encouraged to invest her surplus money wisely in an attempt to build a fund for the education of her growing children. This quest is aided by the author's analysis of many industries in the later chapters.

The single girl can afford to speculate in a rather carefree manner. Ostensibly, the thrill of earning enough to buy a fur coat or a new car is worth the risk of hard-earned capital. It is not clear how this feat should be attempted, but the clues are contained in the copious advice that the author gives throughout the book.

A valuable survey of thirty major industry groups adds to the importance of this book. An introduction to the complex mechanism of choosing by industry selection and company analysis spells out the methodical study that leads to investment success. Some of the industries represented are airlines, electronics, utilities, food, steel, retail, paper, tobacco, drugs, banks, defense, and autos. A list of the leading companies in each industry is offered the reader. Further study and detailed analysis can determine his or her choice of the best company in the group.

The advanced look at companies represents a giant step forward from the fundamental knowledge that is found in this book. A look at over-the-counter trading, bonds, preferred stocks, mutual funds, commodities, and investment clubs fills out most of the well-known areas that are normally discussed in beginner books. A glossary of definitions, "The Language of Investing," at the back of the book is a good source of stock market definitions. It is reprinted by permission of the New York Stock Exchange.

There are no surprises to be found in these pages. An honest attempt has been made to inform women of their obligations in the financial arena. It is a duty which they will have to deal with sooner or later in life. The education which this book offers is an excellent first step for the eager novice. It creates enough excitement for the student to continue with a more intricate and complex study of this difficult and diverse subject.

Levy, Herta Hess
What Every Woman Should Know about Investing Her Money. Chicago: Dartnell, 1968. 222 pp. $6.95

This book lives up to the promise of its title. In a thorough, concise manner, the author prepares the bewildered woman investor for the necessary task of managing her finances. In the process, Mrs. Levy has written a beginner book covering the basic fundamentals of the stock market for all newcomers, male or female.

With the aid of eight pages of photographs and a long chapter on the history and mechanics of the securities market, the reader is prepared for the basic economic facts underlying the motivation of investors who buy and sell stocks. The next step informs the tyro of many sources of information—periodicals, newspapers, financial services, and books on investment.

By this time the reader has reached the point where she is competent enough to establish her objective and set her investment goals. Does she want dividends, growth, or capital gain? The narrative then explains many different areas of investment such as common stocks, preferred stocks, bonds (corporate, convertible, etc.), and investment companies (mutual funds).

The last three chapters explain Wall Street jargon, how to read financial statements, and the work of the professionals who help you in the various areas of finance. These include your broker, banker, accountant, lawyer. The balance of this book is composed of the definitions of terms, "The Language of Investing."

The value of Mrs. Levy's book is obvious. It will have a beneficial effect on the many thousands of readers who want to learn a new way of life. It covers a subject that is now a veritable must for more than 32 million stockholders. Veterans of the peaks and valleys of market action can take a page out of this newcomer's book and bone up on fundamentals. This work by a knowledgeable woman stockbroker can confidently take its place in the library of beginner books which help millions of neophytes in their first unsteady steps into the investment world.

Low, Janet
Understanding the Stock Market. Boston: Little, Brown, 1968. 210 pp. $4.95

As the ranks of stockholders steadily increase with each succeeding year, the need for more information about how the market works has grown apace. The value of Janet Low's guide is that it remains one of the most readable books which analyze, define, and explain the many terms in the lexicon of Wall Street.

While there are many fundamental terms which would only be of interest to the beginner, it would amaze a so-called sophisticated, long-time market trader how many things he could learn of a basic nature that may have escaped his knowledge. For that reason, it would not do any harm to review the subjects in Janet Low's book as a refresher course.

The newcomer to Wall Street must read many books before he can absorb the lessons that lead to an acquaintance with the world of stocks and bonds. This book is an excellent start.

Moore, Colleen
How Women Can Make Money in the Stock Market. Garden City, N.Y.: Doubleday, 1969. 176 pp. $4.95

There is a wealth of important information in Colleen More's book about the stock market. It is not so much a book for women only as a guide for any novice, with lucid explanations of a host of Wall Street's terms and definitions. You can argue the need for another book that generally explains the fundamental knowledge necessary for entry into the market, but this book and many others like it are necessary to instruct the veritable army of newcomers in the jargon of the Street.

There are several things that even the sophisticated investor can learn by reading this book. We sometimes give ourselves too much credit for things we should know but have never bothered to learn. The most valuable part of this book, in the estimation of this reviewer, is the author's evaluation of a company. This is accomplished through a step-by-step reading of a balance sheet, the explanation of which is enhanced by the inclusion of a fold-out sample at the end of the book.

Miss Moore claims that she started out not knowing how to balance her checkbook. She has demonstrated what application and dedication can accomplish. It would undoubtedly please the author if many thousands of women followed her remarkable example and became proficient in the investment area. They must face the unhappy fact that many women outlive their husbands, and that they will have need for financial acumen in that lonesome future.

Rosenberg, Claude N., Jr.
Stock Market Primer. New York: World, 1969. 351 pp. $6.95

Clarifying the mysteries of the stock market and the myriad questions that they pose for the neophyte investor is a king-size order for even the most knowledgeable of counselors. However, the royal treatment is applied to this formidable task in this valuable book.

Rosenberg first prepares the newcomer by explaining how the market works and how to follow it, and by defining the terms that appear on the financial page. The next step in this educational exercise is the examination of a balance sheet which is done to investigate the financial condition and efficiency of a given company. Balance sheet analysis is a prerequisite of open-eyed investing, as opposed to the in-the-dark type. The author emphasizes that there is no substitute for the facts that are available from your broker in deciding whether to buy a particular stock. Precautions such as this take time, but they also remove some of the dangers of uninformed speculation.

The book's most valuable chapter summarizes the pros and cons of forty industries and clearly analyzes their worth in the current market milieu, applying the average p/e ratio that each industry commands. This industry guide is one that security analysts use, and it can be a reference for many years to come.

Having brought the reader to this point, the author closes with an explanation of the explosive potential of the 25–35 age group in the 1970s, and relates the industry approach to the future needs of the country.

While the information contained here is of unquestionable value for the novice investor, the seasoned investor can also glean much useful information from these pages. For example, coverage extends to a list of "bikini stocks" which Rosenberg selects for rapid growth. These are companies with small capitalizations and sizeable potentials.

It is important to understand that learning the fundamentals from a successful investment analyst is not enough to guarantee a successful foray into the stock market's maze. It is the ante that you must pay to enter the game on an equal footing with the other players. When experience is added to knowledge, your chance of winning is considerably improved.

Shinbach, Bruce D.
The Stock Market Made Easy. New York: Vantage Press, 1970. 86 pp. $3.50

The purpose of this book, like so many others of this type, is to inform, and it does that well. It covers the fundamental terms and definitions for the new investor and the old. It lays a basis of understanding which is necessary before an investor can intelligently make a decision.

The author's aim is to explain all those things that people want to know but are afraid to ask because they don't want to display their lack of knowledge.

Shinbach draws on his experience as a stockbroker with a member firm of the New York Stock Exchange to explain the basic language and workings of the stock market with clarity. He writes in a style which is easy to understand and absorb. It prepares the reader for the higher levels of sophistication to be gained from reading other books which explore more difficult areas of the investment process.

Shufro, Edward
The New Investor's Guide to Wall Street. New York: Lion Press, 1970. 159 pp. $4.95

In a particularly well-written book, the author devotes more than half of his time to an interesting and unique explanation of how a company is formed, incorporated, goes public, and eventually makes it to the New York Stock Exchange. The other half of the book deals with the multitude of subjects it is necessary to learn before you can invest profitably. Round lots, odd-lots, symbols, and the role of the specialist are some of the many things covered. A discussion of periodicals to read and of the Dow Jones averages reinforces the need for constant attention to the changes which the market represents. A chapter on how a stockbroker spends his day gives the novice an insight into that part of market routine with which he is most likely to be in contact when he starts his investment career.

The author offers a puzzling formula in his chapter, "Your Financial Future." He prefers that you never buy a stock when it is making new highs. Always buy a stock when it's selling near its low. There is nothing wrong with that advice, although there are many experts who believe that it is not wise because you cannot be sure of how long a stock will hang around the lows or continue to make new lows. When a stock is making new highs it is moving in the right direction and may continue to make new highs for quite some time.

The next bit of intelligence which is hard to grasp is Shufro's statement, "Make it a rule to hold every stock you buy for at least two years." It would really be wonderful if such advice could be followed with a good chance of success. The problem is that when dealing with intangibles you can't state categorically that it will take three years or any other given period of time to meet with success. A perfect example of that is the stirring rise that Syntex had in 1963–1964. It moved up 100 points in three weeks. There was really no need to hold it for more than that period of time to net a fantastic short-term gain.

Shulsky, Sam
The New Stock Buying Guide. Greenwich, Conn.: Fawcett, 1965. 112 pp. $.75

The stock market writer must be careful not to scare off the neophyte with difficult, undecipherable explanations of the basic facts about stocks. This is precisely what Sam Shulsky does not do in his *New Stock Buying Guide.* He asks the obvious questions that puzzle a new investor but proceeds to answer them with the clarity of a newspaper reporter. The subjects that are covered in this book are sufficient to start the investor on the road to financial independence.

The author has spent many years trying to explode the myth that only the rich can afford to buy common stock. He begins with an explanation of what common stock is, why you should own stocks, and how to buy them. It may seem elementary to many readers, but a simple explanation by an expert can allay the ungrounded fear of a newcomer. There is really no reason for the average man to be afraid to own good quality common stocks.

A handful of other chapters describe how the stock market operates, how stocks are bought and sold on the exchange floor and on the over-the-counter market. Shulsky also explains how these various operations are viewed from the boardrooms (branch offices) of the many thousands of brokerage offices. All of these chapters are amply supplemented by illustrative photographs that show the new investor in pictures what he is reading on the pages. They should stimulate the beginner to personally visit the New York and American stock exchanges to actually feel the excitement of the investment process.

The author discusses bonds and debentures, mutual funds, and investment clubs in other chapters. They are all important for the new investor to understand and are elaborated on in more detail in other investment books for those who are interested in further study. There is a glossary at the end of the book which defines many stock market terms and offers a reference for the reader as he continues to increase his stock market sophistication.

This type of book is essential to the education of the millions of new investors who join the shareholder ranks every year. Sam Shulsky as a syndicated columnist answers questions every day in your daily newspaper. He must be crucially aware of the value of this book. The questions which pour in daily can only convince him of the vital need for publications of this kind.

Silverman, Richard
$100 Gets You Started. New York: Macmillan, 1965. 264 pp. $5.95

More than half of this book is a guide to better understanding of the stock market for a beginner. It explains the fundamentals and how to plan an investment program. There are chapters on the margin account and how to use it, its advantages and disadvantages, mutual funds, investment clubs, monthly investment plans, annual reports, and a long discussion on market indicators. This part is at the back of the book as if it were less important than the sensational section which contains thirteen ways to make money in the market starting with as little as $100.

For some reason, the "Foolproof," "Big Money," "Fatten Your Bankroll," and "Automatic Profits" sections, which the author promises in his discussion of the methods described, do not excite the interest sufficiently to warrant an endorsement here. Perhaps it is the miniscule size of the investment. There would be difficulty finding a broker who would handle such a small sum. Many firms will not accept a sale or purchase of less than $750. In fact, you can't open an account for less than $1,000.

Outside of that qualification, there is merit in the author's explanation of warrants, puts and calls, convertible bonds (the margins are much higher now and have lowered the leverage considerably), and convertible preferreds, etc. The neophyte should find this book a valuable guide to the various investment techniques and systems for possible profits in the stock market.

Sterling, Dorothy
Wall Street: The Story of the Stock Exchange. Garden City, N.Y.: Doubleday, 1955. 128 pp. $3.50

In a short, compact book which should not take the average reader more than one hour to read, Dorothy Sterling presents the story of the stock exchange to the neophyte investor.

The growth of Wall Street since 1955 has given substance to the fascination demonstrated by the author for the investment process. She traces Wall Street's history from the time it was the cradle of America until the present day when the canyons of lower Manhattan drill for the oil which lubricates the nation's business, meaning the money which is raised so that new corporations can contribute new jobs and products so that established firms might expand.

Here it all is in a quick and easy way—the way the exchange works, how orders are executed, how the floor brokers operate, etc. This book is a valuable aid for the newcomer to the street, and for those old timers who never had the time or inclination to find out the mechanics of the investment process.

Straley, John A.
What about Common Stocks? New York: Harper & Row, 1962. 150 pp. $3.50

This book is an outline of fundamental stock market facts that every tyro investor must know to enter the market intelligently. It is not, as the author states in the preface, a recipe for quick profits. It is rather a guide to the rewards and pitfalls of investing. For the interested neophyte, Straley describes an approach that is convenient and simple. He cautions that no person should purchase common stock unless he has savings and adequate life insurance to protect his dependents.

At the outset, Straley defines the term common stock and explains how investment nullifies the effect of inflation. The history of the New York Stock Exchange, its operation, and the order process are fully covered. The other exchanges and the over-the-counter market are also briefly mentioned. A discussion of the four basic qualities to look for in a stock are examined next. They are safety, cycles, income, and growth. Straley says that if you expect all four in any one stock, you want the impossible.

In the chapters that follow there is a continuous flow of information on such areas as the monthly investment plan, investment clubs, mutual funds, and dollar-cost averaging. A look at the more exotic and complicated subjects of puts and calls, warrants, short-selling, and convertible securities points the way toward future sophistication for the novice. By this time, his interest should urge him to continue his education in more advanced books on some of the subjects covered here.

This work is a first step in your investment program, one that never stops. The business of stocks is dynamic, and you must continue to learn to keep abreast of new developments and techniques. A beginner must start somewhere; Straley's *What About Common Stocks?* is an ideal place for anyone eager to learn about the stock market.

HOW TO BEAT
THE MARKET

Cattell, Hudson
A Checklist of Stock Market Technics. Springfield, Mass.: John Magee, 1968. 52 pp. $4.00

This slender volume is a worthwhile work and serves a valuable function. It outlines the essential points one has to take into account before making investment decisions.

There is no claim here of infallibility or instant success. In fact, the missing ingredient, by the author's own admission, is the psychological factor which is individual and can't be predicted. This has profound influence on the whole investment process. It can nullify all the beneficial effects of proper selection, timing, etc.

It is obvious that no foolproof method of winning in the market has been discovered, and this checklist is not intended as a guaranteed method for picking winners. It can be a valuable tool in helping the investor put some order into his selection of stocks. As Frank Curto, John Magee's colleague, put it, "The entire strategy of business prediction is a matter of putting one's self in the path of the optimum probabilities."

This is precisely what this checklist does. As a guide for an experienced investor or trader it is extremely valuable and adds immeasurably to the possibility of investment success.

Cobleigh, Ira U.
Happiness Is a Stock that Doubles in a Year. New York: Bernard Geis, 1968. 243 pp. $6.95

In a previous book the author selected forty-five stocks for outstanding performance in the ensuing year. The results were unusual—31 percent of the list doubled in a year, and the whole list gained 64 percent. In this new edition, he has revised his list and once again whets the appetite of the speculative fraternity.

Throughout the body of the book, Cobleigh touches on those industries which have the potential for rapid growth. His discussion includes fundamentals of

121

stock selection, timing, mutual funds, puts and calls, warrants, and other salient subjects. In the chapter, "Bull Markets and Bare Knees," he also documents the theory that skirt lengths go up and down in direct relation to stock market prices.

He lists former doublers on both the New York and American Exchanges to prove that hundreds of stocks have accomplished this feat. There is no attempt on the author's part to convey the impression that it is easy or that it is guaranteed to happen, but his astute observations and lists of doublers prove that it is highly possible.

The speculator who is looking for clues that will help him find those winners should read the chapter that zeroes in on the habitat of the stocks that can double in a year. They are most likely to be found on the American Stock Exchange. The odds favor stocks below 5 on the Amex and below 10 on the Big Board. Management of the target companies should own at least 30 percent of the stock. Capitalizations should be small. Breakthroughs of a dynamic nature in a scientific, technological, commercial, or mineral area help in achieving the desired goal.

There are other important hints that round out Cobleigh's criteria for success in finding doublers that sound most convincing for the eager speculator in his unusual quest for quick success. Of course, the pièce de resistance is the list of forty-five stocks which the author feels have the potential to double within a year. The disclaimers are there, but the crystallization of the whole book and all its helpful clues is wrapped up in the last chapter and the list.

Ira Cobleigh has displayed an eagerness and awe for the potential that speculating in the stock market offers the individual. He has documented the past effectively and has proved the possibility of an enormous gain in a short period of time. He is to be commended for his aggressive treatise, for it once again gives the lie to the public's tired declaration that nobody can make money in the stock market.

Darvas, Nicolas
   The New How I Made $2,000,000 in the Stock Market. New York: Lyle Stuart, 1971. 198 pp. $5.95

This book is a retelling of how an internationally known ballroom dancer tamed the stock market to the tune of $2 million. Nicolas Darvas, after years of trial and error, developed a method for maximizing profits and minimizing losses. Most people in the market realize that it is imperative to do this in order to stay alive. Darvas does it, and what's more, he does it with impersonal precision. The bulk of his orders were sent to his brokers by cable from night clubs all over the world. He was forced to develop a code of communication to be used when he was in such places as Rome, Paris, New Delhi, and Kathmandu. Darvas found that the distance from Wall Street was advantageous since he was not subject to rumors, tips, and well-intentioned information from brokers and friends.

The system selected those stocks that had made historical or all-time highs, with increased volume, and were twice the low of the previous two or three years. A box system was worked out, making it possible for Darvas to place stop-orders. The stops were then constantly moved up as a stock climbed into higher boxes. Darvas substantiates his story with numerous cables and charts of the several stocks that made his fortune. They are augmented by letters from anxious readers who have had questions about his method, questions which he answers simply and clearly.

It seems incredible that all you have to do is watch the list of new highs to find the stocks that lead to fortune. But that is the way it's done. Instead of being overcome by envy, the reader should devote those hours of study and application necessary to dig out the techno-fundamental winners. If you follow the system Darvas explains in this book, success can be yours.

Diamond, Frank B.
The Fine Art of Making Money in the Stock Market. New York: Cornerstone Library, 1968. Distributor: Simon & Schuster. 127 pp. paperback: $1.45

Any attempt to cover all of the many-faceted areas of the securities markets in one book must meet with failure. Frank Diamond has done the next best thing by offering readable explanations of some of the most important and pertinent subjects. His work should serve to enlighten the reader who wants to understand how the stock market works and to help guide him to a more informed attempt at making money in the market.

The author separates the several subjects into those which apply to the investor and those which more aptly aid the speculator. Whether or not there is really a difference between a speculator and an investor is debatable and not a subject for discussion in this account of Diamond's book.

It would be fitting to use the author's own words to sum up the excellence of his work. He has given us a worthwhile evening's lesson in the stock market by dishing up "some brightly colored stones in the speculative mosaic of Wall Street."

Fabricand, Burton P.
Beating the Street: How to Make More Money in the Stock Market. New York: McKay, 1969. 176 pp. $5.95

This book sets out to teach the reader how to acquire an advantage over the other fellow which will help him win in the stock market. The author points out in his opening chapters that a study by Professors L. Fisher and J. H. Lorie of the University of Chicago proved that a portfolio selected in January 1926 by throwing darts at the financial pages of a newspaper would have grown by 1960 at a compounded rate of 9 percent a year. This random method may be effective and satisfactory for some, but not for Fabricand. He has set his sights higher, and proceeds to explain his system for beating the market.

Although the author rules out the roulette wheel and the horses, his repeated references to the races make you squirm with discomfort. The comparison of horses and stocks doesn't give confidence to the reader. In his discussion of gambling he makes the point that the public is always right since their cumulative betting on a horse establishes the favorite. The large take reduces your chances of making real money at the track. Therefore, the author's attention is directed toward the stock market where the commission only averages about 1 percent.

The principle of maximum confusion is the system which Fabricand employs. He contends that there is a time lag between the dissemination of news and the reaction by the public. It is that crucial period which gives the author the chance to make the move that leads to success in his operations. The principle which guides him in his decision is, "Only when surprising changes occur in the conditions affecting stocks is there a chance to do better than the public." Specifically, an earning statement is a surprise if it is at least 10 percent higher than the estimate made by market analysts. The *Value Line*, which follows 1,400 stocks, is used extensively by the author for his earnings estimates. Usually, the unexpected increase causes analysts to revise their estimated earnings sharply upward, and this is the key to the drive for substantial profits. It is so obvious and elementary that most market followers have overlooked its basic importance. Earnings improvement and price/earnings ratios are the prime reason for growth in market value, and the failure to realize the undiscounted nature of newly reported earnings loses the gain that is inherent in that report.

The sell signal that offers you the counter action to the above is when earnings are reported that are 10 percent below your expectations, those of your analyst, or those of the company's officials. It appears that the rules stated here can provide the investor with an intelligent and rational approach to financial gain in an irrational and illogical medium. The many charts, tables, and painstaking explanations by Fabricand provide the proof that it has been done, and his publication of this book puts the system in the public domain. The challenge is therefore joined, and the blame for your failure to use the author's advice can only be the inertia and inflexibility that is always the bane of the stock market trader and investor.

Fisher, Milton
How to Make Money in the Over-the-Counter Market. New York: William Morrow, 1970. 237 pp. $5.95

In this book one can once again find the effluence of enthusiasm for the stock market from a man who has enjoyed the fruits of success that a career in Wall Street can offer. The excitement shows through in the author's attempt to explain the market to the average person who is locked into a humdrum existence on a low-level, unglamourous, predictable future.

Fisher analyzes in a realistic and entertaining way the great potential and challenge of the oldest and largest securities market, the unlisted or over-the-counter market. "Remember," states Fisher, "great oaks from little acorns grow." Those companies which are already listed have had a period of growth that diminishes the possibility of a quantum leap in sales and earnings.

There are valuable chapters on how to buy new issues, how to read and understand a prospectus, and how to trade, invest, and speculate. There are also Fisher's own ideas on when and how to buy and sell.

At the end of the book there is a list of America's fastest growth companies, courtesy of John S. Herold of Greenwich, Conn., illustrating the opportunities for spectacular growth in young, over-the-counter companies. At this point the author states emphatically that America's fastest growing companies can be found in the over-the-counter market.

This book has brought home its point with clarity and proved statistically that big money can be made by buying the small companies. By concentrating on the unlisted market, the author has made it possible to flout the stereotype that over-the-counter stocks should be taboo, are too speculative, and should be avoided. In the author's own words, "The over-the-counter market provides a dramatically different form of investment from listed securities. It provides a fascinating and profitable challenge for the relatively modest investor. It will reward handsomely anyone who takes the time and effort to study and master it."

Floss, Carl William
Market Target. New York: Exposition Press, 1969. 205 pp. $10.00

In a carefully planned study of a broad section of the stock market, the author of this book takes the average investor far down the road toward an intelligent, decision-making process of stock selection. For the many millions of shareholders who use the hit-or-miss method of buying stock and end up missing the hoped-for profit, this book provides an answer to their problems by removing the mystery from the stock market.

Starting with an evaluation of the market and the Dow Jones industrials, Floss rates each stock by measuring the growth rate per month, and thereby determines which are topping out and which are pointing upward. There is no attempt on his part to predict or forecast the future. The numbers express the changing pattern and the direction for each company. This method is a starting point for successful investment in a long-term program. This introduction is followed by an in-depth study of sixteen major industrial groups, including such exotic areas as lasers, pollution control, and oceanography.

In concluding his comments on the efficacy of his method, Floss states that it is not infallible, but is accurate enough to be practical. It competes with other means of selection such as earnings, technical methods, i.e., the use of charts, and demonstrated management capability. However, his techniques will generally provide the earliest warning and will confirm trends that exist and changes which will reverse them.

This careful study on the long-term direction of stocks has placed a valuable tool in the hands of every investor. Those who are wise enough to learn how important it can be will avail themselves of the information that it classifies for their benefit.

Fowler, Elizabeth M.
90 Days to Fortune: How to Make Money in a Bear Market. New York: Ivan Obolensky, 1965. 154 pp. $4.00

It has long been a tenet of experienced investors that one of the attributes needed for success is patience. Elizabeth Fowler lays that tenet to rest with a dramatic story of an amateur who made a fortune in ninety days. What is more, he did it while his professional counterparts were paralyzed by the losses of the bear market of 1962.

Young Jeb Wofford used the option market to make his fortune. He started with $30,000 near the top of the 1961 market. The author claims that there are three ways to make money in a bear market: (1) Sell out and wait for the market to sell off sufficiently and repurchase your stocks near the bottom for the inevitable recovery. Your money will buy you a much larger amount of shares. (2) Sell short or short against the box if you own stock, and the fall in prices will create profits. The lower the market goes, the more money you will make. (3) The use of put options will give you the most leverage and allow you to benefit from the break in the market just as though you were short of it. A put option enables you to sell a stock at a given price for a specified period of time. When the put is exercised at the original price and bought in at a lower price, the difference is a profit.

Elizabeth Fowler has pointed up one of the mysteries of the stock market. She has shown how few investors avail themselves of the opportunities that are present in a bear market. It is a rare investor who sells out his position when the danger signals are obvious. Most stockholders choose to ride out the storm and hope to recover their losses when the market rallies. The optimism that prevails is in contrast to the gloom created by market crashes. A well documented comparison is made between 1929 and 1962 in an attempt to define the causes of each debacle. A chapter that dips into market history looks at the behavior of crowds as explained in *Extraordinary Popular Delusions and the Madness of Crowds* and at the comments of Bernard Baruch who claimed that the book saved him millions.

There is a lesson to be learned from this factual record of success in a bear market, but the tragedy is that its truth will not alter the actions of the majority. The faith and optimism that motivates most Americans to buy stocks in the first place usually causes them to hold on with a religious fervor that denies them the ability to admit that they can lose money when investing in their country.

Greenfield, Samuel C.
The Low-High Theory of Investment: How to Make Money on the Stock Market and Keep It. New York: Coward-McCann, 1968. 183 pp. $4.95

You cannot dispute the age-old market axiom that the surest way to make money is to buy low and sell high. The author of this serious book tells us to do precisely that, and, just in case you doubt him, he proceeds to prove that you can actually buy low and sell high. He has done it for years and advised his clients to do the same.

Samuel Greenfield uses a sound approach based on logic to develop his method of achieving stock market success. The basic tenet of the method is to study the historic trading pattern of a stock as shown in the range, or highs and lows, of the preceding years. This data can be found on the back of the yellow Standard and Poor's Reports. The low-high spread gives the investor the information he needs to determine whether the percentage change is narrow or wide.

The author says, "If the security is purchased near the lower area of its annual range it will probably do well. If it is purchased nearer the high area it will probably do poorly. A red line may be drawn at precisely the area of danger where the risk increases beyond the normal."

The most valid, graphic proof that Greenfield's method has merit is displayed in the chart called "The Low-High Spread Chart From the High of One Year to the Low of the Following Year." Take the same Standard and Poor report and place an oblique line from the low of one year to the high of the next. There is a substantial spread between those two prices, as the author shows with Standard Oil of New Jersey and Zenith.

	Jersey				Zenith		
	LOW	HIGH	PERCENT SPREAD		LOW	HIGH	PERCENT SPREAD
1967	59	71	7	1967	48	72	55
1966	66	84	13	1966	46	89	186
1965	74	90	20	1965	31	61	97
1964	75	93	58	1964	31	44	69
1963	58	77	71	1963	26	42	100
1962	45	60	46	1962	21	38	136
1961	41	52	37	1961	16	41	174
1960	38	51	11	1960	15	22	120
1959	46	59	23	1959	10	23	470
1958	48	60	25	1958	4	12	200
1957	48	69	38	1957	3	4	33
1956	50	63		1956	3	4	

In the example shown it should be noted that the low of one year is always lower than the high of the next year. The author claims that where a security is purchased at or near the low of one year it should show a profit during the following year. The question immediately comes to mind, "How can you know when you are at the low for the year?" The answer is, "You don't!" However, as you approach the fourth quarter or the end of the year you have a fairly good idea when a stock is near its low. This can be determined by watching the list of new lows every day in the *Wall Street Journal* or any other newspaper.

The author explains a system of charts which can be set up to follow your stocks and improve the timing of your purchases. It is obvious that the basis of his whole theory is timing. There are many thick-skinned traders and investors who write off any theory that purports to make money in the stock market. The cynics would do themselves no harm to study this method of buying stocks; the logic it contains cannot be taken lightly.

Mitchell, Samuel
How to Make Big Money in the Stock Market. New York: Frederick Fell, 1968. 243 pp. $5.95

Everyone who has ever tried to make money in the stock market can take heart from the experiences of Samuel Mitchell. Beginning with a little money,

$3,000, and a great deal of patience, fortitude, and loyalty, he now owns millions of dollars of Xerox Corporation stock. I know that the author will forgive me for dwelling on that fantastic story. The rest of the book pales into insignificance beside the wonder of Xerox.

Here is an actual case of a man who ignored the famous Wall Street axiom, "Don't fall in love with a stock," and made it pay off. It wasn't easy. Sam Mitchell didn't fall in love overnight. It must have taken years for his attraction to this company to blossom into a firm, loyal, and durable commitment. It started when Haloid was an over-the-counter company selling at $30 a share. Mitchell heard the company was working on a sensational process, and if it was perfected, the stock would go places. It was not unlike many stories you hear around the boardroom. His broker confirmed that a large company had put some stock away in its pension fund. This appealed to Mitchell, so he decided to buy one hundred shares for $3,000.

After a few years the stock reached $100 a share. Friends of the author badgered him with, "You can't go wrong taking a profit." But Mitchell just became more interested in xerography, the process which Haloid had bought in 1948 from Chester Carlson, the inventor. In time the name of the company was changed to Haloid Xerox, and finally in 1961 to the Xerox Corporation, its present name. The big breakthrough came in 1960 with the introduction of the 914 copier. The rest is history. Xerox is one of the greatest growth companies on the American corporate scene today.

The road to Mitchell's millions was not all smooth. There were times when the skeptics looked right. The years 1962 and 1966 were two difficult bear years when the price of the stock slipped so sharply that even the dedicated Mr. Xerox must have been beset with some doubts about the future. But his courage and persistence prevented him from selling even one share. Today, he admits that Xerox is the brightest star in his constellation of stocks.

There are many other subjects contained in this book such as how to evaluate a purchase, Mitchell's complete portfolio with a short description of each company, and a great deal of other pertinent investment facts and opinions. They all stand in the shadow of Sam Mitchell's big coup—his long ride for the big money with Xerox. It was an almost casual transaction by an amateur which made him a millionaire. It could happen to you.

Owen, Lewis
How Wall Street Doubles My Money Every Three Years. New York: Bernard Geis, 1969. 289 pp. $6.95

If the promise so tantalizingly expressed in the title of this book were possible to fulfill, then all the "little guys" would become "big guys." If you extrapolate the growth of even a small amount of money over a period of years, it would eventually approach the speed of light. This is the first thing that comes to mind when reading Lewis Owen's record of success in the stock market.

In spite of the obvious difficulty of achieving Owen's dream of fortune, it seems fair to say that he has put together an exciting, easy-to-read book for the average investor with a sensible guide for compounding profits and avoiding large losses.

The repetition of certain rules of procedure stands out above the background of a mass of fundamental information about the stock market. "Cut your losses and let your profits run," and, "Buy only those stocks which are active and making new highs." These rules will keep your money working and preserve your principle.

Owen's racy style, newly coined phrases, and poetry make interesting reading, but some of his puns were not appreciated by this reviewer ("caught with their plants down," and, "wearing sackcloth . . . and fallen on their ashes," etc.).

It should be noted that for more than ten years the author made those mistakes that he cautions the reader to avoid, and, in that sense, his thesis presents a well-rounded picture of what not to do as well as what to do in the market. Unfortunately, it is difficult to approach the stock market with the bloodless efficiency of a computer. So, alas, the "specuvestor" will undoubtedly continue to make the same mistakes, selling the good stocks and holding the bad ones, averaging out on the downside instead of pyramiding on the upside.

McLane, Helen J., and Hutar, Patricia
The Investment Club Way to Stock Market Success. Garden City, N.Y.: Doubleday, 1963. 226 pp. paperback: $1.25

The investment club is a new phenomenon which has grown to maturity in the past twenty years and now embraces the hopes and fears of more than 350,000 people. Thousands of social clubs and other groups have changed into financial vehicles helping the novice learn the rudiments of the stock market with a minimum of money, the enjoyment of good company, and possibly some coffee and cake. The authors of this book have put all the essentials surrounding the investment club in perspective so that those who would like to start their own club will know how to get started and profit from the experience of the thousands of clubs now in operation.

At the outset, a group wishing to start an investment club has to set a meeting date. When the charter members assemble, a name is selected, and a limit is set on the amount of members. The frequency of the meetings, the amount of the contribution, and the investment objectives are decided. These are some of the basic decisions necessary before an agreement can be signed and a bank account opened in which the money to be invested is accumulated. Once an agent is chosen by the club and a broker is selected to open the account, the club is ready to do business. Despite the seriousness of the endeavor (you can't be nonchalant when dealing with money), investment club meetings can be lively happenings. They can also lead to clashes and unresolved debates on what to buy. Personality conflicts and other problems arise that are inevitable when men and women are in continuous social contact.

The authors tackle the problem of selecting the best stocks with the finesse of expert analysts as they interpret balance sheets, income statements, and annual reports. The books and portfolio of the club should be managed by competent people, and it is a good idea for all members to add to their investment knowledge through the reading of books, magazines, and other financial periodicals. This will increase their enjoyment of the meetings and allow them to contribute to the success of the club by adding their ideas to the discussion.

The growing-up process can be speedier with the introduction of outside speakers and the assignment of projects or field trips to individuals who can deliver reports on what they have seen and experienced. It all makes for an exciting future where club members can get a financial education, watch their money grow, enjoy a social experience, and achieve a level of sophistication that can help them succeed with their own personal program of common stock investment.

Rudd, Austin G.
You Can Win in Wall Street. Linden, N.J.: Bookmailer, 1964. 83 pp. paperback: $1.00

A retired army colonel has written this guide for anyone who wants to plan an investment program and build an estate for himself and his family. By his own admission, his first twenty-one years were marked by frustration and failure. The last nineteen years of his total of forty were crowned with an enviable success.

Throughout the book there is an obvious excitement and fascination with the stock market and the possibilities which it offers to all. There are many bits of excellent advice gleaned from all his years of experience. The do's and don'ts are valuable for newcomers to that arena where the unpredictable is normal.

The essence of Colonel Rudd's book is the development of a program for accumulating good quality stocks in a portfolio to serve as the backbone of your investments. You may call it "portfolio A." It should consist of 80 percent of your liquid capital. The remaining 20 percent should reside in a semi-investment "B" fund which can include more venturesome companies.

This book is one man's proof that you can win in Wall Street. It is an answer to the cynics who have lost money for whatever reason in their attempt to wrest the riches which abound in the stock market.

Thorp, Edward O., and Sheen, T. Kassouf
Beat the Market: A Scientific Stock Market System. New York: Random House, 1967. 221 pp. $10.00

Contrary to the popular opinion that there is no sure thing in the stock market, this book proves that the authors have developed a mathematically precise method for achieving consistent profits whether the market goes up or down. This basic system can be called "the common stock warrant hedge."

In order to explain the intricate workings of their system, the authors explain the components which make up their recipe for success—warrants, short-selling, and the margin account. This is done in a clear, understandable way. The bulk of the exposition deals with the mechanics of the hedge itself, and how it is possible to alter the mix to maximize profits and minimize risk.

The hedge is accomplished by selling an overpriced warrant short and buying the common long. It is important to use only warrants which are close to expiration so that they will run out of time and therefore recede in price because they become worthless. Most warrants sell at a premium to their conversion into the common, and it is this quality that makes them prey for the short-seller.

The authors have painstakingly worked out a method for calculating the potential risk/gain ratio and show the results of their own transactions. They offer logical reasons as to why they have made their secret known to the world and why millionaires have not flocked to their side. It could be that a large percentage of investors refuse to buy on margin and would rather be burned in oil than sell short. In a revealing chapter, "Can Anything Go Wrong?" it is explained that there are times when a short squeeze can develop in the warrants as happened with Molybdenum warrants in 1962. Another fear is that the American Stock Exchange may ban short sales in warrants at some point before expiration. Obviously, if you are already short, there is no worry on that score.

The warrant hedge has merit as a valid method of effectively pursuing profits while avoiding the risks usually attending stock speculation, but it is highly unlikely that the average investor will try it. The authors can therefore use their method for achieving gains in comparative safety. It is doubtful that they will receive any serious competition from the profit-hungry public.

Weaver, Mark
The Techniques of Short Selling: Making Money on Declines in the Stock Market, rev. ed., with appendix by the eds. of *Indicator Digest.* Palisades Park, N.J.: Investors' Library, 1949–1963. 81 pp. $4.95

Short selling is dealt with in a sober, comprehensive way in one of the few books to examine the subject. It will open the eyes of the most fearful investor. It is a fact that most bulls are too stubborn to admit that there is an alternative to holding stocks during the intermittent disasters called bear markets. Their equity declines sharply, and in many cases they are overcome by fear and sell out near the bottom with huge losses.

Weaver does not take sides in the debate over the value of selling short. He proceeds to give a condensed explanation of all the pertinent information on the subject. A short sale, for example, is one where the stock is borrowed at a certain price and must be bought at some future time and returned to the lender. If the price at which the stock is purchased is lower than the sale price, the transaction is profitable.

There are no restrictions on the length of time one can be short, but the seller must pay any dividends or rights declared during the holding period to the owner of the stock. It is also a little-known fact that although stock is sold short in a margin account, the seller pays no interest. The broker receives the funds from the sale and gives it to the lender of the stock pending the buy-in of the shares, which requires payment of this credit.

The author explains the advantage of selling short against the box, a procedure that locks in an investor's position so that he may protect a profit and carry it into the next taxable year. In this case there is no need to borrow stock since the account is already long the necessary amount. When the buy-in takes place, the investor may deliver his own shares or buy new shares and remain long his original amount.

Weaver discusses tape reading, the Dow Jones averages, business cycles, bull markets, and bear markets. These are all necessary subjects for the prospective short seller to comprehend if he is to understand the conditions that must exist in order to increase his chance for success. The general rules for selection of the best short-sale candidates are: (1) the stock must have had a sharp rise in recent months, preferably an emotional rise with large volume; (2) the stock must have stopped rising for a period of weeks and have shown a period of distribution (large volume without forward movement) and a breakdown in its price; (3) the capitalization must be large and the p/e ratio high; (4) it should have a low short interest; (5) place a buy-stop order above the short-sale price and limit the loss to 10 percent; (6) once you have a profit, keep a trailing buy-stop to insure a profit when the stock turns around and rallies.

As a source book on an important segment of the market, concise coverage of the short-selling technique has limited importance, but with the growing size and sophistication of the investor population, that importance is undoubtedly growing in value. The stock market rises and falls with monotonous regularity, and for those investors who fail to take advantage of the opportunities in a bear market, this book should be an eye-opener.

GENERAL WORKS

Adler, Bill, and Greene, Catherine J., eds.
The Wall Street Reader. New York and Cleveland: World, 1970. 268 pp.
$7.95

Wall Street literature is as diverse and many-faceted as the stock market knowledge it attempts to describe, and this wide-ranging anthology can be the excellent start of a financial education. It is impossible to offer more than just a morsel of each of the twenty-three noted authors' works included in this one volume, but the careful selection of pertinent subject matter has distilled some of the best stock market advice for the fortunate reader.

Gerald M. Loeb, the Dean of Wall Street, is represented with his "ever-liquid account" which succinctly expresses his method of achieving success by concentration, pyramiding an uptrend, and protecting against losses with stop orders. He does not believe in averaging down or too much diversification. He is convinced that diversification is a method of averaging errors or covering up a lack of judgment. Loeb's success is a testament to his good judgment and the soundness of his philosophy of investing as expressed in one of Wall Street's best books, *The Battle for Investment Survival.*

In a chapter from *20,000,000 Careless Capitalists,* Carter Henderson and Albert Lasher take the stockholder to task for his ignorance of the company he buys, its name, the products it makes, and the caliber of management it tolerates. William L. Jiler expounds on "support and resistance" from his book on technical analysis, *How Charts Can Help You in the Stock Market.*

In a diverting discourse that some might take facetiously, Ira U. Cobleigh's chapter, "Bull Markets and Bare Knees," theorizes that skirt lengths vary directly with stock prices, or, simply, that as hemlines go up, so does the market. This essay is only one chapter in that author's *Happiness is a Stock that Doubles in a Year.*

This short review can't possibly reveal all the authors or the contents of their selections, but it should suffice to say that other luminaries such as Adam Smith, Burton Crane, and Louis Engel share their wisdom and experience with the reader. Vital areas of the stock market that are discussed by other authors include mutual funds, the Dow Jones averages, the strategy of investing, and many others.

The editors of this work have culled the highlights of some of Wall Street's best books and served them up to the individual who is eager to learn the techniques and methods of successful investing. The beginning student should make this book a first step in his program, and he might well consider continued self-growth and increased sophistication by reading all the books represented in this anthology.

Baumol, William J.

The Stock Market and Economic Efficiency. New York: Fordham University Press, 1965. 95 pp. $4.00

The contents of this book consist of the Millar Lectures for 1964–1965 which were delivered at Fordham University. The manuscript was written in advance of the lecture series and its oral presentation may have differed slightly.

As can be expected, this book is an intellectual evaluation of the efficiency of the stock market in allocating the nation's capital resources. In the course of the four lectures, Baumol, in an academic prose, intricately details the random nature of stock prices in the short term, the work of the specialist, and the hypothesis that, in the long term, stock prices will ultimately be determined by the record of earnings.

Other interesting subjects discussed by the author include the underutilization of equity as a means of raising capital and the ramification of management's self-serving decisions which fly in the face of stockholders' interests. In sum, there are many hypotheses propounded, and a great many questions raised. This is in keeping with the fact that the stock market is a business of many questions and, unfortunately, an unequal number of answers.

Browne, Harry

How You Can Profit from the Coming Devaluation. New Rochelle, N.Y.: Arlington House, 1970. 189 pp. $5.95

Harry Browne's prediction of a dollar devaluation became a reality one year after his book was published. President Nixon's moves to bolster the economy included an 8 percent devaluation, price and wage controls, and a tax on imports. It is Browne's belief that increasing inflation will ultimately be followed by a major collapse, large-scale bank failures, riots, looting, mass unemployment, and inevitably, wholesale bankruptcies.

While this morbid picture would spell doom for the average man, Browne has prepared a program of action for the four eventualities which he suggests can happen: (1) recession, (2) runaway inflation, (3) devaluation, and (4) depression. His plan for each of these eventualities includes a mixture of some of the following: (1) buying Swiss francs and keeping them in a Swiss bank account; (2) buying bags of silver coins; (3) buying gold stocks; (4) owning a retreat (a place to hide when the riots start), and others.

Such a sobering claim as Harry Browne expounds in his book is enough to scare even the most confident reader as well as the average investor who has his security in the savings bank. If the banks fail, as Browne intimates, and the

Federal Deposit Insurance Corporation is not prepared to cover their deposits, where can the confused public go? An alarmed Congress and an effective administration must actively pursue those policies which can head off the disaster that this book predicts. There is no reason why the richest country in the world has to cower in fear or submit to the deterioration of more than $1 trillion in stock market values. The control over our destiny must be displayed by concerned and confident elected officials if Browne's prediction is to be prevented, and the lid of Pandora's box is to remain closed.

Editors of *Fortune*
Fortune's Guide to Personal Investing. New York: McGraw-Hill, 1963. 216 pp. $5.95

Fortune's editors have compiled this guide to personal investing from a special series which appeared in that excellent business magazine beginning in 1961. This collection of articles is not aimed at the newcomer, but is rather an instructive and informative text for the practicing investor.

The book's theme is cleverly introduced in the first chapter by a provocative essay entitled "What to do with $1,000,000,000,000." This figure represents the assets Americans owned as of 1962. Following chapters go on to explore the many methods through which Americans have attempted to invest that sum wisely.

Coverage is wide and diverse. The articles include hints for success in the areas of foreign stocks, new issues, mutual funds, bonds, and commodities. They examine the efficacy of charts and the Dow Jones, and present a clever interpretation of price multiple buying called "What Price Earnings?"

A trillion dollars is so vast a sum as to be almost incomprehensible to the average investor. It is, however, the total representation of every American's problem in trying to achieve a level of financial success, and *Fortune* has done its part in helping the serious investor reach that goal.

Fried, Sidney
Investing and Speculating with Convertibles. New York: R. H. M. Associates of Delaware, 1968. 86 pp. $3.50

The average investor is completely unaware of any securities except common stocks. His closed mind shuts out many opportunities for enlightenment and useful knowledge. This book opens a new avenue for successful speculation without the addition of risk. It is a perfect example of how the public ignores its own best interest. The subject of this treatise is the investment superiority of the convertible issue of a company over its common stock. Indeed, the author argues that you should never buy a common stock if there is a convertible for the same company. He demonstrates convincingly that the convertible bond offers the investor several advantages over the common.

At the outset he cites four reasons for buying the convertible: (1) you get the same appreciation as the common stock, dollar for dollar, if the common stock goes up; (2) it has a smaller percentage loss than the common stock, dollar for dollar, if the common stock goes down; (3) it gives you a higher yield than the common stock; and (4) it costs less in brokerage commissions. This one-sided list of advantages whets the investor's appetite for the more esoteric uses of the convertible. The intrigue is enhanced by the fact that there is no risk of loss.

The author observes that bonds and preferred stocks are senior securities that receive their interest and dividends before the common stockholder. They also collect their full, stated value in the event of dissolution before the assets of a company accrue to the common. There are advantages of growth which only common stockholders can enjoy if the company's earnings expand. The bondholder is only entitled to his stated interest. When the bond or preferred stock is convertible, it no longer reacts solely to interest rates but has two separate lives. It retains its right to interest and duplicates the movement of the common stock.

An eyebrow raiser is Fried's "convertible hedge." He has developed a completely riskless system for making money in a downside market. Once the reader's doubt is dispelled, it becomes obvious from the examples that the author has a mathematically tight system for winning. "The full hedge" involves buying the senior security and selling short an equal dollar amount of the common stock. We have already found that in a bear market the bond or preferred has a smaller percentage loss than the common. The difference in this loss is the net amount of the gain. If the market moves up, the convertible and common gain in tandem. Therefore the long position in the senior security is cancelled out by the short position in the common stock. Thus we see that a full hedge cannot result in a loss on the upside, and must result in a gain on the downside. A special factor exists that adds spice to this maneuver. If you are long a convertible and short the equivalent dollar amount in its common stock, you don't have to put up any margin to carry the short position.

Fried also discusses "the half hedge." This entails shorting only half of the dollar amount that you buy of the convertible. It produces profits in a strong bull market but can result in minor losses on the downside. The author apologizes for the calculated risk in this process, but no apology is necessary. The half hedge produces profits only in an upside market and cushions the loss in the convertible position on the downside, holding it to a minor percentage of the investment. The risk which a well selected half hedge carries is worth it. There is "much to gain and little to lose," says the author.

One of the components of the various hedges is short selling. This area of the market normally scares the average investor. Fried describes the technique, and he cautions you to sell short first, then buy the convertible. He concludes his discussion with a review of the favorable tax aspects of the convertible. He also analyzes "merger convertibles" which were a popular form of acquisition in the conglomerate growth era of the 1960s.

Everybody is ostensibly in the stock market for the same reason—profit. No investor enjoys losses, and all would rejoice at the thought of a sure-fire method for making money. Sidney Fried has laid it out neatly for everyone to see and understand. There are now 850 convertible issues and a more active and vital market than there was when the author formulated his system over twenty years ago. The adventurous market operator can now apply the lessons of this book and do what everyone thinks is impossible—trade without risk.

Henderson, Carter F., and Lasher, Albert C.
20 Million Careless Capitalists. Garden City, N.Y.: Doubleday, 1967. 287 pp. $5.95

The authors of *20 Million Careless Capitalists* claim that shareholders have a great deal more power with their vote than they realize. It is hard to subscribe to this theory because history has shown that the examples the authors use to point out the power of the proxy are not conclusive evidence of their contention. There is no statistical record of success and failure in proxy fights over the years, but if such a record were kept it would show that in a majority of cases, entrenched management has maintained its power over dissident shareholders. In most cases, the unhappy stockholders are too disorganized and lack the necessary finances for an attempt at dislodging management.

In a rather sketchy final chapter, the authors try to demonstrate how "careful" capitalists protect their money. The Rockefeller billions are watched over by a staff of analysts and a manager who see to it that the assets under their care are growing apace. I trust that this is not an attempt to compare the asset management of the wealthy with the plight of the small stockholder.

In sum, it struck me that the style of writing seemed to be similar to what you see in the *Wall Street Journal.* This is due to the background that each of the authors has with that paper. The plethora of statistical evidence strung together end on end reads like a newspaper article and detracts from the fluency of the story. It can be argued that stockholders are not adequately informed before they buy and are apathetic to the needs of their company. The authors' title can be updated now to read 32 million careless capitalists.

Hirsch, Yale
The 1972 Stock Trader's Almanac. Old Tappan, N.J.: Hirsch Organization, 1971. 160 pp. flexible cover: $6.95

The Stock Trader's Almanac accomplishes a great many things for the harried investor who is invariably pressed for valuable time. It arranges investment information in a unique way, consolidates the wisdom of Wall Street's famous personalities, and provides monthly reminders of the statistical truths of the past, so that you can be alert to the dangers and rewards of its assembled knowledge.

There are forecasts of the years's market action by fifteen distinguished stock market analysts and observers. These studied interpretations of the underlying economic, political, and psychological factors that drive the market in its bull and bear orbit will not confuse the reader. They will rather serve to crystallize the thoughts and opinions that have already formed in his mind. It is a forum of opinions and fearless predictions that is rarely found in this quantity and variety anywhere. This year the fifteen contributors are George Lindsey, Ralph A. Rotnem, Peter L. Bernstein, Monte J. Gordon, Cornelius C. Bond, Jr., Eldon A. Grimm, Claude N. Rosenberg, Jr., Edson Gould, Kenneth Ward, Stanley A. Nabi, Raphael Yavneh, Jack Raphael, George A. Chestnutt, Jr., James Dines, and Larry Williams.

The daily diary found in these pages is handy as an appointment record or for traveling, entertainment, and gift entries for tax purposes. There is a section which helps the investor plan his portfolio, keep track of his buy and sell transactions for the year, and prepare his tax records. Investment information is brought up to date each year, and new techniques are explained for the reader's benefit. In a continuous effort to bring new and better facts to future editions, there is a suggestion box which guarantees that the next almanac will be bigger and better.

Janeway, Eliot
What Shall I Do with My Money? New York: McKay, 1970. 209 pp. $5.95

Contrary to the popular misconception that has arisen through his current bearish posture on the stock market, Eliot Janeway in *What Shall I Do With My Money?* reveals that during the past thirty-seven years he has been bullish most of the time. In the introduction, Janeway offers a prescription for the country's economic ills consisting of three measures: (1) credit controls, (2) a federal sales tax, and (3) a dividend tax credit.

The body of the book is composed of letters from readers of Janeway's syndicated columns. The questions asked on subjects such as cash, stocks, property, bonds, insurance, mutual funds, etc., give the author ample opportunity to develop his point of view on the whole gamut of managing money. The question and answer method is a technique which can adequately cover a wide diversity of needs from that of a fifteen-year-old newsboy to that of a retired couple living on social security.

Among the tenets of the author which stand out are the following:

1. He believes in a cash reserve.
2. Adequate insurance is very important.
3. He likes mutual funds.
4. The stock market is now weak because the yield spread between stocks and bonds is too wide.

There is a great deal to be learned from the answers of the author. He clearly states his views on the economy and the stock market. Janeway offers his advice in a precise and rational way, and does not spread the paralyzing fear and one-sided predictions of doom that the media generally like to attribute to him.

Lundberg, Ferdinand
The Rich and the Super-Rich: A Study in the Power of Money Today. New York: Lyle Stuart, 1968. 883 pp. $15.00

The age-old problem of the unequal distribution of wealth in America is the subject of this tome. In a methodical way it shatters the myth of equality of opportunity through the use of a mountain of statistics and other source materials.

At the outset Lundberg quotes from the Lampman findings for the National Bureau of Economic Research that 1.6 percent of the adult population owned more than 30 percent of all the assets and equities of the personal sector of the economy, 20 percent of the wealth being government-owned. This group owned 82.2 percent of all stock, 100 percent of all state and local (tax-exempt) bonds,

88.5 percent of other bonds, and other assorted assets. In a further study, Dr. Gabriel Kolk, in his "Wealth and Power in America," concludes that, "Since World War II one-tenth of the nation has owned an average of two-thirds of its liquid assets." The power of the argument these two surveys reveal is difficult to refute and lays the basis for the author's further claims.

There have been few new fortunes made since the two world wars, with the exception of the Kennedys, that have played a prominent role in public affairs. Lundberg states that super-wealth is controlled mainly by "the inheritors" and the families which intermarry and cross-fertilize their money and grow wealthier with the years. There follows a more elaborate breakdown of the multi-billion dollar holdings of the du Ponts, Mellons, Rockefellers, and Fords. It is here that the author coins the term "finpol" to describe the financial-political stranglehold that the super-wealthy have on the political life of our country. He compares the country to a "banana republic" controlled by an owning class of no more than 500,000 individuals. Lundberg also sees in the United States today, power centers analogous to those of Medieval Europe where the crown (central government), the nobility (the finpols), and baronage (upper corporate magnates—corp-pols) competed for power against each other. In fact, the finpols and corp-pols appear equal, like prime ministers of a foreign state, when they sit down with the president to discuss the state of the country. Lundberg feels that such a meeting is like a summit conference.

The inequity of the tax laws and the farce which allows foundations to evade millions of dollars in taxes through congressionally dispensed tax loopholes are explored in the Patman Report. The arrogance and contempt shown for a government investigating committee proves that the super-rich feel they are supreme and that the government is an instrument which they can control as they have for generations. The reforms suggested by Patman are vitally necessary and are summed up in a *New York Times* article: "Unfortunately reports filed in New York because of a new law have shown that many charitable foundations are tax dodges that are used for the personal use of their directors."

In their schools and private clubs, the elite rich maintain the contacts that continue their oligarchic control over the corporate and political affairs of the country. In a terse conclusion, Lundberg freely damns the leaders of this country for daring to guarantee peace in a war-torn world when the problems that we face at home are left unsolved. "What is happening as the average citizen looks on in disbelief is that an outworn, patched, politico-economic system is cracking, while no serious steps are taken to ascertain the causes and remedies. The causes of American insufficiency at home and abroad are political, not economic, or at least political before they are economic. Better put they are cultural. Serious problems cannot be solved on the basis of a consensus of value-disoriented dolts."

The author has culled an enormous mountain of facts to prove his point that America is an aristocracy of the rich rather than a democracy. This country, and the constitutional rights it promises to the people, governs with the approval of the "rich and super-rich" who control its corporate wealth and political power. Contrary to the pessimism expressed by Lundberg, however, the interests of all the people and the wealth of the whole country will not be served by "value-disoriented dolts." Instead, the combined intelligence of rich and poor alike will work together for the necessary solutions to preserve our country, our free way of life, and in the process the super-wealth of those who rule us.

Magee, John
Wall Street—Main Street—and You. Springfield, Mass.: John Magee, 1972. 305 pp. $12.00

John Magee displays a new dimension in this book of essays that were written for his weekly advisory service and its allied chart service. He has made profound observations on many subjects that weigh heavily on the quality of man's life, some that only indirectly have an influence on the stock market. They certainly are a far cry from the stereotype of the true chartist who boards up his office to lock out the world, as reported by John Brooks in *Seven Fat Years.* Indeed, it is refreshing to learn more about the thoughts of one of Wall Street's great minds.

Throughout this book Magee evidences a respect and humility toward the stock market, and awe which has been built up from many years of dealing with the vicissitudes and vagaries of its amoebic propensities. The many pieces which the author includes in this work comprise an amalgam of advice and observations on inflation, psychology, trading tactics, timing, investment decisions, philosophy, human foibles, greed, fear, and politics. What stands out most forcefully is John Magee's conservative approach to the market. His experience has taught him to be prepared for the worst while things look their best.

Magee is basically protective or negative. This is because it is more difficult to sell than to buy. If he buys a stock at $7.00 and it drops to $6.00 he'd want to sell fast to avoid a bigger loss. If he buys a stock at $7.00 and it goes up to $70.00, he would sell it if it falls back to $65.00 or $63.00 to protect the major part of his gain.

There are several axioms that deserve to be mentioned here as part of the author's studied advice to the reader. They are only a few of the many observations which have developed from his years of market experience.

"A trend should be assumed to continue in effect until such time as its reversal has been definitely signaled."

"Sell a bad situation."

"Don't sell a good situation too soon."

"Don't go for broke because that's how you'll end up."

"A balanced, diversified portfolio is the best protection."

"A stock should be held as long as it looks strong or firm, and should be sold as soon as it starts to look weak, regardless of whether one has a small profit, a large profit, or a loss at that point."

"Keep your eye on the tape! Never mind what people say about the market. Watch what they're doing."

"Don't try to forecast the future. Be prepared for disappointments, unpredictable moves, and news events that will call for a new look and perhaps radically altered tactics."

"It is necessary to take a stand even when no man knows for certain how circumstances may change."

"The greatest risk is always with the new position. We do not have to worry nearly so much about established trends, where all we are concerned with are protective limits."

"Learn the value of patience."

Although most of the book is directly concerned with the stock market, Magee can't help but comment on the human condition. In one essay he expresses the futility of the major powers wasting their resources in projects that don't solve the world's problems. "They embrace a senseless competition for supremacy that could possibly destroy everything." In another he bemoans the feeling that is obvious to many hapless millions when he asks, "Have we lost track of the main point? What has happened to joy, and to love, and to the sheer fun of life?"

It should be pointed out to the reader of this analysis that an evening with John Magee will not only be a valuable lesson in the stock market, but also a penetrating look at those problems which must be overcome by man in his quest for a better life. John Magee is already well known throughout the world as a famous chartist, the author, with the late Robert D. Edwards, of *Technical Analysis of Stock Trends,* the chartist's bible. It is high time that we had a greater appreciation of John Magee, the man.

Manfrini, J.

Under the Buttonwood Tree (A-Huffin An' A-Puffin). New York: Vantage Press, 1969. 182 pp. $4.50

Manfrini's book reveals a disturbing attitude toward the large nationwide wire houses. The author writes from over forty years of experience, and many of those were spent in the branch offices of Walston and Co. It is apparent to any reader that the "gross" or commission totals were all that management cared about. At least, that is the way Manfrini sees things.

It is an age-old problem on Wall Street which will always be debated pro and con, as long as salesmen get paid commissions for the business they do. How can one determine the honesty of a decision by a registered representative? Does his suggestion reflect a sincere desire to enhance the performance of an account, or is the necessity for more commission the motivating factor? It is obvious that the author believes the management of large wire houses doesn't care. It could be out of personal pique since he was replaced by a younger man as a branch office manager.

The author on a visit to another branch office was obviously upset by the undecorous manner displayed by the new Registered Representatives and a young manager "who did not have a gray hair in his head." It is an unhappy experience for a man who "prided himself on running a branch office with the discipline and dignity befitting a fiduciary business."

Manfrini jumps all over the place as he traces his history, experience, and opinions. It is a free-form expression of a man's walk through the stock market's years of exciting growth, and it is well worth the trip for the curious reader.

Ney, Richard
The Wall Street Jungle. New York: Grove Press, 1970. 348 pp. $7.50

The thrust of this book is a wholesale condemnation of Wall Street, the stock market, the SEC, etc. In a sensational cataloging of the abuses that one must suffer when investing in stocks, Ney singles out the specialist as the main culprit in what he claims is a system "rigged" to the detriment of the average stockholder. The outrage which develops in the narrative would appear more genuine if the author were not shown on the back cover smiling contentedly behind the wheel of a Rolls Royce. This pose does not blend well with the painful bleating of one who has been robbed by the market-makers of Wall Street

The use of terms like "roulette wheel," "rigging," "Machiavelli," "larceny," and "swindle" creates an atmosphere of distrust, apathy, and outright hate that the losing investor is only too happy to seize upon as his own in an effort to blame someone for his market losses. The slanted characterizations of the author reach their zenith of vilification when he refers to the New York Stock Exchange as a "powerful politburo," an oblique attempt to equate America's industrial marketplace with the ruling political entity of Communist Russia. It is a parallel so ludicrous that it is difficult to imagine, let alone accept.

If the reader chooses to believe Ney's thesis that the stock market is rigged and manipulated for the benefit of the specialist and his friends, he would be wise to heed the caution that this book suggests. The author paradoxically unveils a technical system which he alleges can make money by anticipating the actions of the specialist. Can Ney avoid the larceny cooked up by the specialists who control the stock market? Is it possible to win at roulette when the wheel is fixed? Or are the grievances exposed by the author legitimate ones that can be rectified by enlightened stock exchange and SEC officials?

It is worthwhile to spotlight inequities and propose the necessary reforms. Constructive criticism and internal self-regulation have been responsible for the continuing progress the New York Stock Exchange has made since its founding in 1792. Radical iconoclasm and extreme departures from the current form of the financial marketplace are the author's suggestions. It would seem that a rational, intelligent approach, without rancor or sensationalism, would have a more valuable effect on the evolution of the marketplace. It would accrue to the benefit of all people who seek to invest their savings for a secure future.

Sarnoff, Paul
Wall Street Careers. New York: Julian Messner, 1968. 189 pp. $3.95

Sarnoff has spent over three decades in various Wall Street capacities, and this book is a testimonial to his enthusiasm for his way of life. It is a rare book that recommends the financial area as a career with a future for the confused job-seeker.

He starts with a compact look at the history of Wall Street and then quickly shifts into the essence of his book. Sarnoff draws on his extensive personal experience to delineate the abundant possibilities for employment in the financial markets. Production, administration, research, back office, bonds, over-the-counter markets are several of the areas explained in detail by the author with his estimates of educational requirements, experience necessary to qualify, and the salary range for each position.

Two facts make this book especially important and vitally necessary for those people who are seeking entry into the street. The first is that for twenty years, 1930–1950, there was hardly a trickle of new personnel being added to Wall Street's minions. The reasons are obvious—stagnation caused by the depression, no business, World War II, and the subsequent years of transition to a peacetime economy. These facts contributed to the loss of a whole generation in Wall Street, with the result that there was a dearth of young people in key positions of all occupational areas.

The second reason is the phenomenal growth in the stockholding public which has constantly outstripped all predictions. It now stands at 32 million shareholders, with the expectation that there will be 40 million shareholders by 1975 and 50 million by 1980. In view of the above facts, it seems obvious that this book serves a valuable function. It will continue to be a guide to the many thousands of young people who are seeking a career in Wall Street, one which can prove to be demanding but with rewards as unlimited as the eager worker's imagination.

Schultz, Harry D., and Coslow, Samson, eds.
A Treasury of Wall Street Wisdom. Palisades Park, N.J.: Investors' Press, 1966. 392 pp. $6.95

In their attempt to collect all the most important financial writers of the twentieth century into one anthology and to briefly present their thoughts, theories, and practiced philosophies, the authors have truly provided a valuable service to millions of market followers. This treasury will stand as a guide to present and future generations of stock market adherents who hope to learn the distilled knowledge and experience of the past from those recognized experts who have published their findings for all to see and benefit from.

In a field which has such a profound effect on the politics, economics, and the everyday life of the average person, it is tragic that there have been so few commentators and writers throughout the stock market's history. Not until the present time, when 32 million stockholders view the financial scene with such avid interest, has the public spirit been so intimately aligned with the fluctuations of the marketplace.

Schultz and Coslow have been selective in their collection, and start with Charles Dow whom they call the grandfather of technical analysis. The writings of Dow are followed by those of his disciples, Nelson, Hamilton, Rhea, and Russell. The next group of writers made history during the boom of the 1920s. The aftermath of the 1929 crash is explored by the next group, and the 1930s are covered by what the authors call the "Sages of the Thirties." This was rather a dull period during which the public was virtually absent because of the depression and the need to concentrate on making a living. The final section is devoted to contemporary wisdom with selections from Benjamin Graham, Gerald M. Loeb, Edwards and Magee, and others.

It should be pointed out that the selections of each writer are necessarily short and do not adequately cover the total philosophy of the individual. They serve only as an introduction for the reader, who should follow his area of interest by reading the complete works of the author to gain the true meaning of his work. If there is one failing in this collection, aside from the omission of many other excellent financial writers, it is that nowhere in the book have the authors commented on the work of the "keenest minds in Wall Street" and given their opinions as to the contribution made by the individual, and what it means in the whole scope of stock market literature. They can be forgiven, however, for the importanc of this invaluable guide to Wall Street's most renowned writers is truly a treasure for those interested in tracing the history of the stock market from the turn of the century to the present day.

Schwartz, Robert J.
You and Your Stockbroker. New York: Macmillan, 1967. 182 pp. $4.95

It is an astounding fact that billions of dollars change hands each week through the purchase and sale of stocks and bonds without a formal contract. It takes just a short conversation on the telephone, a visit to a broker, or a verbal order to set the wheels in motion. Obviously, there are times when, through a lack of proper communication or a broker's error, a dispute arises between a customer and his registered representative.

The multitude of disputed areas are cataloged here in case-history form in an attempt to enlighten the reader and to clarify the rights and obligations of the respective parties. In most cases the author succeeds in explaining the legal reasons for his conclusion by use of hypothetical questions and answers. The average investor can identify with the commonplace situations such as brokerage errors, orders, executions, and payments. Duties, obligations, and rights pertain to the relationships between a client and his registered representative or the brokerage firm where he is employed.

Margin, dividends, and interest payments are all related to the service of the broker, and the monthly statement plays an important part in providing the information necessary to clarify the current condition of the customer's account. There are other problem areas that can be cleared up by educating the investor in the operational procedure of Wall Street. Transfer and delivery of stock certificates are complicated processes that entail weeks of waiting, and the broker up front usually bears the brunt of the abuse for the delay that is caused by back offices, registrars, and other personnel. Dividend payments are another headache, since the bulk of this nation's stockholders are not aware of the four distinct dates that apply in this area—declaration date, exdividend date, stockholders of record, and payable date.

There are problems specific to married women whose husbands order stock for them. No broker can legally accept an order through an agent. Therefore a broker must receive an order directly from the wife for her own account, or it can be voided. With the high incidence of divorce recently this is a critical area for brokers to watch. There are many legal obstacles confronting the broker in his handling of deceased accounts. The estates, executors, and the legal forms necessary to transfer the deceased account's stock present formidable problems for both broker and customer. The list goes on to include corporations, custodian accounts for minor children, investment clubs, bonds, bankruptcy, and new issues.

It is difficult to generalize about the legal rights of the parties involved in a dispute, but it is fair to say that if you have an altercation with your broker you should find out what your legal rights are before writing to the Securities and Exchange Commission. This book is a necessary reference manual for the investment industry and can clear up a great many problems that arise in the day-to-day business dealings of the average broker and investor.

Schwed, Fred, Jr.
Where Are the Customers' Yachts? Original: Simon & Schuster, 1940. Reprint: Springfield, Mass.: John Magee, 1960. 217 pp. $4.50

Everyone knows that there is no dearth of material in Wall Street which can evoke laughter. In fact the *Bawl Street Journal*, published every year, is an exercise in self-abuse which Wall Streeters themselves look forward to with glee. *Where Are the Customers' Yachts?* is not so much a question as a presumption on the part of the public that Wall Street somehow owes it something. Of course that is not so, and the author doesn't believe it either. The fact is that since the 1970 crash, the question could be joined with,"Where are the brokers' yachts?"

Fred Schwed, Jr., has delighted the reader with an irreverent spoof on Wall Street's hallowed and sanctified truths, and thanks to John Magee, who reprinted it, its timeless wit can entertain many more thousands of investors. Added to the fun are illustrations by Peter Arno. The author flits from one subject area to another distributing his humor as a bee buzzes from flower to flower. His shafts fall gently on their targets, but, in an effort to save himself from total iconoclasm, the author has some kind words for the specialist.

It is obvious to the reader, or it should be, that this book in its attempt to single out the humorous aspects of some of Wall Street's many facets, is not the author's sour grapes at having lost. His introduction clearly reveals that, although he hasn't a Cadillac to his name, he realizes that had he held his stocks long enough, he would have become rich beyond his limited dreams of avarice.

Smith, Adam (George J. W. Goodman)
The Money Game. New York: Random House, 1968. 302 pp. $6.95

It is difficult to determine whether this book was a phenomenal best seller because of the timing of its publication or the excellence of its style and content. Quite possibly it was a combination of both.

Adam Smith (a pseudonym of George J. W. Goodman) has spread the panorama of the stock market before us, all $700 billion of its stock and $600 billion of its bonds. In a delightfully "camp" way he has shown us why he considers the complicated maneuvering that goes on a mere game.

In the process he captures the excitement of the 1960s with the growth of the funds and the youthful managers who created the magnetic appeal which made the industry flourish. The conglomerate movement is explained in rather simplified terms with a look into the accounting methods which helped fuel its growth.

Goodman's friendship with fund managers allows the reader to look behind the scenes into the trading room of the institutions and to learn the problems of the gunslingers of that period.

Any survey of the game would not be complete without examining the antics of the crowd to see why they are almost always wrong. The author shows how the various players act and react in the situations they create for themselves. He also shows how the public sale of a company's stock has been the best way to make big money as opposed to picking a couple of stocks.

The systems, fundamental, technical, and random walk, which compete for public favor are detailed without the author's expressing a preference for any one method. The bias to which the author confesses is concentration in a few issues with small capitalizations which can be carefully watched for the hoped-for quantum jump in market price.

In a philosophical conclusion, the author plumbs the depths of man's conscious desire to pile up wealth for the future which he almost never enjoys. He does not expect the millenium, when wealth will no longer be the measure of social importance, to arrive for at least another one hundred years. So, in Adam Smith's own words, "I wish you the joys of the game."

Springer, John L.
If They're So Smart, How Come You're Not Rich? Chicago: Henry Regnery, 1971. 235 pp. $5.95

There is a common misconception that prevails with regard to the money invested in the stock market. People somehow feel that Wall Street is a Golconda promising to shower them with riches. This book has catered to that myth and fostered its continuance by branding in a one-sided way all those who venture opinions as to the direction of the stock market as a whole or of any stock in particular.

Springer indicts as incompetent the advisory services, brokerage houses and their research departments, market letters, and registered representatives. It would be fair to say that there is much that is true in what the author writes, since most of his statistics are derived from studies, but the indictment is so strong that it would almost indicate that Diogenes and his lantern should not waste time looking in Wall Street.

The investment advisory industry is singled out by Springer who claims that they are incompetent, make promises they cannot fulfill, do not research their recommended stocks adequately, and actually practice fraud upon their customers. As a sensational record of failure among the experts, this book may serve to dispel the belief that it is easy to make money in the stock market and should put the investor on guard against those who would take advantage of him.

The author would admit, if asked, that there are thousands of honest, conscientious people in Wall Street who try their best to serve their customers and to make money for them. It would not serve his purpose in writing this book if the uninformed public should use his indictment of Wall Street advisors as its scapegoat for losing, when the real culprit is its own gullibility and lack of industry. The author himself has made "a not inconsiderable sum of money by working the stock market. But he has done it in a sensible way, through self-education and by making sure that he is well informed about the stocks he is interested in."

Perhaps the author's example will serve to motivate the investor to study the stock market in such a way as to become competent enough to make his own selections. In that way the blame or praise, as the case may be, will remain where it truly belongs.

Zarb, Frank G., and Kerekes, Gabriel T., eds.
The Stock Market Handbook: Reference Manual for the Securities Industry.
Homewood, Ill.: Dow Jones-Irwin, 1970. 1073 pp. $27.50

The proliferation of investment knowledge and the participation in the stock market of 25 million new people since 1952 have made the publication of this book a necessity. The reference material, contributed by authors who are experts in their field, offers a coverage that assures the reader of authentic and specialized knowledge in every area. The securities industry has ballooned in size and importance in the post-World War II years, and this reference manual is an up-to-date look at every aspect of the business.

The opening section of the book is devoted to essays that cover the scope of the securities industry. They deal with government regulation, the investor, investment banking, and underwriting. The history, organization, and purpose of listed exchanges follow. These include the New York Stock Exchange, the American Stock Exchange, and the National Stock Exchange. The regional exchanges and the over-the-counter markets are next with a look at the body that is responsible for their regulation, the National Association of Securities Dealers (NASD).

The next segment examines the various types of securities, federal, municipal and state, and corporate. This exposition is rounded out by a discussion of such subjects as mutual funds, options, margin trading, and arbitrage. The complex subject of the integrated securities firm is then investigated in all its many facets, incorporation, personnel recruitment, personnel training, and compensation. There are essays on sales management, advertising, research, new accounts, and underwriting. Electronic data processing, communications, order room, taxes, legal, employee benefits, and record retention are some of the other departments that are among the responsibilities of the brokerage firm.

There is a survey of the specialty houses that includes nonmember firms, institutional houses, bond houses, specialist firms, odd-lot dealers, and option dealers. This group is growing as fast as any other area of the market. The final chapters are confined to investment decisions that are made by the analyst, computer, investment counselor, and portfolio manager.

The editors, Frank Zarb and Gabriel Kerekes, have taken the vast and amorphous securities industry and given it substance, form, and organization in this excellent reference manual. For all those brokerage firms and individuals who want an encyclopedia of the stock market industry, it is now available in the form of this concentrated and comprehensive tome.

TEXTBOOKS AND REFERENCE WORKS

INVESTMENT TEXTBOOKS

The need for accurate investment information has grown with the rapid rise of investors in the past two decades. Indeed, the population of stockholders has outpaced the available supply of textbook material to such an extent that the 32 million people who should know more about the subject have less than twenty texts from which to gain a financial education. The tragedy is not so much that there are not enough books, but that the average investor is not likely to use the excellent sources which are at his disposal. The college student who takes a course in finance or business and studies the subject matter of these textbooks is certain to develop a well-rounded view of the investment media, the stock exchanges and how they work, and security analysis, and a perspective on investment objectives.

The seventeen textbooks recommended here cover generally the same ground, although the authors have organized and structured the material to stress their own preference as to content and importance. There are many basic subject areas that must be covered; the priority of entry is not critical. For example, the several books on the stock market place their emphasis on the exchanges, their history, organization and membership, floor procedure, round-lot orders, odd-lot orders, the specialist, listing of securities, federal regulation of securities markets, margin, short selling, kinds of orders, and the customer and his broker. The subject matter is concentrated on the securities markets and their functions. There is no doubt as to the importance of this element of financial knowledge.

The majority of the textbooks represented here prefer to take a broader view of the financial area and to concentrate on the total investment picture which includes an introduction to investment, security analysis, portfolio management, and investment principles and practices. A typical book starts with an introduction giving the reader a background in the nature of investment and the risks inherent in the investment process. It then explains the various security instruments such as common stocks, preferred stocks, bonds (corporate, convertible, or municipal), and government securities. This is followed by a look at the security markets, the stock exchanges, their history, how they handle buying and selling of securities, sources of investment information, and the relation of the investor to his broker.

At this point, the valuation of securities and the factors that weigh upon the choice of investments are discussed. Fundamental and technical analysis vie for the investor's favor as the book invariably analyzes balance sheets, income statements, growth stocks, income stocks, investment companies, the insurance industry, public utilities, commercial banks, the electronics industry, the railroads, the airlines, price/earnings ratios, and a host of other basic investment criteria. Portfolio analysis and the need for diversification, timing, professional assistance, taxation and its effect on investment policy find their way into the discussion only after the reader has already absorbed a great deal of basic investment knowledge.

There are many refinements to be learned from years of experience in the actual investment process. There is no substitute for that. But the prerequisite for an intelligent entry into the stock market can only be gained by a thorough study of the fundamental facts which any one of these financial textbooks can offer the investor.

Amling, Frederick
Investments: An Introduction to Analysis and Management, 2nd ed. Englewood Cliffs, N.J.: Prentice-Hall, 1965. 768 pp. $11.50

Badger, Ralph E., and Coffman, Paul B.
The Complete Guide to Investment Analysis. New York: McGraw-Hill, 1967. 504 pp. $14.50

Badger, Ralph E., Torgerson, Harold W., and Guthmann, Harry G.
Investment Principles and Practices, 6th ed. Englewood Cliffs, N.J.: Prentice-Hall, 1969. 748 pp. $13.50

Clendenin, John C., and Christy, George A.
Introduction to Investments, 5th ed. New York: McGraw-Hill, 1969. 691 pp. $9.95

Cohen, Jerome B., and Zinbarg, Edward D.
Investment Analysis and Portfolio Management. Homewood, Ill.: Dow Jones-Irwin, 1967. 778 pp. $13.25

Cooke, Gilbert W.
The Stock Markets, rev. ed. Cambridge, Mass.: Schenkman, 1969. 570 pp. $11.25

Dougall, Herbert E.
Investments, 8th ed. Englewood Cliffs, N.J.: Prentice-Hall, 1968. 586 pp. $11.95

Eiteman, Wilford J., and Dice, Charles A., and Eiteman, David K.
The Stock Market, 4th ed. New York: McGraw-Hill, 1966. 570 pp. $10.50

Graham, Benjamin, Dodd, David L., and Cottle, Sidney, with Tatham, Charles
Security Analysis: Principles and Technique, 4th ed. New York: McGraw-Hill, 1962. 778 pp. $12.50

Hayes, Douglas A.
Investments: Analysis and Management, 2nd ed. New York: Macmillan, 1966. 501 pp. $10.95

Leffler, George L.
The Stock Market, 3rd ed. New York: Ronald Press, 1963. 654 pp. $9.50

Prime, John H.
Investment Analysis, 4th ed. Englewood Cliffs, N.J.: Prentice-Hall, 1967. 432 pp. $11.50

Renwick, Fred B.
Introduction to Investments and Finance: Theory and Analysis. New York: Macmillan, 1971. 517 pp. $11.95

Sauvain, Harry
Investment Management, 3rd ed. Englewood Cliffs, N.J.: Prentice-Hall, 1967. 666 pp. $12.50

Shade, Philip A.
Common Stocks: A Plan for Intelligent Investing. Homewood, Ill.: Richard D. Irwin, 1971. 326 pp. $8.95

Widicus, W. W. and Stitzel, T. E.
Today's Investments for Tomorrow's Security. Homewood, Ill.: Dow Jones-Irwin, 1971. 415 pp. $9.95

Willett, Edward R.
Fundamentals of Securities Markets, rev. ed. New York: Appleton-Century, 1968. 274 pp. $9.95

SELECTED REFERENCE WORKS

Barnes, Leo, founding author
Your Investments, 18th ed. Comp. and ed. by American Research Council. New York: McGraw-Hill, 1970. 226 pp. paperback: $7.95

Dos Passos, John R.
A Treatise on the Law of Stockbrokers and Stock Exchanges. Original: Harper, 1882. Reprint: Westport, Conn.: Greenwood Press, 1968. 1043 pp. $38.00

Encyclopedia of Stock Market Techniques. Larchmont, N.Y.: Investors Intelligence, 1971. 736 pp. $24.95

Fleur, Leo Y.
Selling Securities Successfully. Englewood Cliffs, N.J.: Prentice-Hall, 1966. 204 pp. $7.95

Hirsch, Yale
1972 Stock Trader's Almanac. Old Tappan, N.J.: Hirsch Organization, 1971. 160 pp. flexible cover: $6.95

See annotation, pp. 137–138.

Loll, Leo M., Jr., and Buckley, Julian G.
The Over-the-Counter Securities Markets: A Review Guide, 2nd ed. Englewood Cliffs, N.J.: Prentice-Hall, 1967. 426 pp. $11.50

Loll, Leo M., Jr., and Buckley, Julian G.
Questions and Answers on Securities Markets. Englewood Cliffs, N.J.: Prentice-Hall, 1968. 230 pp. $9.95

Moody, John
The Truth about Trusts: A Description and Analysis of the American Trust Movement. Original: New York: John Moody, 1904. Reprint: Westport, Conn.: Greenwood Press, 1968. 514 pp. $19.75

Rolo, Charles J., and Nelson, George J.
The Anatomy of Wall Street. Philadelphia: Lippincott, 1968. 307 pp. $7.50

Rosen, Lawrence R.
Go Where the Money Is: A Guide to Understanding and Entering the Securities Business. Homewood, Ill.: Dow Jones-Irwin, 1969. 264 pp. $8.50

Samuelson, Paul A.
Economics, 8th ed. New York: McGraw-Hill, 1970. 868 pp. $10.50

Sarnoff, Paul
Wall Street Wisdom. New York: Pocket Books, 1965. 259 pp. paperback: $1.00

Wyckoff, Peter G.
Dictionary of Stock Market Terms. Englewood Cliffs, N.J.: Prentice-Hall, 1964. 301 pp. $5.95

Zarb, Frank G., and Kerekes, Gabriel T.
The Stock Market Handbook: A Reference Manual for the Securities Industry. Homewood, Ill.: Dow Jones-Irwin, 1970. 1073 pp. $27.50

See annotation, p. 147.

SUPPLEMENTARY
RECOMMENDED LIST

The world of Wall Street is dynamic, and so is its literature. Every year many new works are published that add to the fund of knowledge guiding the investor in his quest for stock market success. The main body of 150 analytical abstracts that make up this bibliography represents an attempt to develop some form out of the vast amoebic entity of the market. In a real sense it is a nucleus of important books that are classified into many stock market areas. It will be necessary to build on this foundation in the future and add many other excellent books that were omitted because of the limitations of time and space.

The supplementary list that follows contains some of the classic works of the past that deserve to be on any list of great books. Most of these books were not included in the text because of space limitations. The list also contains recently published books that will make their mark in the years ahead, and deserve mention here. The future will determine their importance in relation to the total sum of market literature.

A truly representative library of significant stock market literature must collect the classics of the past and select the books of the future. The author and his advisors must dedicate themselves to this task if the goal of this bibliography is to be fulfilled.

Angly, Edward
   Oh Yeah: New York: Viking Press, 1931. 64 pp.

Anonymous
   Wiped Out: How I Lost a Fortune while the Averages Were Making New Highs. New York: Simon & Schuster, 1966. 125 pp. $3.50

Asen, Robert, and Asen, R. Scott
   How to Make Money Selling Stock Options. West Nyack, N.Y.: Parker, 1970. 191 pp. $16.95

Baruch, Hurd
Wall Street: Security Risk. Washington, D.C.: Acropolis Books, 1971. 356 pp. $8.95

Bernhard, Arnold
The Evaluation of Common Stocks. New York: Simon & Schuster, 1959. 182 pp. $3.95

Birmingham, Stephen
Our Crowd: The Great Jewish Families of New York. New York: Harper & Row, 1967. 440 pp. $5.95

Bloom, Murray Teigh
Rogues to Riches: The Trouble with Wall Street. New York: Putnam, 1971. 332 pp. $6.95

Bond, Frederick Drew
Success in Security Operations. New York: Chilton Books, 1931. 273 pp.

Brutus (John Spinner)
Confessions of a Stockbroker: A Wall Street Diary. Boston: Little, Brown, 1971. 263 pp. $6.95

Cootner, Paul
The Random Character of Stock Market Prices. Cambridge, Mass.: M.I.T. Press, 1964. 536 pp. paperback: $4.95

Darvas, Nicolas
The Darvas System for Over-the-Counter Profits. New York: Lyle Stuart, 1971. 144 pp. $5.95

Daughen, Joseph R., and Binzen, Peter
The Wreck of the Penn Central. Boston: Little, Brown, 1971. 365 pp. $7.95

Drew, Garfield A.
New Methods for Profits in the Stock Market: With a Critical Analysis of Established Systems. Original: Boston: Metcalf Press, 1955. Reprint: Burlington, Vt.: Fraser, 1966. 382 pp. paperback: $7.50

Durand, John and Miller, A. T.
The Business of Trading in Stocks. Original: New York: Ticker, 1933. Reprint: Burlington, Vt.: Fraser, 1967. 154 pp. paperback: $3.50

Elias, Christopher
Fleecing the Lambs. Chicago: Henry Regnery, 1971. 246 pp. $6.95

Ellis, Charles D.
Institutional Investing. Homewood, Ill.: Dow Jones-Irwin, 1971. 253 pp. $12.50

Finley, Harold M.
The Logical Approach to Successful Investing. Chicago: Henry Regnery, 1971. 252 pp. $5.95

Fraser, James L.
P.S. What Do You Think of the Market? Original: New York: Guenther, 1920. Reprint: Burlington, Vt.: Fraser, 1966. 80 pp. paperback: $2.50

Friend, Irwin, Blume, Marshall, and Crockett, Jean
Mutual Funds and Other Institutional Investors: A New Perspective. New York: McGraw-Hill, 1970. 197 pp. $7.95

Garett, Garet
Where the Money Grows. Original: New York: Harper, 1911. Reprint: Burlington, Vt.: Fraser, 1966. 66 pp. paperback: $2.50

Gartley, Harold M.
Profits in the Stock Market. New York: H. M. Gartley, c. 1930

Granville, Joseph Ensign
Granville's New Key to Stock Market Profits. Englewood Cliffs, N.J.: Prentice-Hall, 1963. 346 pp. $16.95

Griffith, B. Barret
Investing is Adventure! Original: Boston: Barron's, 1949. Reprint: Burlington, Vt.: Fraser, 1965. 156 pp. paperback: $3.50

Guyon, Don (pseudonym)
One-Way Pockets: The Book of Books on Wall Street Speculation. Original: New York: Capstone, 1917. Reprint: Burlington, Vt.: Fraser, 1965. 64 pp. $2.00

Haller, Gilbert
The Haller Theory of Stock Market Trends. West Palm Beach, Fla.: Gilbert Haller, 1965. 179 pp. $5.00

Hazard, John W.
Choosing Tomorrow's Growth Stocks Today. Garden City, N.Y.: Doubleday, 1968. 305 pp. $6.50

Hewett, William S.
Common Stocks for the Uncommon Man. New York: Frederick Fell, 1966. 195 pp. $5.95

Holmes, Gordon A.
Capital Appreciation in the Stock Market: A Handbook of Sophisticated Stock Market Techniques. West Nyack, N.Y.: Parker, 1969. 172 pp. $17.95

Hurst, J. M.
The Profit Magic of Stock Transaction Timing. Englewood Cliffs, N.J.: Prentice-Hall, 1970. 223 pp. $19.95

Jacobs, William Oliver
The Stock Market Profile: How to Invest with the Primary Trend. West Nyack, N.Y.: Parker, 1967. 184 pp. $16.95

Josephson, Matthew
The Robber Barons. Original: New York: Harcourt, 1934. Reprint: New York: Harcourt, Brace, Jovanovich, 1962. 474 pp. paperback: $2.85

Knapp, Paul
The Berengaria Exchange. New York: Dial Press, 1972. 239 pp. $5.95

Larson, Henrietta M.
Jay Cooke: Private Banker. Westport, Conn.: Greenwood Press, 1968. 512 pp. $21.00

Liveright, James
Simple Methods for Detecting Buying and Selling Points in Securities. Original: New York: Ticker, 1926. Reprint: Burlington, Vt.: Fraser, 1968. 133 pp. paperback: $3.50

Livingston, Joseph Arnold
The American Stockholder. Philadelphia: Lippincott, 1958. 290 pp. $4.90

Magazine of Wall Street
Fourteen Methods of Operating in the Stock Market. Original: New York: Ticker, 1924. Reprint: Burlington, Vt.: Fraser, 1968. 157 pp. paperback: $4.00

Manne, Henry G.
Insider Trading and the Stock Market. New York: Free Press, 1966. 274 pp. $6.95

Markstein, David L.
How to Make Money with Mutual Funds. New York: McGraw-Hill, 1969. 258 pp. $7.95

Merritt, Robert D.
Financial Independence through Common Stocks, 7th rev. ed. New York: Simon & Schuster, 1969. 344 pp. $6.50

Moore, William C.
Wall Street: Its Mysteries Revealed: Its Secrets Exposed. Original: William C. Moore, 1921. Reprint: Burlington, Vt.: Fraser, 1969. 144 pp. paperback: $5.00

Raw, Charles, Page, Bruce, and Hodgson, Godfrey
"Do You Sincerely Want to be Rich?" The Full Story of Bernard Cornfeld and IOS. New York: Viking Press, 1971. 400 pp. $8.95

Ripley, William Zebina
Main Street and Wall Street. Boston: Little, 1927. 359 pp.

Rogers, Donald I.
How Not to Buy Common Stocks. New Rochelle, N.Y.: Arlington House, 1972. 219 pp. $7.95

Rosenberg, Claude N., Jr.
Psycho-Cybernetics and the Stock Market: The Key to Maximum Investment Profits and Peace of Mind. Chicago: Playboy Press, 1971. 224 pp. $6.95

Schabacker, Richard W.
Stock Market Profits. Original: New York: B. C. Forbes, 1934. Reprint: Burlington, Vt.: Fraser, 1967, 1970. 340 pp. paperback: $7.50

Schaefer, Edward George
How I Helped More Than 10,000 Investors to Profit in Stocks, rev. ed. Englewood Cliffs, N.J.: Prentice-Hall, 1963. 244 pp. $4.95

Schultz, Harry D.
Panics and Crashes and How You Can Make Money out of Them. New Rochelle, N.Y.: Arlington House, 1972. 520 pp. $7.95

Schulz, John W.
The Intelligent Chartist. New York: WRSM Financial Service, 1962. 275 pp. $10.00

Seamans, George
The Seven Pillars of Stock Market Success. Chicago: Seamans-Blake, 1933.

Sheldon, Michael U.
Plan Your Way to Wall Street Profit. New York: Grosset & Dunlap, 1969. 207 pp. $5.95

Shulman, Morton
Anyone Can Make a Million. New York: McGraw-Hill, 1966. 276 pp. $4.95

Sloan, Alfred P., Jr.
My Years with General Motors. Garden City, N.Y.: Doubleday, 1963. 472 pp. $10.00

Smitley, Robert L.
Popular Financial Delusions. Original: Philadelphia: Roland Swain, 1933. Reprint: Burlington, Vt.: Fraser, 1963. 338 pp. flexible cover: $5.00; hardbound: $7.00

Sparling, Earl
Mystery Men of Wall Street. New York: Greenberg, 1930. 254 pp.

Thiers, Adolphe
The Mississippi Bubble: A Memoir of John Law. Original: W. A. Townsend, 1859. Reprint: Westport, Conn.: Greenwood Press, 1969. 338 pp. $12.50

Tso, Lin
Techniques for Discovering Hidden-Value Stocks. New York: Frederick Fell, 1965. 443 pp. $10.00

Vartan, Vartanig G.
50 Wall Street. New York: McGraw-Hill, 1968. 341 pp. $5.95

Vartan, Vartanig G.
The Dinosaur Fund. New York: McGraw-Hill, 1972. 391 pp. $7.95

Wolf, H. J.
Studies in Stock Speculation: Vol. I. Original: New York: Ticker, 1924. Reprint: Burlington, Vt.: Fraser, 1966. 224 pp. paperback: $3.50

Wolf, H. J.
Studies in Stock Speculation: Vol. II: Ten Cardinal Principles of Trading and Supplemental Discussions of General Interest to Traders and Investors. Original: New York: Ticker, 1926. Reprint: Burlington, Vt.: Fraser, 1967. 184 pp. paperback: $3.50

Zerden, Sheldon
Margin: Key to a Stock Market Fortune. New York: Pilot Books, 1969. 53 pp. paperback: $3.95

Author-Title Index

159

Title-Author Index